Other Books and Series by Jeff Bowen

Applications for Enrollment of Chickasaw Newborn Act of 1905
Volumes I thru VII

Cherokee Intermarried White 1906 Volume I thru X

Applications for Enrollment of Creek Newborn Act of 1905
Volumes I, II, III, IV, V, VI, VII & VIII

Visit our website at **www.nativestudy.com** to learn more about these and other books and series by Jeff Bowen

APPLICATIONS FOR ENROLLMENT OF CREEK NEWBORN ACT OF 1905
VOLUME IX

TRANSCRIBED BY
JEFF BOWEN
NATIVE STUDY
Gallipolis, Ohio
USA

Other Books and Series by Jeff Bowen

1901-1907 Native American Census Seneca, Eastern Shawnee, Miami, Modoc, Ottawa, Peoria, Quapaw, and Wyandotte Indians (Under Seneca School, Indian Territory)

1932 Census of The Standing Rock Sioux Reservation with Births And Deaths 1924-1932

Census of The Blackfeet, Montana, 1897- 1901 Expanded Edition

Eastern Cherokee by Blood, 1906-1910, Volumes I thru XIII

Choctaw of Mississippi Indian Census 1929-1932 with Births and Deaths 1924-1931 Volume I
Choctaw of Mississippi Indian Census 1933, 1934 & 1937, Supplemental Rolls to 1934 & 1935 with Births and Deaths 1932-1938, and Marriages 1936-1938 Volume II

Eastern Cherokee Census Cherokee, North Carolina 1930-1939 Census 1930-1931 with Births And Deaths 1924-1931 Taken By Agent L. W. Page Volume I
Eastern Cherokee Census Cherokee, North Carolina 1930-1939 Census 1932-1933 with Births And Deaths 1930-1932 Taken By Agent R. L. Spalsbury Volume II
Eastern Cherokee Census Cherokee, North Carolina 1930-1939 Census 1934-1937 with Births and Deaths 1925-1938 and Marriages 1936 & 1938 Taken by Agents R. L. Spalsbury And Harold W. Foght Volume III

Seminole of Florida Indian Census, 1930-1940 with Birth and Death Records, 1930-1938

Texas Cherokees 1820-1839 A Document For Litigation 1921

Choctaw By Blood Enrollment Cards 1898-1914 Volumes I thru XVII

Starr Roll 1894 (Cherokee Payment Rolls) Districts: Canadian, Cooweescoowee, and Delaware Volume One
Starr Roll 1894 (Cherokee Payment Rolls) Districts: Flint, Going Snake, and Illinois Volume Two
Starr Roll 1894 (Cherokee Payment Rolls) Districts: Saline, Sequoyah, and Tahlequah; Including Orphan Roll Volume Three

Cherokee Intruder Cases Dockets of Hearings 1901-1909 Volumes I & II

Indian Wills, 1911-1921 Records of the Bureau of Indian Affairs Books One thru Seven;
Native American Wills & Probate Records 1911-1921

Other Books and Series by Jeff Bowen

Turtle Mountain Reservation Chippewa Indians 1932 Census with Births & Deaths, 1924-1932

Chickasaw By Blood Enrollment Cards 1898-1914 Volume I thru V

Cherokee Descendants East An Index to the Guion Miller Applications Volume I
Cherokee Descendants West An Index to the Guion Miller Applications Volume II (A-M)
Cherokee Descendants West An Index to the Guion Miller Applications Volume III (N-Z)

Applications for Enrollment of Seminole Newborn Freedmen, Act of 1905

Eastern Cherokee Census, Cherokee, North Carolina, 1915-1922, Taken by Agent James E. Henderson
    Volume I (1915-1916)
    Volume II (1917-1918)
    Volume III (1919-1920)
    Volume IV (1921-1922)

Complete Delaware Roll of 1898

Eastern Cherokee Census, Cherokee, North Carolina, 1923-1929, Taken by Agent James E. Henderson
    Volume I (1923-1924)
    Volume II (1925-1926)
    Volume III (1927-1929)

Applications for Enrollment of Seminole Newborn Act of 1905 Volumes I & II

North Carolina Eastern Cherokee Indian Census 1898-1899, 1904, 1906, 1909-1912, 1914 Revised and Expanded Edition

1932 Hopi and Navajo Native American Census with Birth & Death Rolls (1925-1931) Volume 1 - Hopi
1932 Hopi and Navajo Native American Census with Birth & Death Rolls (1930-1932) Volume 2 - Navajo

Western Navajo Reservation Navajo, Hopi and Paiute 1933 Census with Birth & Death Rolls 1925-1933

Cherokee Citizenship Commission Dockets 1880-1884 and 1887-1889 Volumes I thru V

Copyright © 2012
by Jeff Bowen

ALL RIGHTS RESERVED
No part of this publication may be reproduced
or used in any form or manner whatsoever
without previous written permission from the
copyright holder or publisher.

Originally published:
Baltimore, Maryland
2012

Reprinted by:

Native Study LLC
Gallipolis, OH
www.nativestudy.com
2020

Library of Congress Control Number: 2020917992

ISBN: 978-1-64968-088-4

Made in the United States of America.

This series is dedicated to the descendants of the
Creek newborn listed in these applications.

DEPARTMENT OF THE INTERIOR.

Commissioner to the Five Civilized Tribes.

NOTICE.

Opening of Land Office at Wewoka,
IN THE SEMINOLE NATION, INDIAN TERRITORY.

Notice is hereby given that on Monday, September 4, 1905, the Commissioner to the Five Civilized Tribes will establish a land office at Wewoka, in the Seminole Nation, Indian Territory, for the purpose of allowing citizens and freedmen of the Seminole Nation to select allotments of land for their minor children enrolled under the Act of Congress approved March 3, 1905 (33 Stat. L 1060), and for the further purpose of allowing citizens and freedmen of the Seminole Nation, whose allotments are incomplete, to select additional land in order to bring the value of their allotments up to the standard of $309.09, as nearly as may be practicable.

Each child whose enrollment in accordance with the Act of March 3, 1905, has been duly approved by the Secretary of the Interior, is entitled to receive an alllotment of forty acres without regard to the character or value of the land selected.

Selection of allotments for minor children must be made by their citizen or freedmen parents or by a duly appointed guardian, or curator, or by a duly appointed administrator.

TAMS BIXBY,
Commissioner.

Muskogee, Indian Territory,
July 29, 1905.

This particular notice makes mention of the Act of 1905. The Creek and Seminole were closely related tribes. Both tribes' notices were like similar in nature.

DEPARTMENT OF THE INTERIOR,
Commission to the Five Civilized Tribes.

Closing of Citizenship Rolls

OF THE MUSKOGEE OR CREEK NATION.

WHEREAS, on June 13, 1904, the Secretary of the Interior, under the authority in him vested by the provisions of the act of Congress approved March 3, 1901, (31 Stat., 1058) ordered that September 1, 1904, be and the same is hereby fixed as the time when the rolls of the Muskogee or Creek Nation shall be closed:

Notice is hereby given that the Commission to the Five Civilized Tribes will, at its office in Muskogee, Indian Territory, up to and inclusive of September 1, 1904, receive applications for the enrollment of citizens and freedmen of the Muskogee or Creek Nation, and that after that date the application of no person whomsoever for enrollment as a citizen or freedman of said nation will be received by the Commission.

Commission to the Five Civilized Tribes,
TAMS BIXBY, Chairman,
T. B. NEEDLES,
C. R. BRECKINRIDGE,
Commissioners.

Muskogee, Indian Territory,
June 25, 1904.

A notice like this was printed in newspapers and posted throughout Indian Territory.

INTRODUCTION

This series concerns Applications for Enrollment of Creek Newborn, National Archive film M-1301 (Act of 1905), as described in the National Archives publication *American Indians*. It falls under the heading Applications for Enrollment of the Commission to the Five Civilized Tribes, 1898-1914, M-1301 and is transcribed from microfilm rolls 414-419. This shows the application forms filled out by individuals applying for enrollment in the Five Civilized Tribes under the Dawes Commission. These applications contain additional information that wasn't abstracted to the census cards that you find in series M-1186. This particular roll (Creek by Birth) contains its own series of numbers separate from M-1186. To find each party's roll number you would have to reference M-1186. On July 25, 1898, there was an Indian Territory Division created in the Office of the Department of Interior. This division was created because of the increased work caused by what was called the Curtis Act, named after Senator Charles Curtis. Basically, this law stated that the tribal rolls needed to be descriptive and pointed out that each tribal roll was without description and had to be redone. At this point there was such a struggle among the Creeks to accept that the Government was going to change their way of life, again, that their leaders were refusing to cooperate in handing over their census information. The Commission had found that enrolling the Creeks was a difficult task not only because the Creek feared what was coming but also because their tribal structure was consistent with being a confederacy with forty-four different bands whose tribesmen lived in different towns of which each had a king that was supposed to keep track of their citizenry. The Commission reported that there was very little evidence of any census that existed and what there was had been kept carelessly. There were attempts and tribal conflicts along the way, but the Curtis Act would make it so they had to do it again no matter what effort from the past. In 1899, Agent Wesley Smith educated Washington to the fact that it was difficult to verify Creek eligibility. The acts passed by the Creeks themselves concerning enrollment since 1893 had been strewn amongst the archives of the Creek Council in Muskogee, I.T., and there was no provision ever approved for the printing of the those enrollments. There was confusion and difficulty let alone the fact that surnames were practically unknown among the Creek. But there was no confusion on March 9, 1905, when the Commission stated they would come to seven towns in the Creek Nation and accept applications that had to be made on a standardized blank form and contain a notarized affidavit from the mother and the attending doctor or midwife. A few by mail, but most of them were offered to a field party led by Commissioner Needles. The Commission took in applications for 2,410 children by the deadline of midnight, May 2, 1905.

This series contains applications and correspondence from 1,171 of those claimants. Realizing there were over 2,400 applicants originally, it is understood that not all were accepted. Also included are names of doctors, lawyers, mid-wives, and others who attended to the Creek Nation before and during this time in history.

Jeff Bowen
Gallipolis, Ohio
NativeStudy.com

Applications for Enrollment of Creek Newborn
Act of 1905   Volume IX

C670
DEPARTMENT OF THE INTERIOR,
COMMISSION TO THE FIVE CIVILIZED TRIBES.
Eufaula, I. T., April 3, 1905.

In the matter of the application for the enrollment of James Wadsworth as a citizen by blood of the Creek Nation.

ELIZA WADSWORTH, being duly sworn, testified as follows:

BY COMMISSION:
Q What is your name? A Eliza Wadsworth.
Q What is your age? A 38.
Q What is your post office address? A Checotah.
Q Are you a citizen of the Creek Nation? A Yes, sir.
Q To what town do you belong? A Arbeka---North Fork or Deep Fork, I do not know which.
Q Do you make application for the enrollment of your minor child, James Wadsworth, as a citizen by blood of the Creek Nation.[sic] *(No answer given)*
Q What is the name of his father? A John Wadsworth.
Q Is he a citizen of the Creek Nation? A He is a Seminole.
Q Is he you lawful husband? Ab[sic] Yes sir.
Q If it should be found that your child James Wadsworth, is entitled to enrollment in either the Creek or Seminole Nation, in which Nation do you desire to have him enrolled? A In the Creek Nation.

I, Drennan C Skaggs, being duly sworn, on oath states, that the above and foregoing is a full and true transcript of my stenographic notes taken in said cause on said date.

DC Skaggs

Subscribed and sworn to before me this sworn to before me this 20th day of July 1905.

J McDermott
Notary Public.

Applications for Enrollment of Creek Newborn
Act of 1905   Volume IX

NC. 670.
Muskogee, Indian Territory, July 15, 1905.

Chief Clerk,
   Seminole Enrollment Division,
      Muskogee, Indian Territory.

Dear Sir:

    April 7, 1905, application was made to the Commission to the Five Civilized Tribes for the enrollment of James Wadsworth, born August 31, 1903, as a citizen by blood of the Creek Nation. It is stated in said application that the father of said child is John Wadsworth, a citizen of the Seminole Nation, and that the mother is Eliza Wadsworth, a citizen of the Creek Nation.

    You are requested to inform the Creek Enrollment Division as to whether application has been made for the enrollment of said James Wadsworth as a citizen of the Seminole Nation, and if so, what disposition has been made of the same.

                      Respectfully,
                                  Commissioner.

DEPARTMENT OF THE INTERIOR.
COMMISSION TO THE FIVE CIVILIZED TRIBES.

Muskogee, Indian Territory, July 19, 1905.

Chief Clerk,
   Creek Enrollment Division.

Dear Sir:

    Receipt is acknowledged of your letter of July 14, 1905 (NC-670) stating that application was made to the Commission to the Five Civilized Tribes for the enrollment of James Wadsworth, born August 31, 1903, child of John Wadsworth, a citizen of the Seminole Nation, and Eliza Wadsworth, a citizen of the Creek Nation, as a citizen by blood of the Creek Nation and requesting to be informed as to whether application was made for the enrollment of said child as a citizen of the Seminole Nation.

    In reply to your letter you are informed that it does not appear from an examination of the records of this office that any application was made to the Commission to the Five Civilized Tribes for the enrollment of said James Wadsworth as a citizen of the Seminole Nation.

                      Respectfully,
                            Tams Bixby   Commissioner.

Applications for Enrollment of Creek Newborn
Act of 1905   Volume IX

NC 670

Muskogee, Indian Territory, November 13, 1906

Chief Clerk,
   Seminole Enrollment Division,
      General Office.

Dear Sir:

     You are hereby advised that the name of James Wadsworth, born August 31, 1903 to John Wadsworth, an alleged citizen of the Seminole Nation and Eliza Wadsworth, a citizen by blood of the Creek Nation, is contained in schedule of minor citizens by blood of the Creek Nation, approved by the Secretary of the Interior, September 27, 1905 opposite Roll number 628.

                        Respectfully,

                                    Commissioner.

BIRTH AFFIDAVIT.

Department of the Interior,
COMMISSION TO THE FIVE CIVILIZED TRIBES.

     IN RE APPLICATION FOR ENROLLMENT, as a citizen of the Creek Nation, of James Wadsworth, born on the 31 day of August, 1903

Name of Father: John Wadsworth   a citizen of the Seminole Nation.
Name of Mother: Eliza Wadsworth   a citizen of the Creek Nation.
Arbeka Town

                       Post-Office: Checotah, Ind. Ter.

AFFIDAVIT OF MOTHER.

                                        Child Present

UNITED STATES OF AMERICA,
   INDIAN TERRITORY,
     Western   District.

     I, Eliza Wadsworth, on oath state that I am about 38 years of age and a citizen by blood, of the Creek Nation; that I am the lawful wife of John Wadsworth, who is a citizen, by blood of the Seminole Nation; that a male child was born to me on 31 day of August, 1903, that said child has been named James Wadsworth, and ~~is now~~ was living. on March 4, 1905.

                                       Eliza Wadsworth

Applications for Enrollment of Creek Newborn
Act of 1905   Volume IX

WITNESSES TO MARK:
{

Subscribed and sworn to before me this 3 day of April, 1905.

Drennan C Skaggs
Notary Public.

AFFIDAVIT OF ATTENDING PHYSICIAN OR MID-WIFE.

UNITED STATES OF AMERICA,
INDIAN TERRITORY,
Western   District.

I, Josephine Berryhill , a mid-wife , on oath state that I attended on Mrs. Eliza Wadsworth , wife of John Wadsworth on the 31 day of August , 1903 ; that there was born to her on said date a male child; that said child is now living and is said to have been named James Wadsworth

Josephine Berryhill

WITNESSES TO MARK:
{

Subscribed and sworn to before me this 3 day of April, 1905.

Drennan C Skaggs
Notary Public.

BIRTH AFFIDAVIT.
DEPARTMENT OF THE INTERIOR.
COMMISSION TO THE FIVE CIVILIZED TRIBES.

IN RE APPLICATION FOR ENROLLMENT, as a citizen of the Creek Nation, of Nancy Tiger, born on the 13 day of Aug , 1903

Name of Father: Cooper Tiger   a citizen of the   Creek   Nation.
(Euchee)
Name of Mother: Salina   "   a citizen of the   Creek   Nation.
(Euchee)

Postoffice   Kellyville

Applications for Enrollment of Creek Newborn
Act of 1905 Volume IX

AFFIDAVIT OF MOTHER.

UNITED STATES OF AMERICA, Indian Territory, }
Western DISTRICT.

Child Present

I, Salina Tiger , on oath state that I am 20 years of age and a citizen by blood , of the Creek Nation; that I am the lawful wife of Cooper Tiger , who is a citizen, by blood of the Creek Nation; that a female child was born to me on 13 day of Aug , 1903 , that said child has been named Nancy Tiger , and was living March 4, 1905.

Salina Tiger

Witnesses To Mark:
{ David Shelby
  Jesse McDermott

Subscribed and sworn to before me this 24 day of April , 1905.

(Seal)

Edw C Griesel
Notary Public.

AFFIDAVIT OF ATTENDING ~~PHYSICIAN~~ OR MID-WIFE.

UNITED STATES OF AMERICA, Indian Territory, }
Western DISTRICT.

I, For-co-wee Yellowhead , a Mid wife , on oath state that I attended on Mrs. Salina Tiger , wife of Cooper Tiger on the 13 day of Aug , 1903 ; that there was born to her on said date a female child; that said child was living March 4, 1905, and is said to have been named Nancy Tiger

Her
For-co-wee x Yellowhead
mark

Witnesses To Mark:
{ David Shelby
  Jesse McDermott

Subscribed and sworn to before me 24 day of April, 1905.

(Seal)

Edw C Griesel
Notary Public.

Applications for Enrollment of Creek Newborn
Act of 1905   Volume IX

BIRTH AFFIDAVIT.

DEPARTMENT OF THE INTERIOR,
COMMISSION TO THE FIVE CIVILIZED TRIBES.

In Re- Application for Enrollment, as a citizen of the Creek Nation, of   Nancy Tiger , born on the 13 day of August , 1903

Name of Father: Cooper Tiger   a citizen of the   Creek   Nation.
Name of Mother: Salina Tiger   a citizen of the   Creek   Nation.

                      Post-office   Bristow Ind Ter

AFFIDAVIT OF MOTHER.

UNITED STATES OF AMERICA,
    INDIAN TERRITORY,
Western   District.

    I, Salina Tiger , on oath state that I am 22 years of age and a citizen by Birth , of the Creek   Nation; that I am the lawful wife of   Cooper Tiger , who is a citizen, by Birth   of the Creek   Nation; that a   female   child was born to me on   13   day of August , 1903 , that said child has been named Nancy Tiger , and is now living.

                                    Salina Tiger
Witnesses To Mark:

    (Name Illegible)

    Subscribed and sworn to before me this 3 day of April, 1905.

                                    E. W. Sims
                                       Notary Public.

AFFIDAVIT OF ATTENDING PHYSICIAN OR MID-WIFE.

UNITED STATES OF AMERICA,
    INDIAN TERRITORY,
Western   District.

    I, Jensen Skeeter , a   Midwife , on oath state that I attended on Mrs. Salina Tiger , wife of Cooper Tiger on the 13 day of August , 1903; that there was born to her on said date a Female child; that said child is now living and is said to have been named Nancy Tiger

Applications for Enrollment of Creek Newborn
Act of 1905 Volume IX

           her
         Jensen x Skeeter
Witnesses To Mark: mark
 { Robert Elder
 { *(Name Illegible)*

Subscribed and sworn to before me this 3 day of April, 1905.

            E. W. Sims
             Notary Public.

NC-672

        Muskogee, Indian Territory, August 14, 1905.

Willis Woods,
  Tulsa, Indian Territory.

Dear Sir:

  In the matter of the application for the enrollment of your minor daughter, Argethel Woods, as a citizen by blood of the Creek Nation (born September 11, 1904), it will be necessary for you to furnish this Office with the affidavits of two disinterested persons as to the birth of said child. Said affidavits must set forth said child's name, the names of her parents, the date of her birth, and whether or not she was living on March 4, 1905.

         Respectfully,
            Acting Commissioner.

AFFIDAVIT OF DISINTERESTED WITNESSES.

United States of America,
  Western District,
   Indian Territory.

  We, the undersigned, on oath state that we are personally acquainted with Cora Woods the wife of Willis Woods ; that there was born to her a female child on or about 11 day of September 1903; that the said child has been named Argethel Woods and was living March 4, 1905.

  We further state that we have no interest in this case.

            R M Govey
            Mrs R M Govey

Applications for Enrollment of Creek Newborn
Act of 1905 Volume IX

Subscribed and sworn to before me this 25 day of April 1906

My Com expires Oct 11. 1906   Walter J Reneau
                                    Notary Public.

BIRTH AFFIDAVIT.
DEPARTMENT OF THE INTERIOR,
COMMISSIONER TO THE FIVE CIVILIZED TRIBES.

IN RE APPLICATION FOR ENROLLMENT, as a citizen of the Creek Nation, of Artethel Woods, born on the 11 day of Sept, 1904

Name of Father: Willis Woods   a citizen of the   U.S.   Nation.
Name of Mother: Cora Woods   a citizen of the   Creek   Nation.

            Postoffice   Tulsa Ind Ter

AFFIDAVIT OF MOTHER.

UNITED STATES OF AMERICA, Indian Territory, }
Western   District.

I, Cora Woods, on oath state that I am 22 years of age and a citizen by Blood, of the Creek Nation; that I am the lawful wife of Willis Woods, who is a citizen, by Birth of the U.S. Nation; that a Female child was born to me on 11 day of September, 1904, that said child has been named Argethel Woods, and was living March 4, 1905.

I further certify that there was   Cora Woods
no one present but my husband
Witness to Mark:
                        }

Subscribed and sworn to before me this 23 day of March, 1905.

                        Robert E. Lynch
                        Notary Public.

AFFIDAVIT OF ATTENDING PHYSICIAN OR MID-WIFE.

UNITED STATES OF AMERICA, Indian Territory, }
Western   District.

I, Willis Woods, a -----, on oath state that I attended on Mrs. Cora Woods, My wife ef *(blank)* on the 11" day of Sept 1904 ; that there was born to her on said

8

Applications for Enrollment of Creek Newborn
Act of 1905   Volume IX

date a   Female   child; that said child was living March 4, 1905, and is said to have been named Argethel Woods   There was no one present but myself and wife

Witness to Mark:

Willis Woods

}

Subscribed and sworn to before me this 23   day of March , 1905.

Com Ex 7/3/1906   Robert E. Lynch
                                                            Notary Public.

BIRTH AFFIDAVIT

DEPARTMENT OF THE INTERIOR,
COMMISSION TO THE FIVE CIVILIZED TRIBES.

IN RE Application for Enrollment, as a citizen of the Creek Nation, of Lillie Woods , born on the 4 day of July , 1901

Name of Father: Willis A Woods   a citizen of the   ~~Cherokee~~   Nation.
Name of Mother: Cora Woods   a citizen of the   Creek   Nation.

Post-office: Dawson I.T.

AFFIDAVIT OF MOTHER.

UNITED STATES OF AMERICA,
INDIAN TERRITORY.
Western   District.

I, Cora Woods , on oath state that I am 20 years of age and a citizen by Birth , of the Creek   Nation; that I am the lawful wife of Willis A. Woods   , who is a citizen, by *(blank)* of the *(blank)* Nation; that a Female   child was born to me on 4 day of July , 1901 , that said child has been named Lillie Woods , and is now living.

                                       Cora Woods
                                       Cora Adams Woods

WITNESSES TO MARK:

{

Subscribed and sworn to before me this 14 *day of* August , 1902.

Com Ex 7/3/1906   Robert E Lynch
                                                           NOTARY PUBLIC.

9

Applications for Enrollment of Creek Newborn
Act of 1905   Volume IX

AFFIDAVIT OF ATTENDING PHYSICIAN OR MID-WIFE.

UNITED STATES OF AMERICA, }
INDIAN TERRITORY.
Western   District.

I, Mrs Barbara Turkey , a Midwife , on oath state that I attended on Mrs. Cora Woods , wife of Willis A Woods on the 4 day of July , 1901 ; that there was born to her on said date a Female child; that said child is now living and is said to have been named Lillie Woods

                                            Mrs. Barbara Turkey
WITNESSES TO MARK:
{

Subscribed and sworn to before me this 14 day of August , 1902.

        Com Ex 7/3/1906   Robert E Lynch
                                          NOTARY PUBLIC.

BIRTH AFFIDAVIT.
DEPARTMENT OF THE INTERIOR,
COMMISSIONER TO THE FIVE CIVILIZED TRIBES.

IN RE APPLICATION FOR ENROLLMENT, as a citizen of the Creek Nation, of Lillie Rosell Woods , born on the 4" day of July , 1901

Name of Father: Willis Woods   a citizen of the U.S.   Nation.
Name of Mother: Cora Woods   a citizen of the Creek Nation.

                Postoffice   Tulsa Ind Ter

AFFIDAVIT OF MOTHER.

UNITED STATES OF AMERICA, Indian Territory, }
Western   District.

I, Cora Woods , on oath state that I am 22 years of age and a citizen by Blood , of the Creek Nation; that I am the lawful wife of Willis Woods , who is a citizen, by Birth of the U.S. Nation; that a Female child was born to me on 4 day of July , 1901 , that said child has been named Lillie Rosell Woods , and was living March 4, 1905.

                                Cora Woods
Witness to Mark:

10

Applications for Enrollment of Creek Newborn
Act of 1905   Volume IX

Subscribed and sworn to before me this 23   day of   March , 1905.

Com Ex 7/3/1906   Robert E Lynch
                                                                Notary Public.

AFFIDAVIT OF ATTENDING PHYSICIAN OR MID-WIFE.

UNITED STATES OF AMERICA, Indian Territory, }
Western   District.

I, Barbara Turkey , a   Midwife , on oath state that I attended on Mrs. Cora Woods , wife of   Willis Woods on the 4 day of July , 1901 ; that there was born to her on said date a   Female   child; that said child was living March 4, 1905, and is said to have been named Lillie Rosell Woods

                                                           Barbara Turkey
Witness to Mark:

}

Subscribed and sworn to before me this 23   day of   March , 1905.

Com Ex 7/3/1906   Robert E Lynch
                                                                Notary Public.

N.C. 945

DEPARTMENT OF THE INTERIOR,
COMMISSIONER TO THE FIVE CIVILIZED TRIBES,
Tulsa, Indian Territory, September 5, 1908.

In the matter of the application for the enrollment of Nora Fanning as a citizen by blood of the Creek Nation.

NANCY JEFFERSON, being duly sworn, testified as follows:

BY COMMISSIONER:

Q What is your name? A Nancy Jefferson. Was Nancy Fanning and enrolled as Nancy Davis.
Q What is your age? A I am thirty three years old.
Q What is your postoffice address? A Broken Arrow.
A Are you a Creek citizen? A Yes sir.
Q Have you a child named Nora Fanning? A Yes sir.
Q When was she born?[sic] A June 13, 1902.
Q Is she living? A Yes sir.

Applications for Enrollment of Creek Newborn
Act of 1905 Volume IX

Q Who is the father of Nora Fanning? A Bob Fanning.
Q Is he a citizen of the Creek Nation? A No sir.
Q Were you lawfully married to him when this child was born? A Yes, he had a marriage license when we married.
Q Have you that license or can get them? A No, I expect not 'cause Bob took them with him when he left here and I don't know where he is.
Q Do you know where he secured the license? A In Muskogee. Bob Lynch was with him when he got it.

The witness is identified opposite Creek Roll No. 2125.

Q Have you married again? A Yes but not lawfully.
Q To whom? A Moses Jefferson.

I, Jesse McDermott, on oath state that the above and foregoing is a full and true transcript of my notes as taken in said cause on said date.

Jesse McDermott

Subscribed and sworn to before me this 5th day of November, 1906.

My Com. expires Dec 12-1906

MB *(Illegible)*
Notary Public.

BIRTH AFFIDAVIT.

DEPARTMENT OF THE INTERIOR.
COMMISSION TO THE FIVE CIVILIZED TRIBES.

IN RE APPLICATION FOR ENROLLMENT, as a citizen of the Creek Nation, of Nora Fanning, born on the 14 day of June, 1902

Name of Father: Bob Fanning   a citizen of the   U.S.   Nation.
Name of Mother: Nancy W. "   a citizen of the   Creek   Nation.
Lochopoka[sic]
                        Postoffice   Tulsa

AFFIDAVIT OF MOTHER.

UNITED STATES OF AMERICA, Indian Territory,
    Western   DISTRICT.

I, Nancy W. Fanning, on oath state that I am 31 years of age and a citizen by blood, of the Creek Nation; that I am the lawful wife of Bob Fanning, who is a

Applications for Enrollment of Creek Newborn
Act of 1905   Volume IX

citizen, by blood of the Creek[sic] Nation; that a female child was born to me on 14 day of June , 1902 , that said child has been named Nora Fanning , and was living March 4, 1905.

              Nancy W. Fanning

Witnesses To Mark:

{

 Subscribed and sworn to before me this 1 day of May , 1905.

 Seal   Edw C Griesel
               Notary Public.

AFFIDAVIT OF ATTENDING PHYSICIAN OR MID-WIFE.

UNITED STATES OF AMERICA, Indian Territory,
  Western   DISTRICT.

 I, Nora Burgess , a Midwife , on oath state that I attended on Mrs. Nancy W Fanning , wife of Bob Fanning on the 14 day of June , 1902 ; that there was born to her on said date a female child; that said child was living March 4, 1905, and is said to have been named Nora Fanning

              Nora Burgess

Witnesses To Mark:

{

 Subscribed and sworn to before me this 1 day of May , 1905.

 Seal   Edw C Griesel
               Notary Public.

BIRTH AFFIDAVIT.

DEPARTMENT OF THE INTERIOR,
COMMISSION TO THE FIVE CIVILIZED TRIBES.

 IN RE Application for Enrollment, as a citizen of the Creek Nation, of Nora Davis , born on the 14" day of June , 1902

Name of Father: J.W. Davis   a citizen of the   U.S.   Nation.
Name of Mother: Nancy W. Davis   a citizen of the   Creek   Nation.

        Post-office: Tulsa Ind Ter

Applications for Enrollment of Creek Newborn
Act of 1905 Volume IX

AFFIDAVIT OF MOTHER.

UNITED STATES OF AMERICA,
INDIAN TERRITORY.
Western District.

I, Nancy W. Davis , on oath state that I am 31 years of age and a citizen by Blood , of the Creek Nation; that I am the ~~lawful~~ Divorced wife of J.W. Davis , who is a citizen, by Birth of the U.S. Nation; that a Female child was born to me on 14 day of June , 1902 , that said child has been named Nora Davis , and is now living.

Nancy W. Davis

WITNESSES TO MARK:

{

Subscribed and sworn to before me this 23 day of March , 1905.

Com Ex 7/3/1906   Robert E Lynch
                              NOTARY PUBLIC.

AFFIDAVIT OF ATTENDING PHYSICIAN OR MID-WIFE.

UNITED STATES OF AMERICA,
INDIAN TERRITORY.
Western District.

I, Nora Burgess , a Midwife , on oath state that I attended on Mrs. Nancy W. Davis , wife of J.W. Davis on the 14 day of June , 1902 ; that there was born to her on said date a Female child; that said child is now living and is said to have been named Nora Davis

Nora Burgess

WITNESSES TO MARK:

{

Subscribed and sworn to before me this 23 day of March , 1905.

Com Ex 7/3/1906   Robert E Lynch
                              NOTARY PUBLIC.

BIRTH AFFIDAVIT.

DEPARTMENT OF THE INTERIOR.
COMMISSION TO THE FIVE CIVILIZED TRIBES.

IN RE APPLICATION FOR ENROLLMENT, as a citizen of the Creek Nation, of Nora Fanning, born on the 14 day of June , 1902

Applications for Enrollment of Creek Newborn
Act of 1905   Volume IX

Name of Father: Bob Fanning   a citizen of the   U.S.   Nation.
Name of Mother: Nancy W.   "   a citizen of the   Creek   Nation.
Lochopocha[sic]
                                Postoffice   Tulsa

AFFIDAVIT OF MOTHER.

UNITED STATES OF AMERICA, Indian Territory,⎫
   Western   DISTRICT.   ⎬

    I, Nancy W. Fanning , on oath state that I am 31 years of age and a citizen by blood , of the Creek Nation; that I am the lawful wife of Bob Fanning , who is a citizen, by ----- of the U.S. Nation; that a female child was born to me on 14 day of June , 1902 , that said child has been named Nora Fanning , and was living March 4, 1905.

                                                    Nancy W. Fanning
Witnesses To Mark:
{

    Subscribed and sworn to before me this 1 day of May , 1905.

    Seal   Edw C Griesel
                                                       Notary Public.

AFFIDAVIT OF ATTENDING PHYSICIAN OR MID-WIFE.

UNITED STATES OF AMERICA, Indian Territory,⎫
   Western   DISTRICT.   ⎬

    I, Nora Burgess , a Midwife , on oath state that I attended on Mrs. Nancy W Fanning , wife of Bob Fanning on the 14 day of June , 1902 ; that there was born to her on said date a female child; that said child was living March 4, 1905, and is said to have been named Nora Fanning

                                                    Nora Burgess
Witnesses To Mark:
{

    Subscribed and sworn to before me this 1 day of May , 1905.

    Seal   Edw C Griesel
                                                       Notary Public.

Applications for Enrollment of Creek Newborn
Act of 1905   Volume IX

BIRTH AFFIDAVIT.
DEPARTMENT OF THE INTERIOR.
COMMISSION TO THE FIVE CIVILIZED TRIBES.

IN RE APPLICATION FOR ENROLLMENT, as a citizen of the Creek Nation, of Nora Fanning, born on the 14 day of June, 1902

Name of Father: Bob Fanning   a citizen of the   U.S.   Nation.
Name of Mother: Nancy Fanning   a citizen of the   Creek   Nation.
Roll #2125
                            Postoffice   Broken Arrow I.T.

AFFIDAVIT OF MOTHER.

UNITED STATES OF AMERICA, Indian Territory, ⎫
   Western   DISTRICT.   ⎬
                                              ⎭
                  now Nancy W. Jefferson
     I, Nancy Fanning (nee W. Davis), on oath state that I am 33 years of age and a citizen by blood, of the Creek Nation; that I ~~am~~ was the lawful wife of Bob Fanning, who is a citizen, by *(blank)* of the U.S. Nation; that a female child was born to me on ~~13~~ 14 day of June, 1902, that said child has been named Nora Fanning, and was living March 4, 1905.
                                 Nancy W. Jefferson
Witnesses To Mark:
{

     Subscribed and sworn to before me this 1 day of May, 1905.

     My Commission   J. McDermott
     Expires July 25" 1907   Notary Public.

NC 945.
                    Muskogee, Indian Territory, October 20, 1905.

Nancy W. Fanning,
     Care Bob Fanning,
          Tulsa, Indian Territory.

Dear Madam:

     In the matter of the application for the enrollment of Nora Fanning, born June 14, 1902, as a citizen by blood of the Creek Nation, this office is unable to identify you on its rolls of citizens of the Creek Nation; you are requested to state your maiden name, the

Applications for Enrollment of Creek Newborn
Act of 1905   Volume IX

names of your parents, the Creek Indian Town to which you belong the numbers which appear on your deeds to land in the Creek Nation.

        Respectfully,
           Commissioner.

NC 945.
        Muskogee, Indian Territory, December 16, 1905

Nancy W. Fanning,
  Care Bob Fanning,
    Tulsa, Indian Territory.

Dear Madam:

  In the matter of the application for the enrollment of Nora Fanning, born June 14, 1902, as a citizen by blood of the Creek Nation, this office is unable to identify you on its rolls of citizens of the Creek Nation, you are advised that this office is unable to identify you on its final rolls of citizens of the Creek Nation.

  You are requested to write this office at an early date giving your maiden name, the names of your parents and other members of your family, the Creek Indian Town to which you belong, and, if possible, your name and roll number as same appear on your allotment certificate or deeds to land in the Creek Nation.

  This matter should receive your immediate attention.

        Respectfully,
           Commissioner.

BIRTH AFFIDAVIT.
DEPARTMENT OF THE INTERIOR.
COMMISSION TO THE FIVE CIVILIZED TRIBES.

IN RE APPLICATION FOR ENROLLMENT, as a citizen of the Creek Nation, of Jennie Big Mosquito, born on the 21st day of February, 1905

Name of Father: Big Mosquito   a citizen of the   Creek   Nation.
Name of Mother: Jensey Big Mosquito   a citizen of the   Creek   Nation.

       Postoffice Bristow, Ind. Ter.

Applications for Enrollment of Creek Newborn
Act of 1905   Volume IX

AFFIDAVIT OF MOTHER.

UNITED STATES OF AMERICA, Indian Territory, }
 Western   DISTRICT.

I, Jensey Big Mosquito , on oath state that I am 32 years of age and a citizen by blood , of the Creek Nation; that I am the lawful wife of Big Mosquito , who is a citizen, by blood of the Creek Nation; that a female child was born to me on 21st day of February , 1905 , that said child has been named Jennie Big Mosquito , and was living March 4, 1905.

                                       her
                              Jensey x Big Mosquito
Witnesses To Mark: mark
 { John W Overstreet
   C C Dan Carlos

Subscribed and sworn to before me this 7th day of Aug , 1905.

                              John W Overstreet
                              Notary Public.

AFFIDAVIT OF ATTENDING PHYSICIAN OR MID-WIFE.

UNITED STATES OF AMERICA, Indian Territory, }
 Western   DISTRICT.

I, Salina Tiger , a mid wife , on oath state that I attended on Mrs. Jensey Big Mosquito , wife of Big Mosquito on the 21st day of February , 1905 ; that there was born to her on said date a female child; that said child was living March 4, 1905, and is said to have been named Jennie Big Mosquito

                              Salina Tiger
Witnesses To ~~Mark~~: Signature
 { John W Overstreet
   c c Dan Carlos

Subscribed and sworn to before me this 7th day of Aug , 1905.

                              John W Overstreet
                              Notary Public.

Applications for Enrollment of Creek Newborn
Act of 1905   Volume IX

BIRTH AFFIDAVIT.

DEPARTMENT OF THE INTERIOR,
COMMISSION TO THE FIVE CIVILIZED TRIBES.

In Re- Application for Enrollment, as a citizen of the Creek Nation, of Jennie Skeeter , born on the 21 day of Feby , 1905

Name of Father: Big Mosketer[sic] a citizen of the Creek Nation.
Name of Mother: Jenson Skeeter a citizen of the Creek Nation.

Post-office   Bristow Ind Tery

AFFIDAVIT OF MOTHER.

UNITED STATES OF AMERICA,
INDIAN TERRITORY,
Western   District.

I, Jenson Skeeter , on oath state that I am 32 years of age and a citizen by Birth , of the Creek Nation; that I am the lawful wife of Big Mosketer[sic] , who is a citizen, by birth of the Creek Nation; that a Female child was born to me on 21 day of Feby , 1905 , that said child has been named Jennie Skeeter , and is now living.

                                            her
                                    Jenson x Skeeter
Witnesses To Mark: mark
   { T.W. Flynn
     L.M. Wolfe

Subscribed and sworn to before me this 3 day of April, 1905.

                                    E.W. Sims
                                    Notary Public.

AFFIDAVIT OF ATTENDING PHYSICIAN OR MID-WIFE.

UNITED STATES OF AMERICA,
INDIAN TERRITORY,
Western   District.

I, Salina Tiger , a Midwife , on oath state that I attended on Mrs. Jenson Skeeter , wife of Big Mosketer on the 21 day of Feby , 1905; that there was born to her on said date a Female child; that said child is now living and is said to have been named Jennie Skeeter

                                   Salina Tiger

Applications for Enrollment of Creek Newborn
Act of 1905 Volume IX

Witnesses To Mark:
{ T.W. Flynn

Subscribed and sworn to before me this 3 day of April, 1905.

E.W. Sims
Notary Public.

NC-675

Muskogee, Indian Territory, August 14, 1905.

Jensey Big Mosquito,
    Care of Big Mosquito,
        Bristow, Indian Territory.

Dear Madam:

In the matter of the application for the enrollment of your minor daughter, Jennie Big Mosquito, as a citizen by blood of the Creek Nation, it will be necessary for you to furnish this Office with a proper proof of the birth of said child. A blank for that purpose which has been properly filled out, is herewith enclosed.

You are requested to appear before a notary public with Salina Tiger, midwife, who attended you at the birth of said child, swear to the affidavit, have the midwife sworn to, and return blank to this Office in the enclosed envelope.

                Respectfully,

                                Acting Commissioner.

JYM-14-2
Env

BIRTH AFFIDAVIT.
DEPARTMENT OF THE INTERIOR.
COMMISSION TO THE FIVE CIVILIZED TRIBES.

IN RE APPLICATION FOR ENROLLMENT, as a citizen of the Creek Nation, of Moses Warrener Drew, born on the 23 day of July, 1901

Name of Father: Clifton C Drew	a citizen of the U.S.	Nation.
Name of Mother: Emma Drew	a citizen of the Creek	Nation.

Applications for Enrollment of Creek Newborn
Act of 1905   Volume IX

Postoffice   Tulsa I.T.

AFFIDAVIT OF MOTHER.

UNITED STATES OF AMERICA, Indian Territory, ⎫
Western   DISTRICT.   ⎬

I, Emma Drew , on oath state that I am 29 years of age and a citizen by Blood , of the Creek Nation; that I am the lawful wife of Clifton C Drew , who is a citizen, by U.S. of the *(blank)* Nation; that a male child was born to me on 23^d day of July, 1901 , that said child has been named Moses Warrner[sic] Drew , and was living March 4, 1905.

Emma Drew

Witnesses To Mark:
{

Subscribed and sworn to before me this 6 day of April , 1905.

Wm *(Illegible)*
MY COMMISSION EXPIRES DEC. 15, 1907.   Notary Public.

AFFIDAVIT OF ATTENDING PHYSICIAN OR MID-WIFE.

UNITED STATES OF AMERICA, Indian Territory, ⎫
Western   DISTRICT.   ⎬

I, Mary E. Pearson , a Mid-wife , on oath state that I attended on Mrs. Emma Drew , wife of Clifton C Drew on the 23d day of July , 1901 ; that there was born to her on said date a male child; that said child was living March 4, 1905, and is said to have been named Moses Warrener Drew

ME Pearson

Witnesses To Mark:
{   *(Name Illegible)*

Subscribed and sworn to before me this 6 day of April , 1905.

Wm *(Illegible)*
MY COMMISSION EXPIRES DEC. 15, 1907.   Notary Public.

Applications for Enrollment of Creek Newborn
Act of 1905 Volume IX

BIRTH AFFIDAVIT.
DEPARTMENT OF THE INTERIOR.
COMMISSION TO THE FIVE CIVILIZED TRIBES.

IN RE APPLICATION FOR ENROLLMENT, as a citizen of the Creek Nation, of Wahnahka Sanger, born on the 6th day of November, 1903

Name of Father: Joseph C. Sanger   a citizen of the   Creek   Nation.
Name of Mother: Gertrude L. Sanger   a citizen of the   Creek   Nation.

Postoffice   Eufaula, Ind. Tery.

AFFIDAVIT OF MOTHER.

UNITED STATES OF AMERICA, Indian Territory,
Western   DISTRICT.

I, Gertrude L. Sanger, on oath state that I am Twenty-one years of age and a citizen by blood, of the Creek Nation; that I am the lawful wife of Joseph C. Sanger, who is a citizen, by blood of the Creek Nation; that a Femail[sic] child was born to me on Sixth day of November, 1903, that said child has been named Wah-nah-ka Sanger, and was living March 4, 1905.

                               Gertrude L Sanger
Witnesses To Mark:
{

Subscribed and sworn to before me this 13 day of March, 1905.

My Commission Expires Jan. 39, 1909.   Frank W Rushing
                                             Notary Public.

AFFIDAVIT OF ATTENDING PHYSICIAN OR MID-WIFE.

UNITED STATES OF AMERICA, Indian Territory,
Western District   DISTRICT.

I, Dr. R.M. Counterman, a Physician, on oath state that I attended on Mrs. Gertrude L. Sanger, wife of Joe C. Sanger on the sixth day of November, 1903 : that there was born to her on said date a female child; that said child was living March 4, 1905, and is said to have been named Wahnahka

                               R.M. Counterman, M.D.
Witnesses To Mark:
{

22

Applications for Enrollment of Creek Newborn
Act of 1905 Volume IX

Subscribed and sworn to before me 1st day of April, 1905.

My Commission Expires Jan. 39, 1909.

Frank W Rushing
Notary Public.

BIRTH AFFIDAVIT.

DEPARTMENT OF THE INTERIOR.
COMMISSION TO THE FIVE CIVILIZED TRIBES.

IN RE APPLICATION FOR ENROLLMENT, as a citizen of the CREEK Nation, of Theodore Adams, born on the 11 day of Jan, 1904

Name of Father: George W. Adams   a citizen of the   Creek   Nation.
Name of Mother: Sarah   "   a citizen of the   "   Nation.

Postoffice   Beggs

(Child present)

AFFIDAVIT OF MOTHER.

UNITED STATES OF AMERICA, Indian Territory,
     WESTERN   DISTRICT.

     I, Sarah Adams, on oath state that I am 34 years of age and a citizen by blood, of the Creek Nation; that I am the lawful wife of George W Adams, who is a citizen, by blood of the Creek Nation; that a male child was born to me on 11 day of Jany, 1904, that said child has been named Theodore Adams, and is now living.

                       Sarah Adams

Witnesses To Mark:

     Subscribed and sworn to before me this 31" day of March, 1905.

                       Edw C Griesel
                       Notary Public.

Applications for Enrollment of Creek Newborn
Act of 1905 Volume IX

AFFIDAVIT OF ATTENDING PHYSICIAN OR MID-WIFE.

UNITED STATES OF AMERICA, Indian Territory, }
Western   DISTRICT.

I, Aggie Washington a ...., on oath state that I attended on Mrs. ...., wife of .... on the .... day of ...., 1.......; that there was born to her on said date a .... child; that said child is now living and is said to have been named ....

Witnesses To Mark:
{ ....
  .... }

Subscribed and sworn to before me this ....day of ...., 1........

Notary Public.

AFFIDAVIT OF ATTENDING PHYSICIAN OR MID-WIFE.

UNITED STATES OF AMERICA, Indian Territory, }
Western   DISTRICT.

I, Maggie Washington , a woman , on oath state that I attended on Mrs. Sarrah Adams , wife of G. Washington Adams on the 11th day of January , 1904 ; that there was born to her on said date a Male child; that said child is now living and is said to have been named Theodore Adams

                                        Maggie Washington
Witnesses To Mark:
{ (Name Illegible)
  Dixon Washington

Subscribed and sworn to before me this fourth day of April, 1905.
My Com Ex
March 28 1907   Earl Brown
                                        Notary Public.

Applications for Enrollment of Creek Newborn
Act of 1905 Volume IX

DEPARTMENT OF THE INTERIOR,
COMMISSION TO THE FIVE CIVILIZED TRIBES.
Eufaula, I. T., April 3, 1905.

In the matter of the application for the enrollment of Tommie Osawah (or Crow) as a citizen by blood of the Creek Nation.

MELISSA OSAWAH 9Or[sic] Crow) being duly sworn, testified as follows:

BY COMMISSION:
Q What is your name? A Melissa Osawah.
Q How old are you? A About thirty-two.
Q What is your post office address? A Mellette.
Q Are you a citizen of the Creek Nation? A Yes, sir.
Q To what town do you belong? A Weogufke.
Q Do you make application for the enrollment of your minor child, Tommie Osawah, as a citizen of the Creek Nation? A Yes, sir.
Q What is the name of his father? A George Osawah or Crow.
Q Is he a citizen of the Creek Nation? A No, sir, Seminole.
Q Is he your lawful husband? A Yes, sir.
Q If it should be found that your child Tommie Osawah, is entitles to enrollment in either the Creek or Seminole Nations, in which nation do you desire to have him enrolled? A In the Creek Nation.

---oooOOOooo---

I, D. C. Skaggs, on oath state that the above and foregoing is a full and true transcript of my stenographic notes as taken in said cause on said date.

DC Skaggs

Subscribed and sworn to before me this 21 day of July, 1905.

J McDermott
Notary Public.

Applications for Enrollment of Creek Newborn
Act of 1905   Volume IX

NC. 679.

Muskogee, Indian Territory, July 15, 1905.

Chief Clerk,
   Seminole Enrollment Division,
     Muskogee, Indian Territory.

Dear Sir:

    April 7, 1905, application was made to the Commission to the Five Civilized Tribes for the enrollment of Tommy Osowah[sic], born December 30, 1903, as a citizen by blood of the Creek Nation. It is stated in said application that the father of said child is George Osowah, a citizen of the Seminole Nation, and that the mother is Melissa Osowah, a citizen of the Creek Nation.

    You are requested to inform the Creek Enrollment Division as to whether application has been made for the enrollment of said Tommy Osowah, as a citizen of the Seminole Nation, and if so, what disposition has been made of the same.

               Respectfully,
                        Commissioner.

DEPARTMENT OF THE INTERIOR.
COMMISSION TO THE FIVE CIVILIZED TRIBES.

Muskogee, Indian Territory, July 19, 1905.

Chief Clerk,
   Creek Enrollment Division.

Dear Sir:

    Receipt is acknowledged of your letter of July 15, 1905 (NC-679) stating that application was made to the Commission to the Five Civilized Tribes for the enrollment of Tommy Osowah, born December 30, 1903, child of George Osowah, a citizen of the Seminole Nation, and Melissa Osowah, a citizen of the Creek Nation, as a citizen by blood of the Creek Nation and requesting to be advised as to whether application has been made for the enrollment of said child as a citizen of the Seminole Nation.

    In reply to your letter you are informed that it does not appear from an examination of the records of this office that any application was made to the Commission to the Five Civilized Tribes for the enrollment of said Tommy Osowah as a citizen of the Seminole Nation.

               Respectfully,
                 Tams Bixby   Commissioner.

Applications for Enrollment of Creek Newborn
Act of 1905 Volume IX

BIRTH AFFIDAVIT.
DEPARTMENT OF THE INTERIOR.
COMMISSION TO THE FIVE CIVILIZED TRIBES.

IN RE APPLICATION FOR ENROLLMENT, as a citizen of the Creek Nation, of Tommy Osawah (or Crow), born on the 30 day of December, 1903

Name of Father: George Osawah (or Crow) a citizen of the Seminole Nation.
Name of Mother: Melissa Osawah (or Crow) a citizen of the Creek Nation.
Weogufky Town
       Postoffice Mellette, Ind. Ter.

AFFIDAVIT OF MOTHER.

UNITED STATES OF AMERICA, Indian Territory, ⎱
 Western DISTRICT. ⎰ Child is present

  I, Melissa Osawah (or Crow), on oath state that I am about 32 years of age and a citizen by blood, of the Creek Nation; that I am the lawful wife of George Osawah (or Crow), who is a citizen, by blood of the Seminole Nation; that a male child was born to me on 30 day of December, 1903, that said child has been named Tommy Osawah (or Crow), and was living March 4, 1905.

          her
       Melissa x Osawah (or Crow)
Witnesses To Mark: mark
 { Alex Posey
  DC Skaggs

  Subscribed and sworn to before me this 3 day of April, 1905.

       Drennan C Skaggs
        Notary Public.

AFFIDAVIT OF ATTENDING PHYSICIAN OR MID-WIFE.

UNITED STATES OF AMERICA, Indian Territory, ⎱
 Western DISTRICT. ⎰

  I, Kizzie Givens, a midwife, on oath state that I attended on Mrs. Melissa Osawah (or Crow), wife of George Osawah (or Crow) on the 30 day of December, 1903 ; that there was born to her on said date a male child; that said child was living March 4, 1905, and is said to have been named Tommy Osawah (or Crow)

Applications for Enrollment of Creek Newborn
Act of 1905 Volume IX

Witnesses To Mark:
{ Alex Posey
  DC Skaggs

her
Kizzie x Givens
mark

Subscribed and sworn to before me 3 day of April, 1905.

Drennan C Skaggs
Notary Public.

_____

NC 679

Muskogee, Indian Territory, November 13, 1906

Chief Clerk,
    Seminole Enrollment Division,
        General Office.

Dear Sir:

    You are hereby advised that the name of Tommy Crow born December 30, 1903 to George Osa wah, an alleged citizen of the Seminole Nation and Melissa Crow, a citizen by blood of the Creek Nation, is contained in schedule of minor citizens by blood of the Creek Nation, approved by the Secretary of the Interior September 27, 1905, opposite Roll number 637.

Respectfully,
Commissioner.

_____

(The letter below typed as given)

Tulsa Sep 6 1905

Hon Tams Bixby

    Please inform me if my daughter Amy Amanda Jack enrollment to file on land has been approved and sented back to you office if so please inform me at once. My roll No. 2788 allotment deed 40 and homestead deed 39 Please sended me Township 19 range 11 township 16 range 11 township 19 range 11 township 14 range 11

Alice Jack

Applications for Enrollment of Creek Newborn
Act of 1905 Volume IX

BIRTH AFFIDAVIT.
DEPARTMENT OF THE INTERIOR,
COMMISSIONER TO THE FIVE CIVILIZED TRIBES.

IN RE APPLICATION FOR ENROLLMENT, as a citizen of the Creek Nation, of Mandy Amy Jack , born on the 8 day of March , 1902

Name of Father: John Jack   a citizen of the   U.S.   Nation.
Name of Mother: Alice Jack   a citizen of the   Creek   Nation.

Postoffice   Tulsa Ind Ter

AFFIDAVIT OF MOTHER.

UNITED STATES OF AMERICA, Indian Territory,
Western   District.

I, Alice Jack , on oath state that I am 27 years of age and a citizen by Blood , of the Creek Nation; that I am the lawful wife of John Jack , who is a citizen, by Blood of the U.S. Nation; that a Female child was born to me on 8 day of March, 1902 , that said child has been named Mandy Amy Jack , and was living March 4, 1905.

Mrs Alice Jack
Witness to Mark:

Subscribed and sworn to before me this 27 day of March , 1905.

Robert E Lynch
Com Ex 7/3/1906   Notary Public.

AFFIDAVIT OF ATTENDING PHYSICIAN OR MID-WIFE.

UNITED STATES OF AMERICA, Indian Territory,
Western   District.

I, Elizabeth Bewley , a Midwife , on oath state that I attended on Mrs. Alice Jack , wife of John Jack on the 8 day of March , 1902 ; that there was born to her on said date a Female child; that said child was living March 4, 1905, and is said to have been named Mandy Amy Jack

Elizabeth Bewley
Witness to Mark:

Subscribed and sworn to before me this 27 day of March , 1905.

Applications for Enrollment of Creek Newborn
Act of 1905 Volume IX

Com Ex 7/3/1906

Robert E Lynch
Notary Public.

BIRTH AFFIDAVIT.

DEPARTMENT OF THE INTERIOR.
COMMISSION TO THE FIVE CIVILIZED TRIBES.

IN RE APPLICATION FOR ENROLLMENT, as a citizen of the Creek Nation, of George McGilbray, born on the 2 day of August, 1904

Name of Father: Jackson McGilbray   a citizen of the   Creek   Nation.
(Illegible)
Name of Mother: Nicey McGilbray   a citizen of the   Creek   Nation.
Tuckabatche
                          Postoffice   Indianola Ind Ter.

AFFIDAVIT OF MOTHER.

UNITED STATES OF AMERICA, Indian Territory,
    Western   DISTRICT.   Child is present

    I, Nicey McGilbray, on oath state that I am 22 years of age and a citizen by blood, of the Creek Nation; that I am the lawful wife of Jackson McGilbray, who is a citizen, by blood of the Creek Nation; that a male child was born to me on 2 day of August, 1904, that said child has been named George McGilbray, and was living March 4, 1905. That no one attended on me as midwife or physician at the birth of the child

                                  her
                          Nicey x McGilbray
Witnesses To Mark: mark
 { Alex Posey
   D C Skaggs

    Subscribed and sworn to before me this 4 day of April, 1905.

                            Drennan C Skaggs
                                Notary Public.

Applications for Enrollment of Creek Newborn
Act of 1905 Volume IX

Acquaintance
AFFIDAVIT OF ~~ATTENDING PHYSICIAN OR MID-WIFE~~.

UNITED STATES OF AMERICA, Indian Territory,
Western DISTRICT.

                                                                  am acquainted with
I, Cooper Holoby, ~~a~~ *(blank)*, on oath state that I attended on Mrs. Nicey McGilbray, wife of Jackson McGilbray ~~on the (blank) day of (blank), 190~~; that there was born to her on said date a male child; that said child was living March 4, 1905, and is said to have been named George McGilbray

                                                                   Cooper Holoby

Witnesses To Mark:
{ Alex Posey
{ DC Skaggs

        Subscribed and sworn to before me 4 day of April, 1905.

                                                        Drennan C Skaggs
                                                        Notary Public.

AFFIDAVIT OF TWO DISINTERESTED WITNESSES.

United States of America, (
Western District,   (ss.
Indian Territory.   (

        I   I am
    ~~We~~, the undersigned, on oath state that ~~we are~~ personally acquainted with Nicey McGilbray the unlawful wife of Jackson McGilbray; that there was born to her a male child on or about the 2^d day of August, 1904; that the child has been named George McGilbray; and that said child was living March 4, 1905.
        I   I
    ~~We~~ further state that ~~we~~ have no interest in this case.

Witnesses to mark.   her
Jesse McDermott   Kizzie x Givens
                                                                   mark

(Name Illegible)

Subscribed and sworn to before me,
this 24 day of January, 1907.
                                                        J McDermott
                       My Commission   Notary Public.
                     Expires July 25' 1907

Applications for Enrollment of Creek Newborn
Act of 1905 Volume IX

BIRTH AFFIDAVIT.
DEPARTMENT OF THE INTERIOR.
COMMISSION TO THE FIVE CIVILIZED TRIBES.

IN RE APPLICATION FOR ENROLLMENT, as a citizen of the Creek Nation, of George McGilbray, born on the 2 day of August, 1904

Name of Father: Jackson McGilbray   a citizen of the Creek Nation.
(Illegible) Town
Name of Mother: Nicey McGilbray (nee Fish)   a citizen of the Creek Nation.
Tuckabatche Town
                     Postoffice   Indianola, Ind. Ter.

AFFIDAVIT OF MOTHER.

UNITED STATES OF AMERICA, Indian Territory,
     Western   DISTRICT.   Child is present

I, Nicey McGilbray, on oath state that I am 22 years of age and a citizen by blood, of the Creek Nation; that I am the lawful wife of Jackson McGilbray, who is a citizen, by blood of the Creek Nation; that a male child was born to me on 2 day of August, 1904, that said child has been named George McGilbray, and was living March 4, 1905. That no one attended on me as midwife or physician at the birth of the child.
                                her
                          Nicey x McGilbray
Witnesses To Mark: mark
{ Alex Posey
{ DC Skaggs

     Subscribed and sworn to before me this 4 day of April, 1905.

                          Drennan C Skaggs
                             Notary Public.

AFFIDAVIT OF ATTENDING PHYSICIAN OR MID-WIFE.

UNITED STATES OF AMERICA, Indian Territory,
     Western   DISTRICT.
                                      am acquainted with
I, Cooper Holoby, a ~~(blank)~~, on oath state that I ~~attended on~~ Mrs. Nicey McGilbray, wife of Jackson McGilbray ~~on the (blank) day of (blank), 190~~; that

Applications for Enrollment of Creek Newborn
Act of 1905   Volume IX

there was born to her on ~~said date~~ August 2, 1904 a male child; that said child was living March 4, 1905, and is said to have been named George McGilbray

Cooper Halepy[sic]

Witnesses To Mark:
{ Alex Posey
  DC Skaggs

Subscribed and sworn to before me 4 day of April, 1905.

Drennan C Skaggs
Notary Public.

NC 681. OCH

DEPARTMENT OF THE INTERIOR,
COMMISSIONER TO THE FIVE CIVILIZED TRIBES.

In the matter of the application for the enrollment of George McGilbray, as a citizen by blood of the Creek Nation.

DECISION.

The record in this case shows that on April 7, 1905, application was made, in affidavit form, for the enrollment of George McGilbray, as a citizen by blood of the Creek Nation, under the provisions of the act of Congress approved March 3, 1905 (33 Stats., 1048. Supplemental affidavit as to the date of birth of said child was filed January 25, 1907.

The evidence and the records of this office show that said George McGilbray is the child of Nicey McGilbray, whose name appears as "Nicey Fish" on a schedule of citizens by blood of the Creek Nation, approved by the Secretary of the Interior March 28, 1902, opposite number 8816, and Jackson McGilbray, whose name appears upon a partial schedule of citizens by blood of the Creek Nation, approved by the Secretary of the Interior March 13, 1902, opposite number 1397.

The evidence further shows that said George McGilbray was born August 2, 1904, and that said child was living on March 4, 1905.

It is, therefore, ordered and adjudged that said George McGilbray is entitled to be enrolled as a citizen by blood of the Creek Nation under the provisions of the Act of Congress approved March 3, 1905 (33 Stat. L., 1048), and the application for her[sic] enrollment as such is accordingly granted.

Tams Bixby COMMISSIONER.

Muskogee, Indian Territory.
FEB 2- 1907

Applications for Enrollment of Creek Newborn
Act of 1905 Volume IX

REFER IN REPLY TO THE FOLLOWING:
NC-681.

DEPARTMENT OF THE INTERIOR,
COMMISSIONER TO THE FIVE CIVILIZED TRIBES.

Muskogee, Indian Territory, August 15, 1905.

Nicey McGilbray,
   c/o Jackson McGilbray,
      Indianola, Indian Territory.

Dear Madam:

    In the matter of the application for the enrollment of your minor son George McGilbray, born August 2, 1904. as a citizen by blood of the Creek Nation, it will be necessary for you to furnish this office with the affidavit of an additional disinterested witness as to the birth of said child. Said affidavit must set forth said child's name, the date of his birth, the names of his parents and whether or not he was living on March 4, 1905.

    You are requested to immediately inform this office as to the names of the parents of your husband Jackson McGilbray, the Creek Indian town to which he belongs and if possible his final roll number as the same appears upon his allotment certificate and deeds. This information is desired in order that he may be identified upon the final roll of citizens by blood of the Creek Nation.

                                          Respectfully,

                                                  Wm. O. Beall
                                                  Acting Commissioner.

NC-681.

                            Muskogee, Indian Territory, October 17, 1905.

Nicey McGilbray,
   c/o Jackson McGilbray,
      Indianola, Indian Territory.

Dear Madam:

    In the matter of the application for the enrollment of your minor son George McGilbray, born August 2, 1904, as a citizen by blood of the Creek Nation, it will be necessary for you to furnish this office with the affidavit of an additional disinterested witness as to the birth of said child. Said affidavit must set forth said child's name, the date of his birth, the names of his parents and whether or not he was living on March 4, 1905.

    You are requested to immediately inform this office as to the name of the parents of your husband, Jackson McGilbray, the Creek Indian town to which he belongs and if possible his final roll number as the same appears upon his allotment certificate and

Applications for Enrollment of Creek Newborn
Act of 1905   Volume IX

deeds. This information is desired in order that he may be identified upon the final roll of citizens by blood of the Creek Nation.

        Respectfully,

            Commissioner.

NC 681.

        Muskogee, Indian Territory, January 14, 1907.

Cooper Holluby,
  Mellette, Indian Territory.

Dear Sir:

  You are requested to deliver the enclosed letter to Nicey McGilbra, same having been returned from Indianola, Indian Territory unclcimed[sic] by her.

  You are further requested to explain the matter to her and urge her to furnish proof therein requested within ten days.

        Respectfully,

            Commissioner.

LM-681.

N C 681.

        Muskogee, Indian Territory, March 7, 1907.

Nicey McGilbray,
  Care of Jackson McGilbray,
    Indianola, Indian Territory.

Dear Madam:

  You are hereby advised that on March 2, 1907 the Secretary of the Interior approved the enrollment of your minor child, George McGilbray, as a citizen by blood of the Creek Nation, and that the name of said child appears upon the roll of New Born citizens by blood of the Creek Nation, enrolled under the Act of Congress approved March 3, 1905, as number 1234.

  This child is now entitled to allotment and application therefor should be made without delay at the Creek Land Office, Muskogee, Indian Territory.

        Respectfully,

            Commissioner.

Applications for Enrollment of Creek Newborn
Act of 1905   Volume IX

BIRTH AFFIDAVIT.

DEPARTMENT OF THE INTERIOR.
COMMISSION TO THE FIVE CIVILIZED TRIBES.

IN RE APPLICATION FOR ENROLLMENT, as a citizen of the CREEK Nation, of Eli Casey, born on the 1 day of Oct, 1904

Name of Father: John Casey   a citizen of the   Creek   Nation.
Name of Mother: Savanah Casey   a citizen of the   Creek   Nation.

         Postoffice   Oktaha[sic], I.T.

AFFIDAVIT OF MOTHER.

UNITED STATES OF AMERICA, Indian Territory, ⎫
     WESTERN   DISTRICT. ⎬

     I, Savanah Casey , on oath state that I am 18 years of age and a citizen by blood, of the Creek Nation; that I am the lawful wife of John Casey , who is a citizen, by blood of the Creek Nation; that a male child was born to me on 1 day of Oct, 1904 , that said child has been named Eli Casey , and is now living.

                                        Savannah Casey
Witnesses To Mark:
{

     Subscribed and sworn to before me this 30 day of March , 1905.

                                        W.A. Cain
                                            Notary Public.

AFFIDAVIT OF ATTENDING PHYSICIAN OR MID-WIFE.

UNITED STATES OF AMERICA, Indian Territory, ⎫
     WESTERN   DISTRICT. ⎬

     I, Lettie Evans , a Midwife , on oath state that I attended on Mrs. Savanah Casey , wife of John Casey on the 1 day of Oct , 1904 ; that there was born to her on said date a male child; that said child is now living and is said to have been named Eli Casey

                                        Lettie Evans
Witnesses To Mark:
{

Applications for Enrollment of Creek Newborn
Act of 1905 Volume IX

Subscribed and sworn to before me this 30 day of March, 1905.

                                 W.A. Cain
                                 Notary Public.

BIRTH AFFIDAVIT.

DEPARTMENT OF THE INTERIOR.
COMMISSION TO THE FIVE CIVILIZED TRIBES.

IN RE APPLICATION FOR ENROLLMENT, as a citizen of the CREEK Nation, of Vera Irene Casey, born on the 7 day of Dec, 1901

Name of Father: John Casey   a citizen of the   *(blank)*   Nation.
Name of Mother: Savanah Casey   a citizen of the   *(blank)*   Nation.

                   Postoffice   Oktaha[sic], I.T.

AFFIDAVIT OF MOTHER.

UNITED STATES OF AMERICA, Indian Territory, ⎫
     WESTERN   DISTRICT. ⎭

     I, Savanah Casey, on oath state that I am 18 years of age and a citizen by blood, of the Creek Nation; that I am the lawful wife of John Casey, who is a citizen, by blood of the Creek Nation; that a Female child was born to me on 7th day of Dec, 1901, that said child has been named Vera Irene Casey, and is now living.

                                   Savannah Casey

Witnesses To Mark:
{

Subscribed and sworn to before me this 30 day of March, 1905.

                                 W.A. Cain
                                 Notary Public.

AFFIDAVIT OF ATTENDING PHYSICIAN OR MID-WIFE.

UNITED STATES OF AMERICA, Indian Territory, ⎫
     WESTERN   DISTRICT. ⎭

     I, Lettie Evans, a Midwife, on oath state that I attended on Mrs. Savanah Casey, wife of John Casey on the 7 day of Dec, 1901; that there was born to her on

Applications for Enrollment of Creek Newborn
Act of 1905 Volume IX

said date a Female child; that said child is now living and is said to have been named Vera Irene Casey

Lettie Evans

Witnesses To Mark:
{

Subscribed and sworn to before me this 30 day of March, 1905.

W.A. Cain
Notary Public.

BIRTH AFFIDAVIT.

DEPARTMENT OF THE INTERIOR.
COMMISSION TO THE FIVE CIVILIZED TRIBES.

IN RE APPLICATION FOR ENROLLMENT, as a citizen of the CREEK Nation, of Alvro Edgar Casey, born on the 29 day of Mar, 1903

Name of Father: John Casey   a citizen of the   Creek   Nation.
Name of Mother: Savanah Casey   a citizen of the   Creek   Nation.

Postoffice   Oktaha[sic], I.T.

AFFIDAVIT OF MOTHER.

UNITED STATES OF AMERICA, Indian Territory, }
    WESTERN   DISTRICT.   }

I, Savanah Casey, on oath state that I am 18 years of age and a citizen by blood, of the Creek Nation; that I am the lawful wife of John Casey, who is a citizen, by blood of the Creek Nation; that a male child was born to me on 29 day of March, 1903, that said child has been named Alvro Edgar Casey, and is now living.

Savannah Casey

Witnesses To Mark:
{

Subscribed and sworn to before me this 30 day of March, 1905.

W.A. Cain
Notary Public.

Applications for Enrollment of Creek Newborn
Act of 1905   Volume IX

AFFIDAVIT OF ATTENDING PHYSICIAN OR MID-WIFE.

UNITED STATES OF AMERICA, Indian Territory,
WESTERN DISTRICT.

I, Lillie Evans , a Midwife , on oath state that I attended on Mrs. Savanah Casey , wife of John Casey on the 29 day of March , 1903 ; that there was born to her on said date a male child; that said child is now living and is said to have been named Alvro Edgar Casey

Lillie Evans

Witnesses To Mark:

{

Subscribed and sworn to before me this 30 day of March , 1905.

W.A. Cain
Notary Public.

NC-683

DEPARTMENT OF THE INTERIOR,
COMMISSIONER TO THE FIVE CIVILIZED TRIBES.
Muskogee, Indian Territory, August 1, 1905.

In the matter of the application for the enrollment of Alex Clark as a citizen by blood of the Creek Nation.

Betsy Phillips, being duly sworn, testified as follows (through Jesse McDermott, Official Interpreter):

EXAMINATION BY THE COMMISSION:
Q What is your name? A Betsy Phillips.
Q How old are you? A I don't know exactly.

Witness seems to be about sixty.

Q What is your postoffice? A Eufaula
Q Do you know Alex Clark, a child of George and Louisa Clark? A Yes sir.
Q Is Alex living? A Yes sir. He was living when I left home.
Q Is he any kin to you? A Yes sir.
Q Grand-son? A Yes sir.
Q Your daughter's child? A Yes sir.
Q Were you the midwife--did you act as midwife when the child was born? A Yes sir.

Applications for Enrollment of Creek Newborn
Act of 1905   Volume IX

Q Well, Betsy, you have executed affidavits here in which the month when this child was born does not agree; in one you say one month and in another you say another month. When was this child born, do you know? A In the first affidavit that I have executed I stated that it was on the 19th day of April, and I know that is correct.
Q In the last affidavit you executed, the one you executed with the father of the child, George, you said April; in the first one you made in the same you year the child was born, you said May. A It must certainly be a mistake of the notary public.
Q You said April four times, but the first time he put it down wrong; is that right?
A Yes, I said April.
Q You remember saying that the first time two years ago; do you re-member[sic] that; how old was the child when you went there? A The child was over a year when he made out--
Q At the time the affidavits were made out by P. F. Turner it was in the same spring that the child was born; are you certain that the child was more than three days old when you went there? A It was over three days old. It was born in the same year, in the same spring.
Q It was over three days old; that is all you remember? A That's all I remember.
Q Your memory of the months is not very good? A No sir.
Q Your daughter, Louisa, is dead now, is she? A Yes sir.
Q She died last year? A Yes sir.

George Clark, being duly sworn, testified as follows:

EXAMINATION BY THE COMMISSION:
Q What is your name? A George Clark.
Q How old are you? A About 26.
Q What is your postoffice? A Eufaula.
Q Are you a citizen of the Creek Nation? A No, sir.
Q Mr. Clark, is your wife, Louisa, dead? A Yes sir.
Q When did she die, to the best of your remembrance? A The first of the year.
Q What year, 1904? A Yes sir.
Q Early part of 1904? A Yes sir.
Q Did you put it down--did you make any record of her death? A No, I have made no record of it.
Q Is your child, Alex Clark, living? A Yes sir.
Q When was he born, to the best of your remembrance? A In April, 1903.
Q Certain of that? A Yes sir.
Q We have here affidavits that say in the month of May, and they were made in the same year that the child was born and before your wife died; and her mother, the midwife here, also stated in the month of May, 1903. You made affidavit stating that the child was born in April, 1903. That was when the baby was young, when it was fresh in their minds. Why are you so positive about April? What makes you know it was in April instead of May? A It is my best recollection.
Q Have you got it down some where? A I have it in my book at home.
Q Did you look before you came here? A Yes sir.

Applications for Enrollment of Creek Newborn
Act of 1905   Volume IX

Q After refreshing your mind, you now say it was in Aril, 1903-- is that right? A Yes sir.
Q Your mother-in-law, that lady, says that she made out an affidavit along with you stating April. She now says it was April. She says she meant to say April when before Notary Public; he put it down May. Where is this child living? A With its grandmother.
Q With this lady, Betsy? A Yes sir.
Q Is she as much as two years old? A Yes sir.
Q You don't exactly know how many months over? A Yes sir.

INDIAN TERRITORY, Western District.,
    I, J. Y. Miller, a stenographer to the Commissioner to the Five Civilized Tribes, do hereby certify that the above and foregoing is a true and complete translation of my notes as same appear in my stenographic report of this case.

                              JY Miller
Sworn to and subscribed before me
this the 3rd day of August, 1905.
                              Edw C Griesel
                              Notary Public.

Cr NC-683
                          Muskogee, Indian Territory, July 19, 1905.

George Clark,
    Eufaula, Indian Territory.

Dear Sir:

    In the matter of the application for the enrollment of your minor child, Alex Clark, as a citizen by blood of the Creek Nation, You are advised that it will be necessary for you and the midwife in attendance at his birth to appear at this office at an early date, for the purpose of being examined under oath.

                            Respectfully,
                                  Commissioner.

    Indian Territory
Western District.

Personally appeared before me a Notary Public of the above named District, Lewis Guinn and W.A. Lawson, who being duly Sworn depose and say; We are well acquainted with Alex. Clark son of George and Louisa Clark, and that he was born on the 19th day of April 19o3[sic], and that he is now living.

Applications for Enrollment of Creek Newborn
Act of 1905 Volume IX

Lewis Guinn
W.H. Lawson

Subscribed and sworn to before me this 19th day of August, 19o3.
Aug 1-1906
Thos. F. *(Illegible)*
Notary Public.

BIRTH AFFIDAVIT.
DEPARTMENT OF THE INTERIOR.
COMMISSION TO THE FIVE CIVILIZED TRIBES.

IN RE APPLICATION FOR ENROLLMENT, as a citizen of the Creek Nation, of Alex Clarke[sic], born on the 19 day of April, 1903

Name of Father: George Clarke   a citizen of the United States Nation.
Name of Mother: Louisa Clarke (nee Phillips)   a citizen of the Creek Nation.
Tuskegee Town
                          Postoffice   Eufaula, Ind. Terr.

AFFIDAVIT OF MOTHER.   Child present.

UNITED STATES OF AMERICA, Indian Territory,
    Western   **DISTRICT.**

I, George Clark, on oath state that I am 26 years of age and a citizen by -----, of the United States Nation; that I ~~am~~ was the lawful ~~wife~~ husband of Louisa Clark, who ~~is~~ was a citizen, by blood of the Creek Nation; that a male child was born to ~~me~~ her on 19 day of April, 1903, that said child has been named Alex Clark, and was living March 4, 1905. That the mother, Louisa Clark, died last December a year ago.

                                his
                        George x Clark
Witnesses To Mark: mark
  { DC Skaggs
  { Alex Posey

Subscribed and sworn to before me this 4 day of April, 1905.

                        Drennan C Skaggs
                        Notary Public.

Applications for Enrollment of Creek Newborn
Act of 1905   Volume IX

AFFIDAVIT OF ATTENDING PHYSICIAN OR MID-WIFE.

UNITED STATES OF AMERICA, Indian Territory,
Western   DISTRICT.

my daughter
I, Betsey Phillips , a mid-wife , on oath state that I attended on ^ Mrs. Louisa Clark , wife of George Clark on the 19 day of April , 1903 ; that there was born to her on said date a male child; that said child was living March 4, 1905, and is said to have been named Alex Clark That the mother, Louisa Clark died in December 1903.

                                     her
                              Betsey x Phillips
Witnesses To Mark: mark
  { DC Skaggs
    Alex Posey

Subscribed and sworn to before me 4 day of April, 1905.

                           Drennan C Skaggs
                           Notary Public.

BIRTH AFFIDAVIT.

DEPARTMENT OF THE INTERIOR,
COMMISSION TO THE FIVE CIVILIZED TRIBES.

In Re Application for Enrollment, as a citizen of the Creek Nation, of Alex Clark, born on the 19 day of May, 1903

Name of Father: George Clark   a citizen of the   U.S.   Nation.
Name of Father: Louisa Clark   a citizen of the   Creek Nation.

                Post-office   Eufaula I T

AFFIDAVIT OF MOTHER.

UNITED STATES OF AMERICA,
INDIAN TERRITORY,
Western   District.

I, Louisa Clark , on oath state that I am 19 years of age and a citizen by blood , of the Creek Nation; that I am the lawful wife of George Clark , who is a citizen, by marriage of the Creek Nation; that a male child was born to me on 19th day of May , 1903 , that said child has been named Alex Clark , and is now living.

                                     her
                           Louisa Clark x
                                   mark

Applications for Enrollment of Creek Newborn
Act of 1905   Volume IX

WITNESSES TO MARK:
{ James B Pike
{ B.W. Tarrey

Subscribed and sworn to before me this 22 day of May , 1903
Aug 1 1906

Thos. F. *(Illegible)*
NOTARY PUBLIC.

AFFIDAVIT OF ATTENDING PHYSICIAN OR MID-WIFE.

UNITED STATES OF AMERICA, }
INDIAN TERRITORY,
Western   District.

I, Betsy Phillips , a Midwife , on oath state that I attended on Mrs. Louisa Clark , wife of George Clark on the 19 day of May , 1903 ; that there was born to her on said date a male child; that said child is now living and is said to have been named Alex Clark

              her
         Betsy Phillips x
WITNESSES TO MARK: mark
{ James B Pike
{ B.W. Tarrey

Subscribed and sworn to before me this 22 day of May , 1903
Aug 1 1906

Thos. F. *(Illegible)*
NOTARY PUBLIC.

NC-684
DEPARTMENT OF THE INTERIOR,
COMMISSIONER TO THE FIVE CIVILIZED TRIBES.

Muskogee, Indian Territory, December 4, 1905

  In the matter of the application for the enrollment of Roley Fixico as a citizen by blood of the Creek Nation.

  Basta Fixico, being duly sworn, testified as follows (through Jesse McDermott, Official Interpreter):

Applications for Enrollment of Creek Newborn
Act of 1905   Volume IX

EXAMINATION BY THE COMMISSIONER:
Q What is your name? A Basta Fixico.
Q What is the name of your father? A Tharlip Harjo.
Q What is your postoffice? A Weleetka.
Q What is the name of your mother? A Sarfarcher Deer.
Q How do you come to be enrolled as Basta Fixico? A There is a man in our family by the name Fixico and they got us down on the pay rolls that way. I guess the Dawes Commission enrolled us that way. My name ought to be Harjo. I was enrolled as Basta Fixico.

       The witness is identified as Bastie Fixico on Creek Indian card, field No. 1443, Roll No. 4579.

Q Have you a child named Roley? A Yes sir.
Q Is he living? A Yes sir. There she is, here.
Q What is the name of the mother of Roley? A Jemima Fixico.
Q You know what her name was before? A Jemima Jones.
Q What was her father's name? A Washington Jones.
Q Mother's name? A Sallie Jones.

       Said mother is identified as Jemima Jones on Creek Indian card, Field No. 4690.

Q Its name is Roley Fixico, is it? A Yes sir.

INDIAN TERRITORY, Western District.
       I, J. Y. Miller, a stenographer to the Commissioner to the Five Civilized Tribes, do hereby certify that the above and foregoing is a true and complete translation of my notes as same appear in my stenographic report of this case.

                            JY Miller
Sworn and subscribed to before me
this the 7th day of December,
1905.   J McDermott
                                    Notary Public.

BIRTH AFFIDAVIT.
DEPARTMENT OF THE INTERIOR.
COMMISSION TO THE FIVE CIVILIZED TRIBES.

       IN RE APPLICATION FOR ENROLLMENT, as a citizen of the Creek Nation, of Roley Harjo, born on the 1st day of February, 1905

Name of Father: Bassta Harjo	a citizen of the	Creek	Nation.
Name of Mother: Jemmima Harjo	a citizen of the	Creek	Nation.

Applications for Enrollment of Creek Newborn
Act of 1905   Volume IX

Postoffice   Weleetka Ind Ter.

AFFIDAVIT OF MOTHER.

UNITED STATES OF AMERICA, Indian Territory, }
Western   DISTRICT.

I, Jemmima Harjo , on oath state that I am 18 years of age and a citizen by blood , of the Creek Nation; that I am the lawful wife of Bassta Harjo , who is a citizen, by blood of the Creek Nation; that a male child was born to me on 1st day of February , 1905 , that said child has been named Roley Harjo , and was living March 4, 1905.

                                                     her
                                   Jemmima x Harjo
Witnesses To Mark: mark
{ HG Malot
  Tupper Dunn

Subscribed and sworn to before me this 24 day of April , 1905.

My Com Exp Aug 19 1908   Tupper Dunn
                                                      Notary Public.

AFFIDAVIT OF ATTENDING PHYSICIAN OR MID-WIFE.

UNITED STATES OF AMERICA, Indian Territory, }
Western   DISTRICT.

I, Sar-farts-cha , a midwife , on oath state that I attended on Mrs. Jemmima Harjo , wife of Bassta Harjo on the 1st day of February , 1905 ; that there was born to her on said date a male child; that said child was living March 4, 1905, and is said to have been named Roley Harjo

                                                    her
                                  Sar-farts-cha x
Witnesses To Mark: mark
{ HG Malot
  Tupper Dunn

Subscribed and sworn to before me this 24 day of April , 1905.

My Com Exp Aug 19 1908   Tupper Dunn
                                                      Notary Public.

Applications for Enrollment of Creek Newborn
Act of 1905 Volume IX

BIRTH AFFIDAVIT.
DEPARTMENT OF THE INTERIOR.
COMMISSION TO THE FIVE CIVILIZED TRIBES.

IN RE APPLICATION FOR ENROLLMENT, as a citizen of the Creek Nation, of Roley Fixico, born on the 1st day of Feb, 1905

Name of Father: Bastie Fixico   a citizen of the Creek   Nation.
Name of Mother: Jemima " nee Jones   a citizen of the Creek   Nation.

Postoffice   Weleetka I.T.

AFFIDAVIT OF MOTHER.

UNITED STATES OF AMERICA, Indian Territory,
    Western   **DISTRICT.**

I, Jemima Fixico, on oath state that I am 18 years of age and a citizen by blood, of the Creek Nation; that I am the lawful wife of Bastie Fixico, who is a citizen, by blood of the Creek Nation; that a male child was born to me on 1st day of February, 1905, that said child has been named Roley Fixico, and was living March 4, 1905.
                                                   her
                                     Jemmima x Fixico
Witnesses To Mark: mark
   { Henry G Hains
   { Jesse McDermott

Subscribed and sworn to before me this 4" day of Dec., 1905.

My Commission expires July 25th 1907   J McDermott
                                             Notary Public.

                                                              HGH

REFER IN REPLY TO THE FOLLOWING: **DEPARTMENT OF THE INTERIOR,**
       NC-684   **COMMISSIONER TO THE FIVE CIVILIZED TRIBES.**

Muskogee, Indian Territory, August 16, 1905.

Jemima Harjo (or Fixico),
    c/o Bastie Harjo (or Fixico),
       Weleetka, Indian Territory.

Dear Madam:

Applications for Enrollment of Creek Newborn
Act of 1905   Volume IX

On April 4, 1905 you filed with the Commission to the Five Civilized Tribes an application for the enrollment of your minor son Roley as a citizen by blood of the Creek Nation. Your name appears in the affidavit relative to the birth of said child as Jemima Harjo and the name of the father of said child appears therein as Bassta Harjo. The said Bassta Harjo is identified upon the final roll of citizens by blood of the Creek Nation as Bastie Fixico. It therefore necessarily follows that if you are lawfully married to him and his correct name is Bastie Fixico your name must be Jemima Fixico and the name of your son must be Roley Fixico and not Roley Harjo.

In order that these discrepancies may be corrected there is inclosed herewith blank for proof of birth, which has been properly filled out, showing your surname and the surname of your said son to be Fixico. You are requested to have said affidavits properly executed and when so executed return the same to this office in the inclosed envelope. Be careful to see that the notary public, before whom the affidavits are sworn to, attached his name and seal to each affidavit. In case any signature is by mark the same must be attested by two disinterested witnesses.

                Respectfully,
                            Wm. O. Beall
                            Acting Commissioner.

CTD-43.
Env.

REFER IN REPLY TO THE FOLLOWING:
NC-684.

DEPARTMENT OF THE INTERIOR,
COMMISSIONER TO THE FIVE CIVILIZED TRIBES.

Muskogee, Indian Territory, October 17, 1905.

Jemima Harjo (or Fixico),
    c/o Bastie Harjo (or Fixico),
        Weleetka, Indian Territory.

Dear Madam:
On April 4, 1905 you filed with the Commission to the Five Civilized Tribes an application for the enrollment of your minor son Roley as a citizen by blood of the Creek Nation. Your name appears in the affidavit relative to the birth of said child as Jemima Harjo and the name of the father of said child appears as Basta Harjo. The said Basta Harjo is identified upon the final roll of citizens by blood of the Creek Nation as Bastie Fixico. It therefore necessarily follows that if you are lawfully married to him and his correct name is Bastie Fixico your name must be Jemima Fixico and the name of your minor son must be Roley Fixico and not Roley Harjo.

In order that these discrepancies may be corrected there is inclosed herewith a blank for proof of birth which has been filled out showing your surname and the surname

Applications for Enrollment of Creek Newborn
Act of 1905   Volume IX

of your said son to be Fixico. You are requested to have said affidavits properly executed and when so executed return the same to this office in the inclosed envelope. Be careful to see that the notary public, before whom the affidavits are sworn to, attached his name and seal to each affidavit. In case any signature is by mark the same must be attested by two disinterested witnesses.

                Respectfully,

                          Tams Bixby
                          Commissioner.

CTD-43.
Env.

HGH

REFER IN REPLY TO THE FOLLOWING:

DEPARTMENT OF THE INTERIOR,
COMMISSIONER TO THE FIVE CIVILIZED TRIBES.

Muskogee, Indian Territory, October 23, 1906.

Jemima Fixico,
    c/o Bassta Fixico,
        Weleetka, Indian Territory.

Dear Madam:

      You are hereby advised that the name of your minor child, Roley Fixico, is contained in the partial list of citizens by blood of the Creek Nation, approved by the Secretary of the Interior October 15, 1906, and that a selection of land in the Creek Nation may now be made for said child at the Creek Land Office in Muskogee, Indian Territory.

      This matter should receive your prompt attention.

                Respectfully,

                          Tams Bixby
                          Commissioner.

Applications for Enrollment of Creek Newborn
Act of 1905   Volume IX

NC-685

Muskogee, Indian Territory, August 14, 1905.

Roxie Ansill,
    Care of Samuel E. Ansill,
        Boynton, Indian Territory.

Dear Madam:

    In the matter of the application for the enrollment of your minor child, Henry F. Ansill, as a citizen by blood of the Creek Nation, it will be necessary for you to furnish this Office with either the original or a certified copy of the marriage license and certificate, showing marriage between you and Samuel E. Ansill, the father of said child.

    It will also be advisable for you to furnish this Office with the affidavit of Samuel E. Ansill as to the birth of said child, and a blank for that purpose, which has been partially filled out, is enclosed herewith.

                Respectfully,

                            Acting Commissioner.

CTD-44

BIRTH AFFIDAVIT.

DEPARTMENT OF THE INTERIOR.
COMMISSION TO THE FIVE CIVILIZED TRIBES.

    IN RE APPLICATION FOR ENROLLMENT, as a citizen of the Creek Nation, of Henry F. Ansill , born on the 22nd day of December, 1904

Name of Father: Samuel E Ansell   a citizen of the   Creek   Nation.
Name of Mother: Roxie Ansell   a citizen of the United StatesNation.

                Postoffice   Boynton, Ind. Ter.

AFFIDAVIT OF MOTHER.

UNITED STATES OF AMERICA, Indian Territory, ⎱
    Western   DISTRICT.   ⎰

    I, Samuel E. Ansell , on oath state that I am 38 years of age and a citizen by blood , of the Creek Nation; that I am the lawful ~~wife of~~ husband of Roxie Ansell , who is a citizen, by *(blank)* of the United States ~~Nation~~; that a male child was born

Applications for Enrollment of Creek Newborn
Act of 1905   Volume IX

to me on   22nd   day of December , 1904 , that said child has been named   Henry F. Ansill[sic] , and was living March 4, 1905.

Samuel E. Ansill

Witnesses To Mark:
{

Subscribed and sworn to before me this 11 day of September , 1905.

Henry G Hains
Notary Public.

BIRTH AFFIDAVIT.

DEPARTMENT OF THE INTERIOR.
COMMISSION TO THE FIVE CIVILIZED TRIBES.

IN RE APPLICATION FOR ENROLLMENT, as a citizen of the Creek Nation, of   Henry F. Ansiel , born on the 22 day of December , 1904

Name of Father: Sam Ansiel   a citizen of the   Creek   Nation.
Hitchitee Town
Name of Mother: Roxie Ansiel   a citizen of the United StatesNation.

Postoffice   Boynton, Ind. Terr.

Child present

AFFIDAVIT OF MOTHER.

UNITED STATES OF AMERICA, Indian Territory, }
   Western   DISTRICT.

I, Roxie Ansiel , on oath state that I am   22   years of age and a citizen by ------ , of the United States   ~~Nation~~; that I am the lawful wife of Sam Ansiel , who is a citizen, by blood of the   Creek   Nation; that a   male   child was born to me on   22   day of   December , 1904 , that said child has been named   Henry F. Ansiel , and was living March 4, 1905.

Roxie Ansiel

Witnesses To Mark:
{

Subscribed and sworn to before me this 4 day of April , 1905.

Drennan C Skaggs
Notary Public.

Applications for Enrollment of Creek Newborn
Act of 1905 Volume IX

AFFIDAVIT OF ATTENDING PHYSICIAN OR MID-WIFE.

UNITED STATES OF AMERICA, Indian Territory,
Western DISTRICT.

I, Jane Tiger , a mid-wife , on oath state that I attended on Mrs. Roxie Ansiel , wife of Sam Ansiel on the 22 day of December , 1904 ; that there was born to her on said date a male child; that said child was living March 4, 1905, and is said to have been named Henry F. Ansiel

Jane Tiger

Witnesses To Mark:

Subscribed and sworn to before me 4 day of April, 1905.

Drennan C Skaggs
Notary Public.

BIRTH AFFIDAVIT.

DEPARTMENT OF THE INTERIOR.
COMMISSION TO THE FIVE CIVILIZED TRIBES.

IN RE APPLICATION FOR ENROLLMENT, as a citizen of the Creek Nation, of Hettie Jane Morrison , born on the 20 day of January , 1905

Name of Father: Hence Morrison   a citizen of the Creek Nation.
Coweta Town
Name of Mother: Nancy Morrison   a citizen of the United StatesNation.

Postoffice   Wetumka, Ind. Ter.

AFFIDAVIT OF MOTHER.

UNITED STATES OF AMERICA, Indian Territory,
Western DISTRICT.   Child is present

I, Nancy Morrison , on oath state that I am 29 years of age and a citizen by *(blank)* , of the United States Nation; that I am the lawful wife of Hence Morrison , who is a citizen, by blood of the Creek Nation; that a female child was born to me

Applications for Enrollment of Creek Newborn
Act of 1905   Volume IX

on 20 day of January, 1905, that said child has been named Hettie Jane Morrison, and was living March 4, 1905.

Nancy Morrison

Witnesses To Mark:
{

Subscribed and sworn to before me this 29 day of March, 1905.

Drennan C Skaggs
Notary Public.

AFFIDAVIT OF ATTENDING PHYSICIAN OR MID-WIFE.

UNITED STATES OF AMERICA, Indian Territory, ⎫
Western   DISTRICT.   ⎭

I, America Atkinson, a midwife, on oath state that I attended on Mrs. Nancy Morrison, wife of Hence Morrison on the 20 day of January this year, (1905); that there was born to her on said date a female child; that said child was living March 4, 1905, and is said to have been named Hettie Jane Morrison

her
America x Atkinson
mark

Witnesses To Mark:
{ Alex Posey
  DC Skaggs

Subscribed and sworn to before me this 29 day of March, 1905.

Drennan C Skaggs
Notary Public.

BIRTH AFFIDAVIT.

DEPARTMENT OF THE INTERIOR.
COMMISSION TO THE FIVE CIVILIZED TRIBES.

IN RE APPLICATION FOR ENROLLMENT, as a citizen of the Creek Nation, of Ernest Morrison, born on the 11 day of March, 1903

Name of Father: Hence Morrison   a citizen of the   Creek   Nation.
Coweta Town
Name of Mother: Nancy Morrison   a citizen of the United StatesNation.

Postoffice   Wetumka, Ind. Ter.

Applications for Enrollment of Creek Newborn
Act of 1905   Volume IX

AFFIDAVIT OF MOTHER.

UNITED STATES OF AMERICA, Indian Territory,
Western   DISTRICT.   Child is present

I, Nancy Morrison , on oath state that I am 29 years of age and a citizen by *(blank)* , of the United States ~~Nation~~; that I am the lawful wife of Hence Morrison , who is a citizen, by blood of the Creek Nation; that a male child was born to me on 11 day of March , 1903 , that said child has been named Ernest Morrison , and was living March 4, 1905.

                                  Nancy Morrison

Witnesses To Mark:
{

Subscribed and sworn to before me this 29 day of March , 1905.

                                  Drennan C Skaggs
                                  Notary Public.

AFFIDAVIT OF ATTENDING PHYSICIAN OR MID-WIFE.

UNITED STATES OF AMERICA, Indian Territory,
Western   DISTRICT.

I, America Atkinson , a midwife , on oath state that I attended on Mrs. Nancy Morrison , wife of Hence Morrison on the 11 day of March, two years ago ; that there was born to her on said date a male child; that said child was living March 4, 1905, and is said to have been named Ernest Morrison

                                  her
                         America x Atkinson

Witnesses To Mark: mark
{ Alex Posey
  DC Skaggs

Subscribed and sworn to before me this 29 day of March , 1905.

                                  Drennan C Skaggs
                                  Notary Public.

Applications for Enrollment of Creek Newborn
Act of 1905   Volume IX

NC-687

Muskogee, Indian Territory, August 14, 1905.

John G. Ansiel,
Eufaula, Indian Territory.

Dear Sir:

In the matter of the application for the enrollment of your minor son, Samuel E. O. Ansiel, as a citizen by blood of the Creek Nation, it will be necessary for you to file with this Office either the original or a certified copy of the marriage license and certificate, showing marriage between you and Lula Ansiel, the non-citizen mother of said child.

It will also be necessary for you, if possible, to supply this Office with your affidavit as to the birth of said child, and a blank for that purpose, which has been partially filled out, is enclosed herewith. You are requested to appear before a notary public, swear to the same, and when sworn to, return it to this Office in the enclosed envelope.

Respectfully,

Acting Commissioner.

CTD-48
Env

CERTIFICATE OF RECORD.

United States of America,
INDIAN TERRITORY,   } ss.
Northern District.

I, *CHARLES A. DAVIDSON*, Clerk of the United States Court in the Northern District, Indian Territory, do hereby certify that the instrument hereto attached was filed for record in my office the   2   day of   December   1901 at ----- M., and duly recorded in Book   L , Marriage Record, Page   383

WITNESS my hand and seal of said Court at Muscogee, in said Territory,
this   3   day of   December   A. D. 1901

Chas A. Davidson   Clerk.
By   (blank)   Deputy.

Applications for Enrollment of Creek Newborn
Act of 1905 Volume IX

MARRIAGE LICENSE

❊❊❊

United States of America,
INDIAN TERRITORY, } ss.   No.   **426**
Northern District.

To Any Person Authorized by Law to Solemnize Marriage---Greeting:

You are Hereby Commanded to Solemnize the Rite and publish the Banns of Matrimony between Mr.   John Ansiel   of   Eufaula , in the Indian Territory, aged   23   years and Miss Lulu Potter   of   Eufaula   in the Indian Territory aged   21   years according to law, and do you officially sign and return this License to the parties therein named.

   WITNESS my hand and official seal at Muscogee Indian Territory this   5"   day of   November   A.D. 190 1
                          Chas. A. Davidson
                               Clerk of the U.S. Court
By   ? M Ford   Deputy

CERTIFICATE OF MARRIAGE.

❊❊

United States of America,
INDIAN TERRITORY, } ss.
Northern District.

   I,   R C McGee   , a Minister of the Gospel, DO HEREBY CERTIFY that on the 10   day of   November   A. D. 1901, I did duly and according to law as commanded in the foregoing License, solemnize the Rite and publish the Banns of Matrimony between the parties therein named.

   WITNESS my hand this   10   day of   November   A. D. 1901

   My credentials are recorded in the office of the Clerk of the United States Court, Indian Territory, Northern District, Book   A , Page   31   .

                          R C McGee
                          A Minister of the Gospel

Applications for Enrollment of Creek Newborn
Act of 1905   Volume IX

Note—This License and Certificate of Marriage must be returned to the Office of the Clerk of the United States Court in the Northern District, Indian Territory, from whence it was issued, within sixty days from the date thereof, or the party to whom the license was issued will be liable in the amount of the One Hundred Dollars ($100.00)

BIRTH AFFIDAVIT.
DEPARTMENT OF THE INTERIOR.
COMMISSION TO THE FIVE CIVILIZED TRIBES.

IN RE APPLICATION FOR ENROLLMENT, as a citizen of the Creek Nation, of Samuel E.O. Ansiel, born on the 4th day of October, 1902

Name of Father: John G. Ansiel   a citizen of the   Creek   Nation.
Name of Mother: Lula Ansiel   a citizen of the United StatesNation.

             Postoffice   Eufaula, Ind. Ter.

AFFIDAVIT OF MOTHER.

UNITED STATES OF AMERICA, Indian Territory,
   Western   DISTRICT.

I, John G. Ansiel, on oath state that I am 28 years of age and a citizen by blood, of the Creek Nation; that I am the lawful ~~wife of~~ husband of Lula Ansiel, who is a citizen, by *(blank)* of the United States ~~Nation~~; that a male child was born to ~~me~~ us on 4th day of October, 1902, that said child has been named Samuel E.O. Ansiel, and was living March 4, 1905.

                                             John G. Ansiel
Witnesses To Mark:
{

Subscribed and sworn to before me this 18 day of August, 1905.

                              (Name Illegible)
                                 Notary Public.
Commission Expires 12/4/1907

Applications for Enrollment of Creek Newborn
Act of 1905 Volume IX

BIRTH AFFIDAVIT.
DEPARTMENT OF THE INTERIOR.
COMMISSION TO THE FIVE CIVILIZED TRIBES.

IN RE APPLICATION FOR ENROLLMENT, as a citizen of the Creek Nation, of Samuel E. O. Ansiel, born on the 4 day of October, 1902

Name of Father: John G. Ansiel   a citizen of the   Creek   Nation.
Hitchitee Town
Name of Mother: Lula Ansiel   a citizen of the United StatesNation.

                Postoffice   Eufaula, Ind. Terr.

AFFIDAVIT OF MOTHER.
                              Child present
UNITED STATES OF AMERICA, Indian Territory,
     Western   DISTRICT.

     I, Lula Ansiel, on oath state that I am 24 years of age and a citizen by *(blank)*, of the United States ~~Nation~~; that I am the lawful wife of John G. Ansiel, who is a citizen, by blood of the Creek Nation; that a male child was born to me on 4 day of October, 1902, that said child has been named Samuel E. O. Ansiel, and was living March 4, 1905.
                               Lula Ansiel
Witnesses To Mark:
{

    Subscribed and sworn to before me this 4 day of April, 1905.

                             Drennan C Skaggs
                               Notary Public.

AFFIDAVIT OF ATTENDING PHYSICIAN OR MID-WIFE.

UNITED STATES OF AMERICA, Indian Territory,
     Western   DISTRICT.

     I, Jane Tiger, a mid-wife, on oath state that I attended on Mrs. Lula Ansiel, wife of John G. Ansiel on the 4 day of October, 1902; that there was born to her on said date a male child; that said child was living March 4, 1905, and is said to have been named Samuel E. O. Ansiel
                               Jane Tiger
Witnesses To Mark:
{

Applications for Enrollment of Creek Newborn
Act of 1905 Volume IX

Subscribed and sworn to before me 4 day of April, 1905.

Drennan C Skaggs
Notary Public.

BIRTH AFFIDAVIT.
DEPARTMENT OF THE INTERIOR.
COMMISSION TO THE FIVE CIVILIZED TRIBES.

IN RE APPLICATION FOR ENROLLMENT, as a citizen of the Creek Nation, of Louisa Thomas, born on the 24 day of December, 1902 and died February 27, 1905

Name of Father: Harley Thomas   a citizen of the   Creek   Nation.
Eufaula Canadian Town
Name of Mother: Lydia Thomas   a citizen of the   Creek   Nation.
Eufaula Canadian Town
                     Postoffice   Eufaula, Ind. Terr.

AFFIDAVIT OF MOTHER.

UNITED STATES OF AMERICA, Indian Territory,
      Western   DISTRICT.

      I, Lydia Thomas, on oath state that I am 29 years of age and a citizen by blood, of the Creek Nation; that I am the lawful wife of Harley Thomas, who is a citizen, by blood of the Creek Nation; that a female child was born to me on 24 day of December, 1902, that said child has been named Louisa Thomas, and ~~was living March 4, 1905~~. died February 27, 1905

                                     Lydia Thomas
Witnesses To Mark:

      Subscribed and sworn to before me this 4 day of April, 1905.

                              Drennan C Skaggs
                              Notary Public.

Applications for Enrollment of Creek Newborn
Act of 1905 Volume IX

AFFIDAVIT OF ATTENDING PHYSICIAN OR MID-WIFE.

UNITED STATES OF AMERICA, Indian Territory, }
Western   DISTRICT.

I, Lucy Wesley, a midwife, on oath state that I attended on Mrs. Lydia Thomas, wife of Harley Thomas on the 24 day of December, 1902 ; that there was born to her on said date a female child; that said child ~~was living March 4, 1905~~ died Feb. 27, 1905, and is said to have been named Louisa Thomas

                                  her
                          Lucy x Wesley
Witnesses To Mark: mark
 { Alex Posey
   DC Skaggs

Subscribed and sworn to before me 4 day of April, 1905.

                          Drennan C Skaggs
                          Notary Public.

NC 688   JLD
DEPARTMENT OF THE INTERIOR,
COMMISSIONER TO THE FIVE CIVILIZED TRIBES.

In the matter of the application for the enrollment of Louisa Thomas, deceased, as a citizen by blood of the Creek Nation.

                . . . .

STATEMENT AND ORDER.

The record in this case shows that on April 7, 1905, application was made, in affidavit form, for the enrollment of Louisa Thomas, deceased, as a citizen by blood of the Creek Nation, under the provisions of the act of Congress approved March 3, 1905.

It appears from the affidavit filed in this matter that said Louisa Thomas, deceased, was born December 24, 1902, and died February 27, 1905.

The Act of Congress approved March 3, 1905, (33 Stats., 1048), provides:

"That the Commission to the Five Civilized Tribes is authorized for sixty days after the date of the approval of this act to receive and consider applications for enrollment, of children, <u>born subsequent to May twenty-fifth, nineteen hundred and one, and prior to March fourth, nineteen hundred and five, and living on said latter date,</u> to citizens of the Creek tribe of Indians whose enrollment has been approved by the Secretary of the Interior prior to the approval of this act; and tc enroll and make allotments to such children."

Applications for Enrollment of Creek Newborn
Act of 1905 Volume IX

It is, therefore, ordered that the application for the enrollment of said Louisa Thomas, deceased, as a citizen by blood of the Creek Nation be, and the same is, hereby dismissed.

Tams Bixby Commissioner.

Muskogee, Indian Territory.
JAN 4 – 1907

NC-689

Muskogee, Indian Territory, August 14, 1905.

Solomon Bullett,
    Hannah, Indian Territory.

Dear Sir:

    In the matter of the application for the enrollment of your minor son, Bailey Bullett, as a citizen by blood of the Creek Nation, it will be necessary for you to furnish this Office with the affidavits of two disinterested persons relative to the birth of said child. Said affidavits must set forth said child's name, the date of its birth, the names of its parents, and whether or not it was living on March 4, 1905.

    This matter should receive your prompt attention.

Respectfully,

Acting Commissioner.

NC-689.

Muskogee, Indian Territory, October 17, 1905.

Solomon Bullett,
    Hannah, Indian Territory.

Dear Sir:

    In the matter of the application for the enrollment of your minor son Bailey Bullett, born June 21, 1904, as a citizen by blood of the Creek Nation you are again advised that it will be necessary for you to furnish this this Office with the affidavits of two disinterested persons relative to the birth of said child. Said affidavits must set forth said child's name, the date of his birth, the names of his parents, and whether or not he was living on March 4, 1905.

Respectfully,

Commissioner.

Applications for Enrollment of Creek Newborn
Act of 1905 Volume IX

NC-689

Muskogee, Indian Territory, December 14, 1905.

Solomon Bullett,
    Hannah, Indian Territory.

Dear Sir:

    In the matter of the application for the enrollment of your minor son, Bailey Bullett, as a citizen by blood of the Creek Nation, it will be necessary for you to furnish this Office with the affidavits of two disinterested persons relative to the birth of said child. Said affidavits must set forth said child's name, the date of its birth, the names of its parents, and whether or not it was living March 4, 1905.

    This matter should receive your prompt attention.

                   Respectfully,
                                  Chairman.

JWH

N C 689

Muskogee, Indian Territory, March 1, 1907.

Millie Bullett,
    c/o Solomon Bullett,
        Hanna, Indian Territory.

Dear Madam :--

    You are hereby advised that on February 15, 1907, the Secretary of the Interior approved the enrollment of your minor child, Bailey Bullett, as a citizen by blood of the Creek Nation, and that the name of said child appears upon the roll of New Born citizens by blood of the Creek Nation, enrolled under the Act of Congress approved March 3, 1905, as number 1163.

    This child is now entitled to allotment and application therefor should be made without delay at the Creek Land Office, Muskogee, Indian Territory.

                   Respectfully,
                                  Commissioner.

Applications for Enrollment of Creek Newborn
Act of 1905 Volume IX

BIRTH AFFIDAVIT.
DEPARTMENT OF THE INTERIOR.
COMMISSION TO THE FIVE CIVILIZED TRIBES.

IN RE APPLICATION FOR ENROLLMENT, as a citizen of the Creek Nation, of Bailey Bullett, born on the 21 day of June, 1904

Name of Father: Solomon Bullett   a citizen of the   Creek   Nation.
Name of Mother: Millie Bullett   a citizen of the   Creek   Nation.

Postoffice   Hanna I.T.

Acquaintance
AFFIDAVIT OF ~~MOTHER~~.

UNITED STATES OF AMERICA, Indian Territory,
Western   DISTRICT.

I, Hattie Harjo , on oath state that I am 18 years of age and a citizen by Blood , of the Creek Nation; that I am ~~the lawful wife of~~ Personally acquainted with Millie Bullett , who is a citizen, by blood of the Creek Nation; that a Male child was born to me on or about 21 day of June , 1904 , that said child has been named Bailey Bullett, and was living March 4, 1905.
                                                                   her
                                                        Hattie x Harjo
Witnesses To Mark: mark
   { JM Bremer
     Wm *(Illegible)*

Subscribed and sworn to before me this 13 day of Dec , 19053

My Commission Expires March 5th, 1908   C C Eskridge
                                                        Notary Public.

Acquaintance
AFFIDAVIT OF ~~ATTENDING PHYSICIAN OR MID-WIFE~~.

UNITED STATES OF AMERICA, Indian Territory,
Western   DISTRICT.

                                          am personally acquainted with
I, Albert Harjo , a *(blank)* , on oath state that I ~~attended on~~ Mrs. Millie Bullett , wife of Solomon Bullett on or about the 21 day of June , 1904 ; that there was born to her on said date a male child; that said child was living March 4, 1905, and is said to have been named Bailey Bullett
                                                      Albert Harjo
Witnesses To Mark:
   {

63

Applications for Enrollment of Creek Newborn
Act of 1905 Volume IX

Subscribed and sworn to before me this 13 day of Dec , 19053

My Commission Expires March 5th, 1908

C C Eskridge
Notary Public.

BIRTH AFFIDAVIT.
DEPARTMENT OF THE INTERIOR.
COMMISSION TO THE FIVE CIVILIZED TRIBES.

IN RE APPLICATION FOR ENROLLMENT, as a citizen of the Creek Nation, of Bailey Bullett, born on the 21 day of June, 1904

Name of Father: Solomon Bullett   a citizen of the   Creek   Nation.
Hillabee Town
Name of Mother: Millie Bullett   a citizen of the   Creek   Nation.
(Illegible) Town

                     Postoffice   Hanna, Ind. Ter.

AFFIDAVIT OF MOTHER.

UNITED STATES OF AMERICA, Indian Territory,
    Western   DISTRICT.   Child is present

     I, Millie Bullett , on oath state that I am about 35 years of age and a citizen by blood , of the Creek Nation; that I am the lawful wife of Solomon Bullett , who is a citizen, by blood of the Creek Nation; that a male child was born to me on 21 day of June, 1904 , that said child has been named Bailey Bullett , and was living March 4, 1905.   her

                                                     Millie x Bullett
                                                              mark

Witnesses To Mark:
   { Alex Posey
   { DC Skaggs

     Subscribed and sworn to before me this 4 day of April , 1905.

                                     Drennan C Skaggs
                                              Notary Public.

Applications for Enrollment of Creek Newborn
Act of 1905 Volume IX

AFFIDAVIT OF ATTENDING PHYSICIAN OR MID-WIFE.

UNITED STATES OF AMERICA, Indian Territory,
Western DISTRICT.

my wife
I, Solomon Bullett, a *(blank)*, on oath state that I attended on ^ Mrs. Millie Bullett, ~~wife of~~ *(blank)* on the 21 day of June, 1904 ; that there was born to her on said date a male child; that said child was living March 4, 1905, and is said to have been named Bailey Bullett

Solomon Bullett

Witnesses To Mark:
{

Subscribed and sworn to before me 4 day of April, 1905.

Drennan C Skaggs
Notary Public.

DEPARTMENT OF THE INTERIOR,
COMMISSION TO THE FIVE CIVILIZED TRIBES.
Holdenville, I. T., March 29, 1905.

In the matter of the application for the enrollment of Johnson and Annie Walker as citizens by blood of the Creek Nation.

MABLE WALKER, being duly sworn, testified as follows:

Through Alex Posey Official Interpreter:

BY COMMISSION:
Q What is your name? A Mable[sic] Walker.
Q How old are you? A I am over thirty.
Q What is your post office address? A Wewoka.
Q Are you a citizen of the Creek Nation? A Yes, sir.
Q To what town do you belong? A Tuckabatche.
Q Do you make application for the enrollment of your children, Johnson and Annie Walker, as citizens of the Creek Nation? A Yes, sir.
Q What is the name of the father of these children? A Jeff Walker.
Q Is he a citizen of the Creek Nation? A He is a Seminole.
Q Is he your lawful husband? a[sic] We were married under Indian law.
Q Do you live together as man and wife? A Yes, sir.

Applications for Enrollment of Creek Newborn
Act of 1905   Volume IX

Q If it should be found that your children, Johnson and Annie Walker, are entitled to be enrolled in either the Creek or Seminole Nations in which nation do you desire to have them enrolled? A In the Creek Nation.

---oooOOOooo---

I, D. C. Skaggs, on oath state that the above and foregoing is a full and true transcript of my stenographic notes as taken in said cause on said date.

DC Skaggs

Subscribed and sworn to before me this 19" day of July, 1905.

Edw C Griesel
Notary Public.

BIRTH AFFIDAVIT.   Supplemental testimony taken.
                    DEPARTMENT OF THE INTERIOR.
          COMMISSION TO THE FIVE CIVILIZED TRIBES.

IN RE APPLICATION FOR ENROLLMENT, as a citizen of the Creek Nation, of Annie Walker, born on the 4 day of February , 1904

Name of Father: Jeff Walker   a citizen of the Seminole   Nation.
Name of Mother: Mabel Walker (nee Lindsey) a citizen of the   Creek   Nation.
Tuckabatche
                            Postoffice   Wewoka, Ind. Ter.

AFFIDAVIT OF MOTHER.

UNITED STATES OF AMERICA, Indian Territory, ⎫
       Western   DISTRICT.   ⎭   Child is present

I, Mabel Walker , on oath state that I am over 30 years of age and a citizen by blood , of the Creek   Nation; that I am the lawful wife of Jeff Walker , who is a citizen, by blood of the Seminole   Nation; that a female   child was born to me on 4 day of February , 1904 , that said child has been named Annie Walker , and was living March 4, 1905.   her
                                    Mabel x Walker
Witnesses To Mark: mark
   ⎰ Alex Posey
   ⎱ DC Skaggs

Applications for Enrollment of Creek Newborn
Act of 1905 Volume IX

Subscribed and sworn to before me this 29 day of March, 1905.

          Drennan C Skaggs
          Notary Public.

AFFIDAVIT OF ATTENDING PHYSICIAN OR MID-WIFE.

UNITED STATES OF AMERICA, Indian Territory, }
  Western   DISTRICT.

  I, Hepsey McGirt, a midwife, on oath state that I attended on Mrs. Mabel Walker, wife of Jeff Walker on the 4 day of February, 1904; that there was born to her on said date a female child; that said child was living March 4, 1905, and is said to have been named Annie Walker   her
            Hepsey x McGirt
Witnesses To Mark: mark
 { Alex Posey
  DC Skaggs

  Subscribed and sworn to before me this 29 day of March, 1905.

          Drennan C Skaggs
          Notary Public.

               NC. 691.

      Muskogee, Indian Territory, July 15, 1905.

Chief Clerk,
  Seminole Enrollment Division,
    Muskogee, Indian Territory.

Dear Sir:

  March 31, 1905, application was made to the Commission to the Five Civilized Tribes for the enrollment of John Walker, born January 2, 1902, and Annie Walker, born February 4, 1904, as citizens by blood of the Creek Nation. It is stated in said application that the father of said children is Jeff Walker, a citizen of the Seminole Nation, and that the mother is Mabel Walker, a citizen of the Creek Nation.

  You are requested to inform the Creek Enrollment Division as to whether application has been made for the enrollment of said children, as citizens of the Seminole Nation, and if so, what disposition has been made of the same.

Applications for Enrollment of Creek Newborn
Act of 1905 Volume IX

Respectfully,

Commissioner.

DEPARTMENT OF THE INTERIOR.
COMMISSION TO THE FIVE CIVILIZED TRIBES.

Muskogee, Indian Territory, July 19, 1905.

Chief Clerk,
  Creek Enrollment Division.

Dear Sir:

Receipt is acknowledged of your letter of July 15, 1905 (NC-691) stating that application was made to the Commission to the Five Civilized Tribes for the enrollment of Johnson Walker, born January 2, 1902, and Annie Walker, born February 4, 1904, children of Jeff Walker, a citizen of the Seminole Nation, and Mabel Walker, a citizen of the Creek Nation, as citizens by blood of the Creek Nation and requesting to be informed as to whether application was made for the enrollment of said child as a citizen of the Seminole Nation. as to whether application was made for the enrollment of said children as citizens of the Seminole Nation.

In reply to your letter you are advised that it does not appear from an examination of the records of this office that any application was ever made for the enrollment of said Johnson Walker and Annie Walker as citizens of the Seminole Nation.

Respectfully,

Tams Bixby   Commissioner.

NC 691

Muskogee, Indian Territory, November 13, 1906

Chief Clerk,
  Seminole Enrollment Division,
    General Office.

Dear Sir:

You are hereby advised that the names of Johnson and Annie Walker, children of Jeff Walker, an alleged citizen of the Seminole Nation and Mabel Walker, a citizen by blood of the Creek Nation, are contained in schedule of minor citizens by blood of the Creek Nation, approved by the Secretary of the Interior, September 27, 1905, opposite Roll numbers 646 and 647.

Respectfully,

Commissioner.

Applications for Enrollment of Creek Newborn
Act of 1905   Volume IX

BIRTH AFFIDAVIT.   Supplemental testimony taken.
DEPARTMENT OF THE INTERIOR.
COMMISSION TO THE FIVE CIVILIZED TRIBES.

IN RE APPLICATION FOR ENROLLMENT, as a citizen of the Creek Nation, of Johnson Walker, born on the 2 day of January, 1902

Name of Father: Jeff Walker   a citizen of the   Seminole   Nation.
Name of Mother: Mabel Walker (nee Lindsey)   a citizen of the   Creek   Nation. Tuckabatche
                                Postoffice   Wewoka, Ind. Ter.

AFFIDAVIT OF MOTHER.

UNITED STATES OF AMERICA, Indian Territory, ⎫
    Western   DISTRICT.   ⎬   Child is present
                                          ⎭

I, Mabel Walker, on oath state that I am over 30 years of age and a citizen by blood, of the Creek Nation; that I am the lawful wife of Jeff Walker, who is a citizen, by blood of the Seminole Nation; that a male child was born to me on 2 day of January, 1902, that said child has been named Johnson Walker, and was living March 4, 1905.
                                                her
                                        Mabel x Walker
Witnesses To Mark: mark
   ⎰ Alex Posey
   ⎱ DC Skaggs

Subscribed and sworn to before me this 29 day of March, 1905.

                        Drennan C Skaggs
                        Notary Public.

AFFIDAVIT OF ATTENDING PHYSICIAN OR MID-WIFE.

UNITED STATES OF AMERICA, Indian Territory, ⎫
    Western   DISTRICT.   ⎬
                                          ⎭

I, Hepsey McGirt, a midwife, on oath state that I attended on Mrs. Mabel Walker, wife of Jeff Walker on the 2 day of January, 1902; that there was born to her on said date a male child; that said child was living March 4, 1905, and is said to have been named Johnson Walker
                                                her
                                        Hepsey x McGirt
                                              mark

Applications for Enrollment of Creek Newborn
Act of 1905 Volume IX

Witnesses To Mark:
{ Alex Posey
{ DC Skaggs

Subscribed and sworn to before me this 29 day of March, 1905.

Drennan C Skaggs
Notary Public.

DEPARTMENT OF THE INTERIOR,
COMMISSION TO THE FIVE CIVILIZED TRIBES.
Eufaula, I. T., April 4, 1905.

In the matter of the application for the enrollment of Arthur Manley, deceased, as a citizen by blood of the Creek Nation.

MILLIE MANLEY, being duly sworn, testified as follows:

Through Alex Posey Official Interpreter:

BY COMMISSION:
Q What is your name? A Millie Manley.
Q How old are you? A About twenty.
Q What is your post office address? A Eufaula.
Q Are you a citizen of the Creek Nation? A Yes, sir.
Q To what town do you belong? A Tuskege[sic].
Q Do you make application for the enrollment of your, deceased, child, Arthur Manley, as a citizen of the Creek Nation? A Yes, sir.
Q What is the name of the child's father? A Thomas Manley.
Q Is he dead? A Yes, sir.
Q Was he your lawful husband? A Yes, sir.
Q When did he die? A He has been dead a little over a month.
Q Was he a citizen of the Creek Nation? A Yes, sir.
Q To what town did he belong? A Eufaula Canadian.
Q When was Arthur born? A June 26, 1904.
Q When did he die? A March 15, 1905.
Q How long has he been dead? A I think it has been about four weeks.
Q According to your affidavit the child has been dead only about three weeks? A I was only guessing at it and may be mistaken.
Q It is desired that you be positive in your answers? A No response.
Q On what day of the week did the child die? A Wednesday night.
Q Who was present when the child died? A Dick Greenwood and his wife.

Applications for Enrollment of Creek Newborn
Act of 1905   Volume IX

Q Are you positive that your child, Arthur, was born June 26, 1904, and died March 15, 1905? A Yes, sir.

DICK GREENWOOD, being duly sworn, testified as follows:
Through Alex Posey Official Interpreter:

BY COMMISSION:
Q What is your name? A Dick Greenwood.
Q How old are you? A I am about sixty-two years old.
Q What is your post office address? A Eufaula.
Q Are you a citizen of the Creek Nation? A Yes, sir, Hickory Ground.
Q Do you know Thomas Manley and his wife Millie Manley? A Yes, sir.
Q Are they both living? A No, sir, Thomas is dead.
Q Do you know when he died? A I cannot be exact but he died on or about the 25 day of February this year.
Q Do you know a child of theirs named Arthur Manley? A Yes, sir.
Q Do you know when that child died? A On the 15th of March, this year.
Q Were you present when the child died? A Yes, sir.
Q What relation was the child to you? A My grandchild.
Q Was there a record made of the child's death? A I made a record.
Q Have you that record with you? A Yes, sir.

Witness present a pocket memorandum book containing various entries. On the last page, written in the Creek Language appears the following entry:
"Arthur Manley died March 15, 1905."

Q When did you make this record? A The day after the child died.

Following the above entry appears another entry as follows:
"Child born February 14 died February 16."

Q To whom does this record refer? A To a different child.
Q Whose child? A Another child of Millie Manley's. It was born in 1903 and only lived two days, and for whom the mother has made no application.
Q On what day of the week did Arthur Manley die? A Wednesday evening.

---oooOOOooo---

I, D. C. Skaggs, on oath state that the above and foregoing is a full and true transcript of my stenographic notes as taken in said cause on said date.
DC Skaggs

Subscribed and sworn to before me this 21 day of July, 1905.
J McDermott
Notary Public.

Applications for Enrollment of Creek Newborn
Act of 1905   Volume IX

NC-692

DEPARTMENT OF THE INTERIOR,
COMMISSIONER TO THE FIVE CIVILIZED TRIBES.

Muskogee, Indian Territory, November 28, 1905.

In the matter of the application for the enrollment of Arthur Manley as a citizen by blood of the Creek Nation.

Lewis Greenwood, being duly sworn, testified as follows:

EXAMINATION BY THE COMMISSIONER:
Q What is your name? A Lewis Greenwood.
Q How old are you? A I am about 30.
Q What is your postoffice? A Eufaula.
Q Do you know Millie Manley and Thomas Manley? A Yes sir.
Q Do you know their child, Arthur Manley? A Yes sir.
Q Is Arthur living? A No sir, he died.
Q When did he die? A Died about the 15th of March, I think.
Q This last March? A Yes sir.
Q How old was he when he died? A I don't remember about; I wasn't there when he was born.
Q Do you know when he was born? (No answer)
Q Do you know about when he was born? A I think about the 15th--born in May, somewhere around there.
Q Of 1904? A Yes sir.
Q How do you remember so well when he died? A I was out there when he died; I was living in town all the time.
Q Do you know when March fourth comes? A Yes sir.
Q Did he die after that? A The 15th of March.
Q About eleven days after the fourth of March? A Yes sir.
Q Do you know whether any record was made anywhere--in a church book--written down anywhere about his death? A I think the Indians always made a piece of board and stick it under the head.
Q You think there is a board over his grave? A Yes sir.
Q Your impression is, then, that he was living March fourth of this year? A Yes sir.
Q You are positive of that--sure of that? A Yes sir.
Q We have some difficulty in identifying the mother of this child. Was she ever known by any other name than Millie? A Mary is her proper name.
Q She is sometimes called Millie? A No, just called. The Indians call Mary Meelie.
Q And that is the way the notary public understood? A Yes sir.
Q Do you know the name of her father? A No, I don't.
Q The name of her mother? A Yes sir.
Q What is it? A Hannah.
Q Did she have a child before? A She's there, living.

Applications for Enrollment of Creek Newborn
Act of 1905   Volume IX

Q What is the name of one? [sic] Mary has a child named Osie Waita. It is by a different father. She has another child living.

The mother is said Arthur Manley is identified as Mary Manley, on Creek Indian card, field No. 3726, opposite Roll No. 8840.

Dick Greenwood, being duly sworn, testified as follows (through Alex Posey, Official Interpreter):

Q What is your name? A Dick Greenwood.
Q You testified before in this case, have you? A Yes, sir.
Q What is the name of the mother of Arthur Manley? A Mary.
Q What was her father's name? A Jimpsey?[sic]
Q Do you know the name of her mother? A Hannah Jimpsey
Q Thomas Manley, the father of this child, is dead, is he? A Yes sir.

INDIAN TERRITORY, Western District.
I, J. Y. Miller, a stenographer to the Commission to the Five Civilized Tribes, do hereby certify that the above and foregoing is a true and complete translation of my notes as same appear in my stenographic report of this case.

JY Miller

Sworn to and subscribed before me
this the 28th day of November,
1905.

J McDermott
Notary Public.

AFFIDAVIT OF DISINTERESTED WITNESSES.

United States of America,
    Indian Territory,
    Western District.

We, the undersigned, on oath state that we are personally acquainted with Mary Manley   wife of   Thomas Manley , that there was born to her on or about the 21   day of   June , 190 4 , a   male   child; that said child was living March 4, 1905, and is said to have been named   Arthur Manley .

We further state that we have no interest in this case.

Dick Greenwood

Lewis Greenwood

Applications for Enrollment of Creek Newborn
Act of 1905   Volume IX

(2) Witnesses to mark:

_____

_____

Subscribed and sworn to before me this 28 day of November, 1905.

           Alex Posey
             Notary Public.

BIRTH AFFIDAVIT.
        DEPARTMENT OF THE INTERIOR.
     COMMISSION TO THE FIVE CIVILIZED TRIBES.

  IN RE APPLICATION FOR ENROLLMENT, as a citizen of the Creek Nation, of Arthur Manley, born on the 26 day of June, 1904 and died March 15, 1905.

Name of Father: Thomas Manley (deceased) a citizen of the Creek Nation.
Eufaula Canadian Town
Name of Mother: Millie Manley (nee Jimsey) a citizen of the Creek Nation.
Tuskegee Town
          Postoffice Eufaula, Ind. Ter.

        AFFIDAVIT OF MOTHER.

UNITED STATES OF AMERICA, Indian Territory,
  Western   **DISTRICT.**

  I, Millie Manley, on oath state that I am about 20 years of age and a citizen by blood, of the Creek Nation; that I am the lawful wife of Thomas Manley, deceased, who is a citizen, by blood of the Creek Nation; that a male child was born to me on 26 day of June, 1904, that said child has been named Arthur Manley, and was living March 4, 1905. That no one attended on me at the birth of the child except my husband who is now dead.   her
           Millie x Manley
Witnesses To Mark: mark
 { Alex Posey
 { DC Skaggs

  Subscribed and sworn to before me this 4 day of April, 1905.

           Drennan C Skaggs
            Notary Public.

Applications for Enrollment of Creek Newborn
Act of 1905 Volume IX

NC-692

Muskogoe[sic], Indian Territory, August 14, 1905.

Millie Manley,
    Care of Dick Greenwood,
        Eufaula, Indian Territory.

Dear Madam:

    In the matter of the application for the enrollment of your minor son, Arthur Manley, as a citizen by blood of the Creek Nation, it will be necessary for you to furnish this Office with the affidavits of two disinterested persons as to the birth of said child. Said affidavits must set forth said child's name, the date of his birth, the names of his parents and whether or not he was living on March 4, 1905.

    You are also requested to inform this Office as to the name under which you are finally enrolled, the names of your parents and other members of your family, and, and if possible, your roll number as the same appears upon your allotment certificates and deeds. This information is desired in order that you may be identified upon the final roll of citizens by blood of the Creek Nation.

        Respectfully,

                Acting Commissioner.

NC-692.

Muskogee, Indian Territory, October 18, 1905.

Millie Manley,
    c/o Dick Greenwood,
        Eufaula, Indian Territory.

Dear Madam:

    In the matter of the application for the enrollment of your minor son, Arthur Manley, born June 26, 1904, as a citizen by blood of the Creek Nation, you are again advised that it will be necessary for you to furnish this Office with the affidavits of two disinterested persons as to the birth of said child. Said affidavits must set forth said child's name, the date of his birth, the names of his parents and whether or not he was living on March 4, 1905.

    You are also requested to inform this Office as to the name under which you are finally enrolled, the names of your parents and other members of your family and and if possible your roll number as the same appears upon your allotment certificates and deeds. This information is desired in order that you may be identified upon the final roll of citizens by blood of the Creek Nation.

        Respectfully,

                Commissioner.

Applications for Enrollment of Creek Newborn
Act of 1905 Volume IX

NC.693.

Muskogee, Indian Territory, July 15, 1905.

Chief Clerk,
    Cherokee Enrollment Division,
        Muskogee, Indian Territory.

Dear Sir:

    April 7, 1905, application was made to the Commission to the Five Civilized Tribes for the enrollment of William T. Watts, Jr., born September 11, 1902, as a citizen by blood of the Creek Nation. It is stated in said application that the father of said child is William T. Watts, a citizen of the Cherokee Nation, and that the mother is Anna H. Watts, a citizen of the Creek Nation.

    You are requested to inform the Creek Enrollment Division as to whether application for the enrollment of said William T. Watts, Jr., has been made as a citizen of the Cherokee Nation, and if so, what disposition has been made of the same.

        Respectfully,
                Commissioner.

REFER IN REPLY TO THE FOLLOWING:

DEPARTMENT OF THE INTERIOR,
COMMISSIONER TO THE FIVE CIVILIZED TRIBES.

Muskogee, Indian Territory, July 18, 1905.

Chief Clerk,
    Creek Enrollment Division,
        Muskogee, Indian Territory.

Dear Sir:

    Replying to your letter of July 15, 1905, (NC. 693) asking to be advised whether or not any application has ever been made for the enrollment as a citizen of the Cherokee Nation of William T. Watts Jr., a child of William T. Watts, a citizen of the Cherokee Nation, and Anna H. Watts, a citizen of the Creek Nation, you are advised that from an examination of the records of the Cherokee Enrollment Division it does not appear that any application has ever been made for the enrollment of said child as a citizen of that nation.

        Respectfully,
                Tams Bixby   Commissioner.

GHL

Applications for Enrollment of Creek Newborn
Act of 1905   Volume IX

NC 693

Muskogee, Indian Territory, November 13, 1906.

Chief Clerk,
Cherokee Enrollment Division,
General Office.

Dear Sir:

You are hereby advised that the name of William T. Watts, Jr. born September 11, 1902 to William T. Watts, and alleged citizen of the Cherokee Nation and Anna H. Watts a citizen by blood of the Creek Nation, is contained in schedule of minor citizens by blood of the Creek Nation, approved by the Secretary of the Interior, September 27, 1905 opposite Roll number 648.

Respectfully,

Commissioner.

BIRTH AFFIDAVIT.

DEPARTMENT OF THE INTERIOR.
COMMISSION TO THE FIVE CIVILIZED TRIBES.

IN RE APPLICATION FOR ENROLLMENT, as a citizen of the Creek or Muskogee Nation, of William T. Watts Jr, born on the 11 day of Sept, 1902

Name of Father: William T. Watts   a citizen of the   Cherokee   Nation.
Name of Mother: Anna H. Watts (deceased) a citizen of the   Creek   Nation.
Okfusky[sic] Canadian or
Coweta Towns   Postoffice   Texanna I.T.

Father
AFFIDAVIT OF MOTHER.

UNITED STATES OF AMERICA, Indian Territory, ⎱
Western   DISTRICT.   ⎰   Child not present

I, William T. Watts, on oath state that I am 29 years of age and a citizen by blood, of the Cherokee Nation; that I am the lawful ~~wife~~ husband of Anna H. Watts (deceased), who is a citizen, by blood of the Creek Nation; that a male child was born to ~~me~~ her on 11 day of September, 1902, that said child has been named William T. Watts, Jr., and was living March 4, 1905.

William T. Watts

Applications for Enrollment of Creek Newborn
Act of 1905   Volume IX

Witnesses To Mark:

Subscribed and sworn to before me this 4 day of April, 1905.

Drennan C Skaggs
Notary Public.

AFFIDAVIT OF ATTENDING PHYSICIAN OR MID-WIFE.

UNITED STATES OF AMERICA, Indian Territory,
Western   DISTRICT.

I, S.H. Hamilton, a physician, on oath state that I attended on Mrs. Anna H. Watts, wife of W.T. Watts on the 11 day of September, 1902; that there was born to her on said date a male child; that said child was living March 4, 1905, and is said to have been named William T. Watts

SH Hamilton M.D.

Witnesses To Mark:

Subscribed and sworn to before me 3 day of April, 1905.

Joseph C. Morton
Notary Public.

My Commission Expires Feb 29 1908

BIRTH AFFIDAVIT.
DEPARTMENT OF THE INTERIOR.
COMMISSION TO THE FIVE CIVILIZED TRIBES.

IN RE APPLICATION FOR ENROLLMENT, as a citizen of the Creek Nation, of Harper Givens, born on the 18 day of August, 1903

Name of Father: William Givens   a citizen of the   Creek   Nation.
Tuckabatche Town
Name of Mother: Annie Givens (nee McGilbra) a citizen of the Creek Nation.
Tulmochussee Town

Postoffice   Mellette, Ind. Ter.

Applications for Enrollment of Creek Newborn
Act of 1905   Volume IX

AFFIDAVIT OF MOTHER.

UNITED STATES OF AMERICA, Indian Territory,
Western DISTRICT.   Child is present

I, Annie Givens, on oath state that I am 25 years of age and a citizen by blood, of the Creek Nation; that I am the lawful wife of William Givens, who is a citizen, by blood of the Creek Nation; that a male child was born to me on 18 day of August, 1903, that said child has been named Harper Givens, and was living March 4, 1905.

                                                             her
                                           Annie x Givens

Witnesses To Mark: mark
{ Alex Posey
{ DC Skaggs

Subscribed and sworn to before me this 4 day of April, 1905.

                                      Drennan C Skaggs
                                      Notary Public.

AFFIDAVIT OF ATTENDING PHYSICIAN OR MID-WIFE.

UNITED STATES OF AMERICA, Indian Territory,
Western DISTRICT.

I, Bettie Davis, a midwife, on oath state that I attended on Mrs. Annie Givens, wife of William Givens on the 18 day of August, 1903; that there was born to her on said date a male child; that said child was living March 4, 1905, and is said to have been named Harper Givens
                                           her
                                       Bettie x Davis

Witnesses To Mark: mark
{ Alex Posey
{ DC Skaggs

Subscribed and sworn to before me 4 day of April, 1905.

                                      Drennan C Skaggs
                                      Notary Public.

Applications for Enrollment of Creek Newborn
Act of 1905   Volume IX

C 695.
DEPARTMENT OF THE INTERIOR,
COMMISSION TO THE FIVE CIVILIZED TRIBES.
Holdenville, I. T., March 29, 1905.

In the matter of the application for the enrollment of Timmie Barnett Wolf as a citizen of the Creek Nation.

SUKEY WOLF, being duly sworn, testified as follows:

Through Alex Posey Official Interpreter:

BY COMMISSION:
Q What is your name? A Sukey Wolf.
Q How old are you? A 19.
Q What is your post office address? A Tidmore.
Q Are you a citizen of the Creek Nation? A Yes, sir.
Q To what town do you belong? A Tuskegee.
Q Do you make application for the enrollment of your minor child, Timmie Barnett Wolf as a citizen of the Creek Nation? A Yes, sir.
Q What is the name of the father of this child? A Jackson Wolf.
Q Is he a citizen of the Creek Nation? A No, sir, he is a Seminole.
Q Is he your lawful husband? A Yes, sir.
Q If it should be found that your child, Timmie Barnett Wolf, is entitled to be enrolled in either the Creek or Seminole Nations in which nation do you desire to have him enrolled?
A In the Creek Nation.

---oooOOOooo---

I, D. C. Skaggs, on oath state that the above and foregoing is a full and true transcript of my stenographic notes as taken in said cause on said date.

D.C. Skaggs

Subscribed and sworn to before me this 19" day of July, 1905.

Edw C Griesel
Notary Public.

Applications for Enrollment of Creek Newborn
Act of 1905 Volume IX

BIRTH AFFIDAVIT.

Supplemental testimony taken.
DEPARTMENT OF THE INTERIOR.
COMMISSION TO THE FIVE CIVILIZED TRIBES.

IN RE APPLICATION FOR ENROLLMENT, as a citizen of the Creek Nation, of Timmie Barnett Wolf, born on the 29 day of August, 1902

Name of Father: Jackson Wolf   a citizen of the   Seminole   Nation.
Name of Mother: Sukey Wolf (nee Foster)   a citizen of the   Creek   Nation.
Tuskegee Town
                  Postoffice   Tidmore, Ind. Ter.

AFFIDAVIT OF MOTHER.

UNITED STATES OF AMERICA, Indian Territory, ⎱
    Western   DISTRICT.   ⎰   Child is present

     I, Sukey Wolf, on oath state that I am 19 years of age and a citizen by blood, of the Creek Nation; that I am the lawful wife of Jackson Wolf, who is a citizen, by blood of the Creek[sic] Nation; that a male child was born to me on 29 day of August, 1902, that said child has been named Timmie Barnett Wolf, and was living March 4, 1905.   her
                                    Sukey x Wolf
Witnesses To Mark: mark
  ⎰ Alex Posey
  ⎱ DC Skaggs

     Subscribed and sworn to before me this 29 day of March, 1905.

                               Drennan C Skaggs
                               Notary Public.

AFFIDAVIT OF ATTENDING PHYSICIAN OR MID-WIFE.

UNITED STATES OF AMERICA, Indian Territory, ⎱
    Western   DISTRICT.   ⎰

     I, Betsey Foster, a midwife, on oath state that I attended on Mrs. Sukey Wolf, wife of Jackson Wolf on the 29 day of August, 1902 ; that there was born to her on said date a male child; that said child was living March 4, 1905, and is said to have been named Timmie Barnett Wolf   her
                                   Betsey x Foster
                                         mark

Applications for Enrollment of Creek Newborn
Act of 1905   Volume IX

Witnesses To Mark:
{ Alex Posey
  DC Skaggs

Subscribed and sworn to before me 29 day of March, 1905.

Drennan C Skaggs
Notary Public.

NC. 695.

Muskogee, Indian Territory, July 15, 1905.

Chief Clerk,
  Seminole Enrollment Division,
    Muskogee, Indian Territory.

Dear Sir:

March 31, 1905, application was made to the Commission to the Five Civilized Tribes for the enrollment of Timmie Barnett Wolf, born August 29, 1902, as a citizen by blood of the Creek Nation. It is stated in said application that the father of said child is Jackson Wolf, a citizen of the Seminole Nation, and that the mother is Sukey Wolf, a citizen of the Creek Nation.

You are requested to inform the Creek Enrollment Division as to whether application has been made for the enrollment of said Timmie Barnett Wolf, as a citizen of the Seminole Nation, and if so, what disposition has been made of the same.

Respectfully,
Commissioner.

W.F.

DEPARTMENT OF THE INTERIOR.
COMMISSION TO THE FIVE CIVILIZED TRIBES.

Muskogee, Indian Territory, July 19, 1905.

Chief Clerk,
  Creek Enrollment Division.

Dear Sir:

Receipt is acknowledged of your letter of July 15, 1905 (NC-695) stating that application was made to the Commission to the Five Civilized Tribes for the enrollment

Applications for Enrollment of Creek Newborn
Act of 1905 Volume IX

of Timmie Barnett Wolf, born August 28, 1902, child of Jackson Wolf, a citizen of the Seminole Nation, and Sukey Wolf, a citizen of the Creek Nation, as a citizen by blood of the Creek Nation and requesting to be informed as to whether application has been made for the enrollment of said Timmie Barnett Wolf as a citizen of the Seminole Nation.

Respectfully,

Tams Bixby Commissioner.

NC 695

Muskogee, Indian Territory, November 13, 1906

Chief Clerk,
Seminole Enrollment Division.
General Office.

Dear Sir:

You are hereby advised that the name of Timmie Barnett Wolf, born August 29, 1902 to Jackson Wolf an alleged citizen of the Seminole Nation and Sukey Wolf, a citizen by blood of the Creek Nation, is contained in schedule of minor citizens by blood of the Creek Nation, approved by the Secretary of the Interior, September 27, 1905, opposite Roll number 650.

Respectfully,

Commissioner.

BIRTH AFFIDAVIT.
DEPARTMENT OF THE INTERIOR.
COMMISSION TO THE FIVE CIVILIZED TRIBES.

IN RE APPLICATION FOR ENROLLMENT, as a citizen of the Creek Nation, of Eddielinie Goat , born on the 3 day of February , 1904

Name of Father: Wadley Goat   a citizen of the   Creek   Nation.
Tulsa L.R. Town
Name of Mother: Minnie Goat (nee Sullivan)   a citizen of the   Creek   Nation.
Tuckabatche

Postoffice   Holdenville, Ind. Ter.

Applications for Enrollment of Creek Newborn
Act of 1905   Volume IX

AFFIDAVIT OF MOTHER.

UNITED STATES OF AMERICA, Indian Territory, }
Western   DISTRICT.   Child is present

I, Minnie Goat , on oath state that I am about 32 years of age and a citizen by blood , of the Creek Nation; that I am the lawful wife of Wadley Goat , who is a citizen, by blood of the Creek Nation; that a female child was born to me on 3 day of February , 1904 , that said child has been named Eddielinie Goat , and was living March 4, 1905.

Minnie Goat

Witnesses To Mark:
{

Subscribed and sworn to before me this 29 day of March , 1905.

Drennan C Skaggs
Notary Public.

AFFIDAVIT OF ATTENDING PHYSICIAN OR MID-WIFE.

UNITED STATES OF AMERICA, Indian Territory, }
Western   DISTRICT.

I, Lillie Miller , a midwife , on oath state that I attended on Mrs. Minnie Goat , wife of Wadley Goat on the 3 day of February , 1904 ; that there was born to her on said date a female child; that said child was living March 4, 1905, and is said to have been named Eddielinie Goat

Lillie Miller

Witnesses To Mark:
{

Subscribed and sworn to before me 29 day of March, 1905.

Drennan C Skaggs
Notary Public.

Applications for Enrollment of Creek Newborn
Act of 1905   Volume IX

C 697
DEPARTMENT OF THE INTERIOR,
COMMISSION TO THE FIVE CIVILIZED TRIBES.
Eufaula, I. T., Aril 4, 1905.

In the matter of the application for the enrollment of Jimmie Loney as a citizen by blood of the Creek Nation.

LIZZIE WILLINGHAM, being duly sworn, testified as follows:

Through Alex Posey Official Interpreter:

BY COMMISSION:
Q What is your name? A Lizzie Willingham.
Q How old are you? A About nineteen.
Q What is your post office address? A Lenna.
Q Are you a citizen of the Creek Nation? A Yes, sir.
Q To what town do you belong? A Cussehta.
Q Do you make application for the enrollment of your minor child, Jimmie Loney, as a citizen by blood of the Creek Nation? A Yes, sir?
Q What is the name of the child's father? A Sam Loney.
Q Is Sam Loney your lawful husband? A No, sir.
Q Is he living? A Yes, sir.
Q Were you ever married to him? A No, sir.
Q Does he acknowledge Jimmie Loney as his son? A Yes, sir.
Q Does he contribute anything towards the support of this child? A No, sir.
Q Did he ever contribute anything for the support of the child? A No, sir, I turned the child over to Joe McCombs and his wife, to raise.

---oooOOOooo---

I, D. C. Skaggs, on oath state that the above and foregoing is a full and true transcript of my stenographic notes as taken in said cause on said date.

DC Skaggs

Subscribed and sworn to before me this 21 day of July, 1905.

J McDermott
Notary Public.

Applications for Enrollment of Creek Newborn
Act of 1905 Volume IX

N.C. 107.

DEPARTMENT OF THE INTERIOR,
COMMISSIONER TO THE FIVE CIVILIZED TRIBES.
Stidham, IT. Sept. 22, 1905.

In the matter of the application for the enrollment of Jimmie McCombs as a citizen by blood of the Creek Nation.

LIZZIE WILLINGHAM, being duly sworn, testified as follows:

Through Alex Posey Official Interpreter:

BY THE COMMISSIONER:
Q What is your name? A Lizzie Willingham.
Q How old are you? A About twenty.
Q What is your post office address? A Lenna.
Q Are you a citizen of the Creek Nation? A Yes, sir.
Q To what town do you belong? A Cussehta.
Q Have you a child named Jimmie McCombs? A Yes, sir. Joe McCombs has adopted the child and it has been named after him instead of its own father, Sam Loney.
Q To what town does Sam Loney belong? A Tallahassoche.
Q The child is living is it? A Yes, sir.
Q Is Sam Loney your lawful husband? A No, sir.
Q Jimmie is an illegitimate child is he? A Yes, sir.
Q Dows Sam Loney recognize Jimmie as his child? A Yes, sir.
Q Does he contribute towards the support of the child? A No, sir. The child was adopted by Joe McCombs while very young.
Q Did Joe McCombs adopte[sic] the child according to law? A No, sir. I just gave him the child to raise without any form of law.
Q Did Rachael Loney attend on you at the birth of the child? A Yes, sir.
Q The date of the child's birth as given in the affidavit executed by you and Rachael Loney is correct is it? A Yes, sir.

---oooOOOooo---

I, D. C. Skaggs, on oath state that the above and foregoing is a full and true transcript of my stenographic notes as taken in said cause on said date.

DC Skaggs

Subscribed and sworn to before me this 29" day of Sept, 1905.

(Name Illegible)
Notary Public.

(The above affidavit given again)

Applications for Enrollment of Creek Newborn
Act of 1905 Volume IX

BIRTH AFFIDAVIT.
DEPARTMENT OF THE INTERIOR.
COMMISSION TO THE FIVE CIVILIZED TRIBES.

IN RE APPLICATION FOR ENROLLMENT, as a citizen of the Creek Nation, of Jimmie Loney, born on the 13 day of November, 1902

Name of Father: Sam Loney   a citizen of the   Creek   Nation.
Tullahosoche Town
Name of Mother: Lizzie Willingham   a citizen of the   Creek   Nation.
Cusheta Town
                     Postoffice   Lenna, Ind. Ter.

AFFIDAVIT OF MOTHER.   Child present

UNITED STATES OF AMERICA, Indian Territory,}
     Western   DISTRICT.

I, Lizzie Willingham, on oath state that I am about 19 years of age and a citizen by blood, of the Creek Nation; that I am not the lawful wife of Sam Loney, who is a citizen, by blood of the Creek Nation; that a male child was born to me on 13 day of November, 1902, that said child has been named Jimmie Loney, and was living March 4, 1905. That the mid-wife in attendance on me at the birth of the child is unable to appear for the purpose of so executing an affidavit on account of illness.

                                   her
                          Lizzie x Willingham
Witnesses To Mark: mark
{ DC Skaggs
   Alex Posey

     Subscribed and sworn to before me this 4 day of April, 1905.

                           Drennan C Skaggs
                              Notary Public.

Applications for Enrollment of Creek Newborn
Act of 1905   Volume IX

BIRTH AFFIDAVIT.
DEPARTMENT OF THE INTERIOR.
COMMISSION TO THE FIVE CIVILIZED TRIBES.

IN RE APPLICATION FOR ENROLLMENT, as a citizen of the Creek Nation, of Jimmie McCombs, born on the 13 day of Nov. , 1903

Name of Father: Sam Loney　　　　　a citizen of the　Creek　　Nation.
Tullahosoche Town
Name of Mother: Lizzie Willingham　　a citizen of the　Creek　　Nation.
Cusshela Town
　　　　　　　　　　　Postoffice　　Lenna, I.T.

AFFIDAVIT OF MOTHER.

UNITED STATES OF AMERICA, Indian Territory, ⎱
　　Western　　　DISTRICT.　　　　　　⎰

I, Lizzie Willingham , on oath state that I am about 20 years of age and a citizen by blood , of the Creek Nation; that I am not the lawful wife of Sam Loney , who is a citizen, by blood of the *(blank)* Nation; that a male child was born to me on 13 day of Nov. , 1903 , that said child has been named Jimmie McCombs , and was living March 4, 1905.
　　　　　　　　　　　　　　her
　　　　　　　　　　Lizzie x Willingham
Witnesses To Mark:　　　mark
　⎰ DC Skaggs
　⎱ Alex Posey

　　Subscribed and sworn to before me this 22 day of Sept , 1905.

　　　　　　　　　　Drennan C Skaggs
　　　　　　　　　　　Notary Public.

AFFIDAVIT OF ATTENDING PHYSICIAN OR MID-WIFE.

UNITED STATES OF AMERICA, Indian Territory, ⎱
　　Western　　　DISTRICT.　　　　　　⎰

I, Rachael Loney , a mid-wife , on oath state that I attended on Mrs. Lizzie Willingham , ~~wife of~~ *(blank)* on the 13 day of Nov. , 1903 ; that there was born to her on said date a male child; that said child was living March 4, 1905, and is said to have been named Jimmie McCombs

Applications for Enrollment of Creek Newborn
Act of 1905 Volume IX

Witnesses To Mark:
{

Rachael Loney

Subscribed and sworn to before me 6 day of Sept, 1905.

           Drennan C Skaggs
           Notary Public.

BIRTH AFFIDAVIT.
DEPARTMENT OF THE INTERIOR.
COMMISSION TO THE FIVE CIVILIZED TRIBES.

IN RE APPLICATION FOR ENROLLMENT, as a citizen of the CREEK Nation, of Jimmie McCombs, born on the ----- day of Nov. , 1902

Name of Father: {Sam Loney   a citizen of the   Creek   Nation.
 not married
Name of Mother: Lizzie Willingham   a citizen of the   Creek   Nation.

      Postoffice   Lenna, I.T. (P.O.)

     AFFIDAVIT OF MOTHER.   Acquaintance

UNITED STATES OF AMERICA, Indian Territory, }
  WESTERN   DISTRICT.

  I, Joe McCombs , on oath state that I am 53 years of age and a citizen by blood , of the Creek Nation; that I am the lawful wife of not related to Lizzie Willingham , who is a citizen, by blood of the Creek Nation; that a male child was born to me her on ----- day of Nov. , 1902 , that said child has been named Jimmie McCombs , and is now living.

           Joe McCombs

Witnesses To Mark:
{

Subscribed and sworn to before me this 9 day of March , 1905.

           Edw C Griesel
           Notary Public.

Applications for Enrollment of Creek Newborn
Act of 1905   Volume IX

BIRTH AFFIDAVIT.
DEPARTMENT OF THE INTERIOR.
COMMISSION TO THE FIVE CIVILIZED TRIBES.

IN RE APPLICATION FOR ENROLLMENT, as a citizen of the Creek Nation, of James Loney, born on the 13 day of November, 1902

Name of Father: Sam Loney	a citizen of the Creek	Nation.
Name of Mother: Lizzie Willingham	a citizen of the Creek	Nation.

Postoffice   Lenna, I.T.

AFFIDAVIT OF MOTHER.

UNITED STATES OF AMERICA, Indian Territory, }
  DISTRICT.
My Commission Expires July 20, 1907.

I, Lizzie Willingham, on oath state that I am 22 years of age and a citizen by Blood, of the Creek Nation; that I am the un lawful wife of Sam Loney, who is a citizen, by Blood of the Creek Nation; that a Male child was born to me on the 13 day of November, 1902, that said child has been named James Loney, and was living March 4, 1905.

                                            her
                       Lizzie Willingham   x
Witnesses To Mark: mark
{ Lewis Collins
{ F.B. Phillips

Subscribed and sworn to before me this 23 day of May, 1905.

                            Henry A McDaniel
                            Notary Public.

AFFIDAVIT OF ATTENDING PHYSICIAN OR MID-WIFE.

UNITED STATES OF AMERICA, Indian Territory, }
  Western   DISTRICT.

I, Rachael Loney, a mid-wife, on oath state that I attended on Mrs. Lizzie Willingham, ~~wife of~~ unlawful wife Sam Loney on the 13 day of November, 1902; that there was born to her on said date a male child; that said child was living March 4, 1905, and is said to have been named James Loney

                            Rachael Loney

Applications for Enrollment of Creek Newborn
Act of 1905 Volume IX

Witnesses To Mark:
{ F.B. Phillips

Subscribed and sworn to before me this 23 day of May, 1905.

My Commission Expires July 20, 1907.

Henry A McDaniel
Notary Public.

NC 107.

Muskogee, Indian Territory, May 17, 1905.

Joe McCombs,
    Lenna, Indian Territory.

Dear Sir:

    The Commission is in receipt of an affidavit executed by you relative to the birth of Jimmie McCombs, minor child of Sam Loney and Lizzie Willingham. You are advised that the affidavits of the mother of said child and of the midwife or physician in attendance at its birth should be supplied.

    There is herewith enclosed a blank form of birth affidavit, and in executing same care should be exercised to see that all blanks are properly filled, all names written in full and in the event that either of the persons signing the affidavit is unable to write, signatures by mark must be attested by two witnesses. Each affidavit must be executed before a Notary Public and the notarial seal and signature of the officer must be attached to each separate affidavit.

                    Respectfully,

                                  Chairman.

BC.

NC.107.

Muskogee, Indian Territory, July 18, 1905.

Lizzie Willingham,
    Lenna, Indian Territory.

Dear Madam:

    In the matter of the application for the enrollment of your minor child, Jimmie McCombs, as a citizen by blood of the Creek Nation, you are advised that this office

Applications for Enrollment of Creek Newborn
Act of 1905   Volume IX

requires your affidavit and the affidavit of the midwife or physician in attendance at the birth of said child.

There is herewith enclosed a blank form of birth affidavit, and in executing same care should be exercised to see that all blanks are properly filled, all names written in full and in the event that either of the persons signing the affidavit is unable to write, signatures by mark must be attested by two witnesses. Each affidavit must be executed before a Notary Public and the notarial seal and signature of the officer must be attached to each separate affidavit.

                              Respectfully,
                                                  Commissioner.
1 BC

C698
DEPARTMENT OF THE INTERIOR,
COMMISSION TO THE FIVE CIVILIZED TRIBES.
Eufaula, I. T., April 4, 1905.

In the matter of the application for the enrollment of Minnie Watson as a citizen of the Creek Nation.

LENA MARRISON[sic], being duly sworn, testified as follows:

Through Alex Posey Official Interpreter:

BY COMMISSION:
Q What is your name? A Lena Morrison.
Q How old are you? A Twenty-five.
Q What is your post office address? A Lenna.
Q Are you a citizen of the Creek Nation? A Yes, sir.
Q To what town do you belong? A Tuskegee.
Q Do you make application for the enrollment of your minor child, Minnie Watson, as a citizen of the Creek Nation? A Yes, sir.
Q Who is her father? A Sandy Watson.
Q Is he your lawful husband? A No, sir.
Q Were you ever married to him? A No, sir.
Q Does Sandy Watson recognize Minnie as his child? A Yes, sir.
Q Does he contribute to the support of the child? A No, sir.
Q Did he ever contribute anything for the support of the child? A No, sir.
Q Is Sandy Watson a citizen of the Creek Nation? A Yes, sir.
Q To what town does he belong? A Okchiye.
Q What was your name at the time the child was born? A Lena McCombs.
Q Are you now married? A Yes, sir.
Q Who is your present husband? A John Morrison, Jr.

Applications for Enrollment of Creek Newborn
Act of 1905 Volume IX

---oooOOOooo---

I, D. C. Skaggs, on oath state that the above and foregoing is a full and true transcript of my stenographic notes as taken in said cause on said date.

DC Skaggs

Subscribed and sworn to before me this 21 day of July, 1905.

J McDermott
Notary Public.

BIRTH AFFIDAVIT.
DEPARTMENT OF THE INTERIOR.
COMMISSION TO THE FIVE CIVILIZED TRIBES.

IN RE APPLICATION FOR ENROLLMENT, as a citizen of the Creek Nation, of Minnie Watson, born on the 23 day of August, 1901

Name of Father: Sandy Watson   a citizen of the Creek Nation. Okchiye Town
Name of Mother: Lena Morrison (nee McCombs) a citizen of the Creek Nation. Tuskegee Town

Postoffice   Lenna, Ind. Ter.

AFFIDAVIT OF MOTHER.

UNITED STATES OF AMERICA, Indian Territory, }
Western   DISTRICT. }   Child is present

I, Lena Morrison (nee McCombs), on oath state that I am 25 years of age and a citizen by blood, of the Creek Nation; that I am not the lawful wife of Sandy Watson, who is a citizen, by blood of the Creek Nation; that a female child was born to me on 23 day of August, 1901, that said child has been named Minnie Watson, and was living March 4, 1905.

Mr.[sic] Lena Morrison

Witnesses To Mark:
{

Subscribed and sworn to before me this 4 day of April, 1905.

Drennan C Skaggs
Notary Public.

93

Applications for Enrollment of Creek Newborn
Act of 1905 Volume IX

AFFIDAVIT OF ATTENDING PHYSICIAN OR MID-WIFE.

UNITED STATES OF AMERICA, Indian Territory,
Western DISTRICT.

I, Millie McCombs , a midwife , on oath state that I attended on Mrs. Lena Morrison (nee McCombs) not the lawful , wife of Sandy Watson on the 23 day of August , 1901 ; that there was born to her on said date a female child; that said child was living March 4, 1905, and is said to have been named Minnie Watson

                                       her
                              Millie x McCombs
Witnesses To Mark: mark
   { Alex Posey
     DC Skaggs

Subscribed and sworn to before me 4 day of April, 1905.

                             Drennan C Skaggs
                             Notary Public.

NC-699

                         Muskogee, Indian Territory, August 15, 1905.

James H. Simpson,
     Eufaula, Indian Territory.

Dear Sir:

      In the matter of the application for the enrollment of your minor daughter, Catherine Elizabeth Simpson, as a citizen by blood of the Creek Nation, it will be necessary for you to file with this Office either the original or a certified copy of the marriage license and certificate, showing marriage between you and Alice M. Simpson, the mother of said child.

      You are also requested to furnish this Office with your affidavit as to the birth of said child, and a blank for that purpose, properly filled out, is enclosed herewith.

                          Respectfully,
                                       Acting Commissioner.

CTD-46

**Applications for Enrollment of Creek Newborn
Act of 1905 Volume IX**

CERTIFICATE OF RECORD.

United States of America,⎫
   INDIAN TERRITORY,   ⎬ ss.
   Western District.   ⎭

     I, *ROBERT P. HARRISON*, *Clerk of the United States Court in the Western District, Indian Territory, do hereby certify that the instrument hereto attached was filed for record in my office the*   17 *day of* Feb.   *1903 at* 2 *P. M., and duly recorded in Book* O , *Marriage Record, Page* 157

     WITNESS my hand and seal of said Court at Muscogee, in said Territory, this 17   *day of*   Feb.   *A. D. 1903*

                                     R P Harrison   Clerk.
By   R.A. Bayne   *Deputy.*

MARRIAGE LICENSE.
••••••••

United States of America,⎫
   Indian Territory,   ⎬ ss.   *No.* **79**
   Western District.   ⎭

To Any Person Authorized by Law to Solemnize Marriage---Greeting:

     You are Hereby Commanded *to Solemnize the Rite and Publish the Banns of Matrimony between Mr.*   James H Simpson   *of*   Eufaula , *in the Indian Territory, aged* 20 *years and Miss* Allye Crites   *of*   Eufaula   *in the Indian Territory aged* 20 *years according to law, and do you officially sign and return this License to the parties therein named.*

     WITNESS my hand and official seal at Muscogee Indian Territory this   27th
day of January   *A.D. 190* 3

                                       R.P. Harrison
                                    Clerk of the U.S. Court
By C. E. Wilcox   *Deputy*

Applications for Enrollment of Creek Newborn
Act of 1905 Volume IX

CERTIFICATE OF MARRIAGE.

•••••

𝔘niteb States of America,
INDIAN TERRITORY, } ss.
Western District.

I, A. Lee Boyd , *a Minister of the Gospel, DO HEREBY CERTIFY that on the* 29 *day of* Jan. *A. D. 1903, I did duly and according to law as commanded in the foregoing License, solemnize the Rite and publish the Banns of Matrimony between the parties therein named.*

WITNESS my hand this 29 *day of* January *A. D. 1903*

My credentials are recorded in the office of the Clerk of the United States Court, Indian Territory, Western District, Book (blank) *, Page* (blank) .

A. Lee Boyd
A Minister of the Gospel

Note—This License and Certificate of Marriage must be returned to the Office of the Clerk of the United States Court in the Northern District, Indian Territory, from whence it was issued, within sixty days from the date thereof, or the party to whom the license was issued will be liable in the amount of the One Hundred Dollars ($100.00)

Commission to the Five Civilized Tribes

In Re Application for enrollment of Catherine Elizabeth Simpson, born on 5th. day November 1903. Name of father James H. Simpson, a citizen by blood of the Creek Nation. Name of mother Alice M. Simpson. Post Office address Eufaula, Indian Territory.

Affidavit of mother.

Indian Territory
Western District

Alice M. Simpson, being duly sworn on oath states; that I am 22 years of age; that I am the lawful wife of James H. Simpson, a citizen by blood of the Creek Nation: that on the 5th day of November 1903 there was born unto me a female child; that said child is now living and has been named Catherine Elizabeth Simpson.

Alice M. Simpson
April
Sworn and subscribed to before me this 3 day of ~~March~~ 1905.

MM Washington
My Commission Expires July 8th, 1906.   Notary Public

Applications for Enrollment of Creek Newborn
Act of 1905 Volume IX

Affidavit of Physician

Indian Territory
Western District

R. M. Counterman, a physician, being duly sworn on oath states that I attended on Mrs Alice M. Simpson, wife of James H. Simpson on the 5th. day of November 1903; that there was born unto her on the said date a female child; that said child is now living and has been named Catherine Elizabeth Simpson.

R.M. Counterman

Sworn and subscribed to before me this 7th day of March 1905.

Edwin G. Bedford
My Commission   Notary Public
Expires May 15th 1907

BIRTH AFFIDAVIT.
DEPARTMENT OF THE INTERIOR.
COMMISSION TO THE FIVE CIVILIZED TRIBES.

IN RE APPLICATION FOR ENROLLMENT, as a citizen of the Creek Nation, of Catherine Elizabeth Simpson, born on the 5th day of November, 1903

Name of Father: James H. Simpson   a citizen of the   Creek   Nation.
Name of Mother: Alice M. Simpson   a citizen of the United States Nation.

Postoffice   Eufaula, I.T.

AFFIDAVIT OF MOTHER.

UNITED STATES OF AMERICA, Indian Territory,
Western   DISTRICT.

I, James H. Simpson, on oath state that I am 22 years of age and a citizen by blood, of the Creek Nation; that I am the lawful ~~wife of~~ husband of Alice M. Simpson, who is a citizen, ~~by~~ *(blank)* of the United States Nation; that a female child was born to ~~me~~ us on 5th day of November, 1903, that said child has been named Catherine Elizabeth Simpson, and was living March 4, 1905.

James H. Simpson

Witnesses To Mark:

Applications for Enrollment of Creek Newborn
Act of 1905 Volume IX

Subscribed and sworn to before me this 16 day of August, 1905.

F. L. Moss
Notary Public.

Western Judicial District
Indian Territory.

I the undersigned Sam'l C Davis a citizen of the "Creek Nation" and of lawful age, do hereby certify that there was born to them about two years ago, a girl baby which is now living and named "Louina Hickory"

Saml C. Davis

On this the 3" day of April 1905 personally appeared before me Sam'l C. Davis who first being duly sworn says the foregoing statements are true.

Robert E. Lynch
My Com Expires July 3" 1906   Notary Public

BIRTH AFFIDAVIT.
DEPARTMENT OF THE INTERIOR,
COMMISSIONER TO THE FIVE CIVILIZED TRIBES.

IN RE APPLICATION FOR ENROLLMENT, as a citizen of the Creek Nation, of Louina Hickory , born on the 15 day of May , 1903

Name of Father: Thomas Hickory   a citizen of the   Creek   Nation.
Name of Mother: Jennie Hickory   a citizen of the   Creek   Nation.

Postoffice   Tulsa IT

AFFIDAVIT OF MOTHER.

UNITED STATES OF AMERICA, Indian Territory,
Western   District.

I, Jennie Hickory , on oath state that I am 27 years of age and a citizen by Blood, of the Creek Nation[sic] Nation; that I am the lawful wife of Thomas Hickory , who is a citizen, by Blood of the Creek Nation[sic] Nation; that a Female child was born to me on 15 day of May , 1903 , that said child has been named Louina Hickory, and was living March 4, 1905.

Applications for Enrollment of Creek Newborn
Act of 1905 Volume IX

Witness to Mark:
JL Kennedy
Saml C Davis

her
Jennie x Hickory
mark

Subscribed and sworn to before me this 3rd day of April , 1905.

Com Ex 7/3/1906　　　　　　　Robert E Lynch
　　　　　　　　　　　　　　　Notary Public.

AFFIDAVIT OF ATTENDING PHYSICIAN OR MID-WIFE.

UNITED STATES OF AMERICA, Indian Territory,
Western District.

I, Thomas Hickory , a *(blank)* , on oath state that I ~~attended on Mrs~~. The Husband of Jennie Hickory and there was no one present but myself when our daughter was born on the 15 day of May , 1903; that there was born to her on said date a Female child; that said child was living March 4, 1905, and is said to have been named Louina Hickory

His
Thomas x Hickory
mark

Witness to Mark:
JL Kennedy
Saml C Davis

Subscribed and sworn to before me this 3" day of April , 1905.

Com Ex 7/3/1906　　　　　　　Robert E Lynch
　　　　　　　　　　　　　　　Notary Public.

BIRTH AFFIDAVIT.

DEPARTMENT OF THE INTERIOR.
COMMISSION TO THE FIVE CIVILIZED TRIBES.

IN RE APPLICATION FOR ENROLLMENT, as a citizen of the Creek Nation, of Vera Oma Duckworth , born on the 11 day of March , 1903

Name of Father: Robert D. Duckworth　　a citizen of the United States Nation.
Name of Mother: Ruth E Duckworth (Hardage) a citizen of the　Creek　Nation.
Big Springs or Hitchitee Town

　　　　　　　　　　　Postoffice　　Holdenville, I.T.

Applications for Enrollment of Creek Newborn
Act of 1905 Volume IX

AFFIDAVIT OF MOTHER.

Child present

UNITED STATES OF AMERICA, Indian Territory, }
Western   DISTRICT.

I, Ruth E. Duckworth, on oath state that I am 23 years of age and a citizen by blood, of the Creek Nation; that I am the lawful wife of Robert D Duckworth, who is a citizen, by *(blank)* of the United States Nation; that a female child was born to me on 11 day of March, 1903, that said child has been named Vera Oma Duckworth, and was living March 4, 1905.

Ruth E Duckworth

Witnesses To Mark:
{

Subscribed and sworn to before me 24 day of March, 1905.

Drennan C Skaggs
Notary Public.

AFFIDAVIT OF ATTENDING PHYSICIAN OR MID-WIFE.

UNITED STATES OF AMERICA, Indian Territory, }
Western   DISTRICT.

I, Nancy R. Hardage, a *(blank)*, on oath state that I assisted the physician who attended on my daughter Mrs. Ruth E. Duckworth, wife of Robert D Duckworth on the 11 day of March, 1903; that there was born to her on said date a female child; that said child was living March 4, 1905, and is said to have been named Vera Oma Duckworth

Nancy R. Hardage

Witnesses To Mark:
{

Subscribed and sworn to before me 24 day of March, 1905.

Drennan C Skaggs
Notary Public.

Applications for Enrollment of Creek Newborn
Act of 1905 Volume IX

NC. 702.

Muskogee, Indian Territory, July 15, 1906.

Chief Clerk,
Cherokee Enrollment Division,
Muskogee, Indian Territory.

Dear Sir:

April 7, 1905, application was made to the Commission to the Five Civilized Tribes for the enrollment of Walter Lee Coodey, born September 28, 1903, as a citizen by blood of the Creek Nation. It is stated in said application that the father of said child is Wm. S. Coodey, a citizen of the Creek Nation, and that the mother is Luvena Coodey, a citizen of the Creek[sic] Nation.

You are requested to inform the Creek Enrollment Division as to whether application has been made for the enrollment of said Walter Lee Coodey as a citizen of the Cherokee Nation, and if so, what disposition has been made of the same.

Respectfully,

Commissioner.

REFER IN REPLY TO THE FOLLOWING:

DEPARTMENT OF THE INTERIOR,
COMMISSIONER TO THE FIVE CIVILIZED TRIBES.

Muskogee, Indian Territory, July 18, 1905.

Chief Clerk,
Creek Enrollment Division,
Muskogee, Indian Territory.

Dear Sir:

Replying to your letter of July 15, 1905, (NC. 702) asking to be advised whether or not any application has ever been made for the enrollment, as a citizen of the Cherokee Nation, of Walter Lee Coodey, a child of Wm. S. Coodey, a citizen of the Creek Nation, and Luvena Coodey, a citizen of the Creek[sic] Nation, you are advised that from an examination of the records of the Cherokee Enrollment Division it does not appear that any application has ever been made for the enrollment of said child as a citizen of that nation.

Respectfully,

GHL Tams Bixby Commissioner.

Applications for Enrollment of Creek Newborn
Act of 1905 Volume IX

NC-702

Muskogee, Indian Territory, August 15, 1905.

Levena Coodey,
    Care of William S. Coodey,
        Eufaula, Indian Territory.

Dear Madam:

    In the matter of the application for the enrollment of your minor son, Walter Lee Coodey, as a citizen by blood of the Creek Nation, it will be necessary for you to furnish this Office with either the original or a certified copy of the marriage license and certificate, showing marriage between you and William S. Coodey, the father of said child.
    It will also be necessary for you to furnish this Office with the affidavit of the said William S. Coodey relative to the birth of the child, and a blank for that purpose, which has been partially filled out, is herewith enclosed.

                Respectfully,

                              Acting Commissioner.

CTD-47

CERTIFICATE OF RECORD.

UNITED STATES OF AMERICA, ⎫
   INDIAN TERRITORY,   ⎬ ss.
Northern District. ⎭
    Chas. A. Davidson
    I, ~~JAMES A. WINSTON~~, Clerk of the United States Court in the Northern District, Indian Territory, do hereby certify that the instrument hereto attached was filed for record in my office the   11"   day of   May   1901 at .... M., and duly recorded in Book   K   , Marriage Record, Page   358

                WITNESS my hand and seal of said Court at Muscogee, in said Territory, this   16"   day of   May   A. D. 1901

                        Chas. A. Davidson   Clerk.
              By   Deputy.

Applications for Enrollment of Creek Newborn
Act of 1905 Volume IX

UNITED STATES OF AMERICA,
INDIAN TERRITORY } ss.   No.
Northern District.

TO ANY PERSON AUTHORIZED BY LAW TO SOLEMNIZE MARRIAGE, GREETING:

You are Hereby Commanded to Solemnize the Rite and publish the Banns of Matrimony between Mr. W. S. Coodey of Eufaula in the Indian Territory, aged 27 years and Miss Lavina Gaylor of Wagoner in the Indian Territory aged 18 years according to law, and do you officially sign and return this license to the parties therein named.

WITNESS my hand and official seal at Wagoner, Indian Territory this 29 day of Jan A.D. 1901

Chas A Davidson
Clerk of the U S Court.
By R. O. Hunter   Deputy.

CERTIFICATE OF MARRIAGE.

UNITED STATES OF AMERICA,
INDIAN TERRITORY } ss.
Northern District.

I, R C Grace, a Minister of the Gospel, DO HEREBY CERTIFY that on the 29th day of January A. D. 1901 I did duly and according to law as commanded in the foregoing License, solemnize the Rite and publish the Banns of Matrimony between the parties therein named.

WITNESS my hand this 4th day of February A. D. 1901

My credentials are recorded in the office of the Clerk of the United States Court, Indian Territory Northern District Book A Page 84

R.C. Grace
A Minister of the Gospel.

Note This license and certificate of marriage must be returned to the office of the Clerk of the United States court in the Western District Indian Territory from whence it was issued within sixty days from the date thereof of the party to whom the license was issued will be liable in the amount of the one hundred dollars ($100.00)

Applications for Enrollment of Creek Newborn
Act of 1905   Volume IX

BIRTH AFFIDAVIT.
DEPARTMENT OF THE INTERIOR.
COMMISSION TO THE FIVE CIVILIZED TRIBES.

IN RE APPLICATION FOR ENROLLMENT, as a citizen of the Creek Nation, of Walter Lee Coodey, born on the 28th day of September, 1903

Name of Father: William S. Coodey   a citizen of the   Creek   Nation.
Name of Mother: Levena Coody[sic]   a citizen of the   Cherokee   Nation.

Postoffice   Eufaula, I.T.

AFFIDAVIT OF MOTHER.

UNITED STATES OF AMERICA, Indian Territory,
Western   DISTRICT.

I, William S. Coodey, on oath state that I am *(blank)* years of age and a citizen by blood, of the Creek Nation; that I am the lawful ~~wife of~~ husband of Levena Coodey, who is a citizen, by blood of the Cherokee Nation; that a male child was born to ~~me~~ us on 28th day of September, 1903, that said child has been named Walter Lee Coodey, and was living March 4, 1905.

William S. Coodey

Witnesses To Mark:

Subscribed and sworn to before me this 16 day of August, 1905.

F. L. Moss
My Commission expires Jan. 20th, 1908.   Notary Public.

104

Applications for Enrollment of Creek Newborn
Act of 1905 Volume IX

BIRTH AFFIDAVIT.
DEPARTMENT OF THE INTERIOR.
COMMISSION TO THE FIVE CIVILIZED TRIBES.

IN RE APPLICATION FOR ENROLLMENT, as a citizen of the Creek Nation, of Walter Lee Coodey , born on the 28 day of September , 1903

Name of Father: W.M.S. Coodey   a citizen of the   Creek   Nation.
Coweta Town
Name of Mother: Levena Coodey   a citizen of the   Cherokee   Nation.

Postoffice   Eufaula, I. T.

AFFIDAVIT OF MOTHER.   Child present

UNITED STATES OF AMERICA, Indian Territory,
    Western   DISTRICT.

     I, Levena Coodey , on oath state that I am 22 years of age and a citizen by blood , of the Cherokee Nation; that I am the lawful wife of W.M.S. Coodey , who is a citizen, by blood of the Creek Nation; that a male child was born to me on 28 day of September , 1903 , that said child has been named Walter Lee Coodey , and was living March 4, 1905.

                                     Levena Coodey
Witnesses To Mark:
{

     Subscribed and sworn to before me this 3 day of April , 1905.

                                   Drennan C Skaggs
                                       Notary Public.

AFFIDAVIT OF ATTENDING PHYSICIAN OR MID-WIFE.

UNITED STATES OF AMERICA, Indian Territory,
    Western   DISTRICT.

     I, W.A. Tolleson , a physician , on oath state that I attended on Mrs. Levena Coodey , wife of W.M.S. Coodey on the 28 day of September , 1903 ; that there was born to her on said date a male child; that said child was living March 4, 1905, and is said to have been named Walter Lee Coodey

                                     W.A. Tolleson M.D.
Witnesses To Mark:
{

Applications for Enrollment of Creek Newborn
Act of 1905 Volume IX

Subscribed and sworn to before me 3 day of April, 1905.

>Drennan C Skaggs
>Notary Public.

NC 702

Muskogee, Indian Territory, November 13, 1906

Chief Clerk,
    Cherokee Enrollment Division,
        General Office.

Dear Sir:

    You are hereby advised that the name of Walter Lee Coodey, born September 28, 1903 to William S. Coodey, a citizen by blood of the Creek Nation and Levena Coodey, an alleged citizen of the Cherokee Nation, is contained in schedule of minor citizens by blood of the Creek Nation, approved by the Secretary of the Interior, September 27, 1905 opposite Roll number 657.

>Respectfully,
>Commissioner.

NC
~~En~~. 704.

DEPARTMENT OF THE INTERIOR,
COMMISSIONER TO THE FIVE CIVILIZED TRIBES.
Muskogee, Indian Territory. February 28, 1906.

    In the matter of the application for the enrollment of Kizzie Colbert as a citizen by blood of the Creek Nation.

    ELLEN COLBERT, being duly sworn testified as follows through Jesse McDermott official interpreter.

Q What is your name? A Ellen Colbert.
Q What is your post-office address? A Eufaula.
Q What is your age? A I am about 39.
Q Have you a new born child? A Yes.
Q What is it's[sic] name? A Kizzie.
Q When was Kizzie born? A December 14.
Q What year A 1903.

Applications for Enrollment of Creek Newborn
Act of 1905   Volume IX

Q   There is on file at this office an affidavit executed by you relative to the birth of Kizzie on August 16, 1905, in said affidavit you have signed your name as Ella, is that your correct name? A   The Notary Public in making out the affidavit spelled my name Ella, but my correct name is Ellen.
Q   There is another affidavit on file executed by you before Drennan C. Skaggs, and your name in that affidavit is spelled Ellen, is that correct? A   Yes.
Q   To what Creek Indian town do you belong? A   Tulsa Canadian.

   Witness is identified on Creek Indian card 3345 opposite roll number 8547.

   I, Harriett E. Arbuckle, on oath state that the above and foregoing is a true and correct transcript of my stenographic notes as taken in said cause on said date.

                                       Harriett E. Arbuckle
Subscribed and sworn to before me
this 1 day of March 1906.
                                       J. McDermott
                                            Notary Public.

NC-704
                              Muskogee, Indian Territory, August 15, 1905.
Thompson Colbert,
      Eufaula, Indian Territory.

Dear Sir:

   In the matter of the application for the enrollment of your minor daughter, Kizzie Colbert, as a citizen by blood of the Creek Nation (born December 14, 1903), it will be necessary for you to file with this Office the affidavits of two disinterested persons relative to the birth of said child. Said affidavits must set forth said child's name, the date of her birth, the names of her parents, and whether or not she was living on March 4, 1905.
                              Respectfully,
                                       Acting Commissioner.

NC-704.
                              Muskogee, Indian Territory, October 18, 1905.
Thompson Colbert,
      Eufaula, Indian Territory.

Dear Sir:

   In the matter of the application for the enrollment of your minor daughter Kizzie Colbert, born December 14, 1903, as a citizen by blood of the Creek Nation you

Applications for Enrollment of Creek Newborn
Act of 1905 Volume IX

state in your affidavit, executed August 16, 1905, that there was no midwife or physician in attendance on your wife, Ellen Colbert, at the birth of said child.

It will be necessary for you to file with this office, in lieu of the affidavit of an attending physician or midwife, the affidavits of two disinterested persons. Said affidavits must set forth said child's name, the date of her birth, the names of her parents, and whether or not she was living on March 4, 1905.

        Respectfully,
            Commissioner.

NC-704

        Muskogee, Indian Territory, December 14, 1905.

Thompson Colbert,
  Eufaula, Indian Territory.

Dear Sir:

  In the matter of the application for the enrollment of your minor child, Kizzie Colbert, born December 14, 1903, as a citizen by blood of the Creek Nation, you are again advised that it will be necessary for you to file with this Office the affidavit of two disinterested persons relative to said child's birth. A blank for that purpose is herewith enclosed.

    This matter should have your prompt attention.

        Respectfully,
            Commissioner.

Dis

Indian Territory)
) SS
Western District)

  We, the undersigned, on oath state that we are personally acquainted with Ellen Colbert wife of Thompson Colbert and that on or about the 14 day of Dec , 1903, a female child was born to them and has been named Kizzie Colbert ; that said child was living March 4, 1905.

        Wm McCombs

        Sarah McCombs

Applications for Enrollment of Creek Newborn
Act of 1905 Volume IX

Witnesses to mark:

Subscribed and sworn to before me this 28" day of Feb 1906.

J McDermott
Notary Public.

BIRTH AFFIDAVIT.
DEPARTMENT OF THE INTERIOR.
COMMISSION TO THE FIVE CIVILIZED TRIBES.

IN RE APPLICATION FOR ENROLLMENT, as a citizen of the Creek Nation, of Kizzie Colbert, born on the 14th. day of December, 1903

Name of Father: Thompson Colbert   a citizen of the   Creek   Nation.
Name of Mother: Ella Colbert   a citizen of the   Creek   Nation.

         Postoffice   Eufaula Ind. Tery.

AFFIDAVIT OF MOTHER.

UNITED STATES OF AMERICA, Indian Territory, ⎤
    Western   DISTRICT.   ⎦

     I, Ella Colbert, on oath state that I am Thirty nine years of age and a citizen by blood, of the Creek Nation; that I am the lawful wife of Thompson Colbert, who is a citizen, by blood of the Creek Nation; that a female child was born to me on the 14th. day of December 1903, ~~190~~, that said child has been named Kizzie Colbert, and was living March 4, 1905.

                                       Ella Colbert

Witnesses To Mark:
{

Subscribed and sworn to before me this 16th. day of August, 1905.

                                   Frank W Rushing
                                       Notary Public.
My Commission Expires Jan. 30, 1909.

Applications for Enrollment of Creek Newborn
Act of 1905   Volume IX

AFFIDAVIT OF ATTENDING PHYSICIAN OR MID-WIFE.

UNITED STATES OF AMERICA, Indian Territory, }
Western   DISTRICT.

I, Thompson Colbert, a *(blank)*, on oath state that I attended on Mrs. Ella Colbert (My wife), wife of In the sickness when our baby Kizzie was born. We had no physician at all. on the 14th. day of December, 1903 ; that there was born to her on said date a female child; that said child was living March 4, 1905, and is said to have been named Kizzie Colbert

             his
         Thompson x Colbert
Witnesses To Mark: mark
{ Arthur E. Raiford
{ Frank W Rushing

Subscribed and sworn to before me this 16th. day of August, 1905.

        Frank W Rushing
         Notary Public.

My Commission Expires Jan. 30, 1909.

BIRTH AFFIDAVIT.

DEPARTMENT OF THE INTERIOR.
COMMISSION TO THE FIVE CIVILIZED TRIBES.

IN RE APPLICATION FOR ENROLLMENT, as a citizen of the Creek Nation, of Kizzie Colbert, born on the 14 day of December, 1903

Name of Father: Thompson Colbert   a citizen of the   Creek   Nation.
Tulsa Canadian
Name of Mother: Ellen Colbert   a citizen of the   Creek   Nation.
Tulsa Canadian Town
      Postoffice   Eufaula Ind. Terr.

AFFIDAVIT OF MOTHER.

UNITED STATES OF AMERICA, Indian Territory, }
Western   DISTRICT.

I, Ellen Colbert, on oath state that I am 35 years of age and a citizen by blood, of the Creek Nation; that I am the lawful wife of Thompson Colbert, who is a citizen, by blood of the Creek Nation; that a female child was born to me on the 14 day of December, 1903, that said child has been named Kizzie Colbert, and was living March 4, 1905. That no one attended on me as midwife or physician at the birth of the child

Applications for Enrollment of Creek Newborn
Act of 1905   Volume IX

Ellen Colbert
Witnesses To Mark:
{

Subscribed and sworn to before me this 3 day of April, 1905.

Drennan C Skaggs
Notary Public.

AFFIDAVIT OF ATTENDING PHYSICIAN OR MID-WIFE.

UNITED STATES OF AMERICA, Indian Territory, }
Western   DISTRICT.

my wife
I, Thompson Colbert , a (blank) , on oath state that I attended on ^ Mrs. Ellen Colbert , wife of (blank) on the 14 day of December, 1903 ; that there was born to her on said date a female child; that said child was living March 4, 1905, and is said to have has been named Kizzie Colbert

his
Thompson x Colbert
Witnesses To Mark: mark
{ Alex Posey
{ DC Skaggs

Subscribed and sworn to before me this 3 day of April, 1905.

Drennan C Skaggs
Notary Public.

BIRTH AFFIDAVIT.
DEPARTMENT OF THE INTERIOR.
COMMISSION TO THE FIVE CIVILIZED TRIBES.

IN RE APPLICATION FOR ENROLLMENT, as a citizen of the Creek Nation, of Lucy Lewallen , born on the 3 day of October, 1902

Name of Father: John Lewallen   a citizen of the United States Nation.
Name of Mother: Louisa Lewallen (nee Grayson)a citizen of the   Creek   Nation.
Arbeka Deep fork Town
Postoffice   Brushhill, Ind. Terr.

Applications for Enrollment of Creek Newborn
Act of 1905 Volume IX

AFFIDAVIT OF MOTHER. Child present.

UNITED STATES OF AMERICA, Indian Territory,
Western DISTRICT.

I, John Lewallen , on oath state that I am 27 years of age and a citizen ~~by~~ ~~(blank)~~ , of the United States Nation; that I ~~am~~ was the lawful ~~wife~~ husband of Louisa Lewallen , who ~~is~~ was a citizen, by blood of the Creek Nation; that a female child was born to ~~me~~ her on the 3 day of October , 1902 , that said child has been named Lucy Lewallen , and was living March 4, 1905. That the mother, Louisa Lewallen, is dead.

John Lewallen

Witnesses To Mark:

Subscribed and sworn to before me this 3 day of April , 1905.

Drennan C Skaggs
Notary Public.

Grandmother
AFFIDAVIT OF ~~ATTENDING PHYSICIAN OR MID-WIFE~~.

UNITED STATES OF AMERICA, Indian Territory,
Western DISTRICT.

I, Winey Grayson , a mid-wife , on oath state that I attended on Mrs. Louisa Lewallen , wife of John Lewallen on the 3 day of October , 1902 ; that there was born to her on said date a female child; that said child was living March 4, 1905, and is said to have been named Lucy Lewallen her

Winey x Grayson
Witnesses To Mark: mark
{ DC Skaggs
  Alex Posey

Subscribed and sworn to before me 3 day of April, 1905.

Drennan C Skaggs
Notary Public.

Applications for Enrollment of Creek Newborn
Act of 1905 Volume IX

BIRTH AFFIDAVIT.
DEPARTMENT OF THE INTERIOR.
COMMISSION TO THE FIVE CIVILIZED TRIBES.

IN RE APPLICATION FOR ENROLLMENT, as a citizen of the Creek Nation, of Charlie Lewallen, born on the 15 day of October, 1904

Name of Father: John Lewallen   a citizen of the United States Nation.
Name of Mother: Louisa Lewallen (nee Grayson) a citizen of the   Creek   Nation.
Arbeka Deepfork Town
                         Postoffice   Brushhill, I.T.

AFFIDAVIT OF MOTHER.

UNITED STATES OF AMERICA, Indian Territory,
     Western   DISTRICT.

     I, John Lewallen, on oath state that I am 27 years of age and a citizen ~~by~~ *(blank)*, of the United States ~~Nation~~; that I ~~am~~ was the lawful ~~wife~~ husband of Louisa Lewallen, who ~~is~~ was a citizen, by blood of the Creek Nation; that a male child was born to ~~me~~ her on the 15 day of October, 1904, that said child has been named Charlie Lewallen, and was living March 4, 1905.

                                 John Lewallen
Witnesses To Mark:

     Subscribed and sworn to before me this 3 day of April, 1905.

                                 Drennan C Skaggs
                                   Notary Public.

AFFIDAVIT OF ATTENDING PHYSICIAN OR MID-WIFE.

UNITED STATES OF AMERICA, Indian Territory,
     Western   DISTRICT.

     I, Winey Grayson, a mid-wife, on oath state that I attended on Mrs. Louisa Lewallen, wife of John Lewallen on the 5 day of October, 1904; that there was born to her on said date a male child; that said child was living March 4, 1905, and is said to have been named Charlie Lewallen
                                   her
                          Winey x Grayson
                                mark

**Applications for Enrollment of Creek Newborn
Act of 1905 Volume IX**

Witnesses To Mark:
{ DC Skaggs
{ Alex Posey

    Subscribed and sworn to before me 3 day of April, 1905.

                              Drennan C Skaggs
                              Notary Public.

**DEPARTMENT OF THE INTERIOR.
COMMISSION TO THE FIVE CIVILIZED TRIBES.**

    In the matter of the death of Charlie Lewallen a citizen of the Creek Nation, who formerly resided at or near Brush Hill , Ind. Ter., and died on the 26 day of December , 1904

AFFIDAVIT OF RELATIVE.

UNITED STATES OF AMERICA, Indian Territory, }
    Western   DISTRICT.

    I, John Lewallen , on oath state that I am 27 years of age and a citizen by (blank) , of the United States Nation; that my postoffice address is Brush Hill , Ind. Ter.; that I am the father of Charlie Lewallen who was a citizen, by blood , of the Creek Nation and that said Charlie Lewallen died on the 26 day of December , 1904
                              John Lewallen
Witnesses To Mark:
{

    Subscribed and sworn to before me this 3 day of April, 1905.

                              Drennan C Skaggs
                              Notary Public.

AFFIDAVIT OF ACQUAINTANCE.

UNITED STATES OF AMERICA, Indian Territory, }
    Western   DISTRICT.

    I, Winey Grayson , on oath state that I am about 48 years of age, and a citizen by blood of the Creek Nation; that my postoffice address is Brush Hill , Ind. Ter.; that I was personally acquainted with Charlie Lewallen who was a citizen,

Applications for Enrollment of Creek Newborn
Act of 1905 Volume IX

by blood , of the Creek Nation; and that said Charlie Lewallen died on the 26
day of December , 1904 her
Witnesses To Mark: Winey x Grayson
{ DC Skaggs mark
  Alex Posey

Subscribed and sworn to before me this 3 day of April, 1905.

Drennan C Skaggs
Notary Public.

NC 705 JLD
DEPARTMENT OF THE INTERIOR,
COMMISSIONER TO THE FIVE CIVILIZED TRIBES.

In the matter of the application for the enrollment of Charlie Lewallen, deceased, as a citizen by blood of the Creek Nation.

STATEMENT AND ORDER.

The record in this case shows that on April 7, 1905, application was made, in affidavit form, for the enrollment of Charlie Lewallen, deceased, as a citizen by blood of the Creek Nation, under the provisions of the Act of Congress approved March 3, 1905.
It appears from the affidavit filed in this matter that said Charlie Lewallen, deceased, was born October 15, 1904, and died December 27, 1904.
The Act of Congress approved March 3, 1905, (33 Stats., 1048), provides:
"That the Commission to the Five Civilized Tribes is authorized for sixty days after the date of the approval of this act to receive and consider applications for enrollment, of children, born subsequent to May twenty-fifth, nineteen hundred and one, and prior to March fourth, nineteen hundred and five, and living on said latter date, to citizens of the Creek tribe of Indians whose enrollment has been approved by the Secretary of the Interior prior to the approval of this act; and to enroll and make allotments to such children."
It is, therefore, ordered that the application for the enrollment of Charlie Lewallen, deceased, as a citizen by blood of the Creek Nation be, and the same is, hereby dismissed.

Tams Bixby Commissioner.
Muskogee, Indian Territory.
JAN 4 – 1907

Applications for Enrollment of Creek Newborn
Act of 1905   Volume IX

BIRTH AFFIDAVIT.
DEPARTMENT OF THE INTERIOR.
COMMISSION TO THE FIVE CIVILIZED TRIBES.

    IN RE APPLICATION FOR ENROLLMENT, as a citizen of the Creek Nation, of Alice Sukey Goat, born on the 7 day of November, 1904

Name of Father: Alfred Goat   a citizen of the   Creek   Nation.
Tulsa L. R. Town
Name of Mother: Racheal[sic] Goat   a citizen of the   Creek   Nation.
Coweta Town
                         Postoffice   Holdenville, Ind. Ter.

AFFIDAVIT OF MOTHER.

UNITED STATES OF AMERICA, Indian Territory, ⎫
     Western   **DISTRICT.**   ⎭   Child is present

    I, Racheal Goat, on oath state that I am about 35 years of age and a citizen by blood, of the Creek Nation; that I am the lawful wife of Alfred Goat, who is a citizen, by blood of the Creek Nation; that a female child was born to me on 7 day of November, 1904, that said child has been named Alice Sukey Goat, and was living March 4, 1905.   her
                                       Racheal x Goat
Witnesses To Mark: mark
  ⎰ Alex Posey
  ⎱ DC Skaggs

    Subscribed and sworn to before me this 28 day of March, 1905.

                                 Drennan C Skaggs
                                       Notary Public.

AFFIDAVIT OF ATTENDING PHYSICIAN OR MID-WIFE.

UNITED STATES OF AMERICA, Indian Territory, ⎫
     Western   **DISTRICT.**   ⎭

    I, Minnie Goat, a midwife, on oath state that I attended on Mrs. Racheal Goat, wife of Alfred Goat on the 7 day of November, 1904; that there was born to her on said date a female child; that said child was living March 4, 1905, and is said to have been named Alice Sukey Goat
                               Minnie Goat

Applications for Enrollment of Creek Newborn
Act of 1905 Volume IX

Witnesses To Mark:
{

Subscribed and sworn to before me this 29 day of March, 1905.

Drennan C Skaggs
Notary Public.

BIRTH AFFIDAVIT.
DEPARTMENT OF THE INTERIOR.
COMMISSION TO THE FIVE CIVILIZED TRIBES.

IN RE APPLICATION FOR ENROLLMENT, as a citizen of the Creek Nation, of Angeline Goat, born on the 19 day of July, 1902

Name of Father: Alfred Goat   a citizen of the   Creek   Nation.
Tulsa L. R. Town
Name of Mother: Racheal[sic] Goat   a citizen of the   Creek   Nation.
Coweta Town
                 Postoffice   Holdenville, Ind. Ter.

AFFIDAVIT OF MOTHER.

UNITED STATES OF AMERICA, Indian Territory,
     Western   DISTRICT. }   Child is present

     I, Racheal Goat, on oath state that I am about 35 years of age and a citizen by blood, of the Creek Nation; that I am the lawful wife of Alfred Goat, who is a citizen, by blood of the Creek Nation; that a female child was born to me on 19 day of July, 1902, that said child has been named Angeline Goat, and was living March 4, 1905.
                                             her
                                    Racheal x Goat
Witnesses To Mark: mark
{ Alex Posey
   DC Skaggs

     Subscribed and sworn to before me this 28 day of March, 1905.

Drennan C Skaggs
Notary Public.

Applications for Enrollment of Creek Newborn
Act of 1905 Volume IX

AFFIDAVIT OF ATTENDING PHYSICIAN OR MID-WIFE.

UNITED STATES OF AMERICA, Indian Territory, }
Western   DISTRICT.

I, Minnie Goat , a midwife , on oath state that I attended on Mrs. Racheal Goat, wife of Alfred Goat on the 19 day of July , 1902 ; that there was born to her on said date a female child; that said child was living March 4, 1905, and is said to have been named Angeline Goat

Minnie Goat

Witnesses To Mark:
{

Subscribed and sworn to before me this 29 day of March , 1905.

Drennan C Skaggs
Notary Public.

---

707 N.C.

Muskogee, Indian Territory, September 2, 1905

Jennie Greenwood,
    Care Lewis Greenwood,
        Eufaula, Indian Territory.

Dear Madam:

In the matter of the application for the enrollment of your minor child, Effie Belle Greenwood, as a citizen of the Creek Nation, you are advised that you will be allowed tens days within which to appear before the Commissioner to the Five Civilized Tribes at Muskogee, Indian Territory, for the purpose of being examined under oath.

Respectfully,
Commissioner.

Applications for Enrollment of Creek Newborn
Act of 1905 Volume IX

N.C.707.

DEPARTMENT OF THE INTERIOR,
COMMISSIONER TO THE FIVE CIVILIZED TRIBES.
Eufaula, I. T., September 23, 1905.

In the matter of the application for the enrollment of Effie Belle Greenwood as a citizen by blood of the Creek Nation.

JENNIE GREENWOOD, being duly sworn, testified as follows:

Through Alex Posey Official Interpreter:

BY THE COMMISSIONER:
Q What is your name? A Jennie Greenwood.
Q How old are you? A I do not know my age. I suppose I am about twenty-three.
Q What is your post office address? A Eufaula.
Q Are you a citizen of the Creek Nation? A Yes, sir.
Q To what town do you belong? A Quasarte No. 1.
Q Have you made application for the enrollment of your minor child, Effie Belle Greenwood? A Yes, sir.
Q Are you known by any name other than Jennie Greenwood? A No, sir.
Q Under what name are you enrolled? A I am enrolled as Lizzie McIntosh.

Witness presents deeds to Homestead and Surplus Allotment, Commission numbers 22198 and 22199, issued to lizzie McIntosh, Creek Indian Roll No. 7618, delivered March 1, 1904.

Q What is the name of your mother? A Hepsey McIntosh.
Q Have you any brothers and sisters? A Yes, sir.
Q Name them? A Nancy Scott, Bettie Scott, Henry, Leah and Dave McIntosh.
Q Were you never known as Lizzie? A No, sir. I was enrolled in my town by Billy Barnett, Town King, and he enterred[sic] my name on the roll wrong. Jennie is my proper name and I am known by no other name.
Q There is no one in your family living or dead named Lizzie? A No, sir.
Q What is the name of your husband? A Lewis Greenwood.
Q To what town does he belong? A Hickory Ground.

---oooOOOooo---

I, D. C. Skaggs, on oath state that the above and foregoing is a full and true transcript of my stenographic notes as taken in said cause on said date.

DC Skaggs

Applications for Enrollment of Creek Newborn
Act of 1905 Volume IX

Subscribed and sworn to before me this 29th day of Sept 1905.

J.C. Smock
Notary Public.

(The above Affidavit given again.)

BIRTH AFFIDAVIT.

DEPARTMENT OF THE INTERIOR.
COMMISSION TO THE FIVE CIVILIZED TRIBES.

IN RE APPLICATION FOR ENROLLMENT, as a citizen of the Creek Nation, of Effie Belle Greenwood, born on the 27 day of July, 1903

Name of Father: Lewis Greenwood   a citizen of the   Creek   Nation.
Hickory Ground   (nee McIntosh)
Name of Mother: Jennie Greenwood   a citizen of the   Creek   Nation.
Quasarte No. 1
                        Postoffice   Eufaula, Ind. Ter.

AFFIDAVIT OF MOTHER.

UNITED STATES OF AMERICA, Indian Territory, ⎫
     Western   DISTRICT.   ⎭

     I, Jennie Greenwood, on oath state that I am 23 years of age and a citizen by blood, of the Creek Nation; that I am the lawful wife of Lewis Greenwood, who is a citizen, by blood of the Creek Nation; that a female child was born to me on 27 day of July, 1903, that said child has been named Effie Belle Greenwood, and was living March 4, 1905.

                                           Jennie x Greenwood
Witnesses To Mark:
   ⎰ Alex Posey
   ⎱ DC Skaggs

     Subscribed and sworn to before me this 3 day of April, 1905.

                                     Drennan C Skaggs
                                          Notary Public.

Applications for Enrollment of Creek Newborn
Act of 1905 Volume IX

AFFIDAVIT OF ATTENDING PHYSICIAN OR MID-WIFE.

UNITED STATES OF AMERICA, Indian Territory,
Western DISTRICT.

    I, Hepsey McIntosh , a midwife , on oath state that I attended on Mrs. Jennie Greenwood, wife of Lewis Greenwood on the 27 day of July , 1903 ; that there was born to her on said date a female child; that said child was living March 4, 1905, and is said to have been named Effie Belle Greenwood

                                           her
                                Hepsey x McIntosh
Witnesses To Mark: mark
   { Alex Posey
     DC Skaggs

    Subscribed and sworn to before me 3 day of April, 1905.

                          Drennan C Skaggs
                          Notary Public.

NC-708

                       Muskogee, Indian Territory, August 15, 1905.

Alice V. Minugh,
      Care of Clarence E. Minugh,
          Muskogee, Indian Territory.

Dear Madam:

    In the matter of the application for the enrollment of your minor son, Jesse L. Minugh, born August 25, 1902, as a citizen by blood of the Creek Nation, it will be necessary for you to furnish this Office with the affidavit of the attending physician or midwife relative to the birth of said child, and a blank for that purpose is enclosed herewith.

    Please give this matter your immediate attention.

                      Respectfully,
                                    Acting Commissioner.
1 B C
Env

Applications for Enrollment of Creek Newborn
Act of 1905 Volume IX

AFFIDAVIT OF ATTENDING PHYSICIAN OR MID-WIFE.

UNITED STATES OF AMERICA, Indian Territory, }
Western DISTRICT.

I, J L Blakeman , a physician , on oath state that I attended on Mrs. (Elmer) Alice V. Minugh , wife of C.E. Minugh on the 25th day of Aug , 1902 ; that there was born to her on said date a male child; that said child was living March 4, 1905, and is said to have been named Jesse Lee Minugh

JL Blakeman

Witnesses To Mark:
{

Subscribed and sworn to before me 18 day of Aug, 1905.

Thos H Owen
Notary Public.

BIRTH AFFIDAVIT.

DEPARTMENT OF THE INTERIOR.
COMMISSION TO THE FIVE CIVILIZED TRIBES.

IN RE APPLICATION FOR ENROLLMENT, as a citizen of the CREEK Nation, of Jesse L. Minugh , born on the 25 day of Aug , 1902

Name of Father: C.E. Minugh	a citizen of the U.S.	Nation.
Name of Mother: Alice V. "	a citizen of the Creek	Nation.

Postoffice Muskogee

Child Present - MAR 31 1905

AFFIDAVIT OF MOTHER.

UNITED STATES OF AMERICA, Indian Territory, }
WESTERN DISTRICT.

I, Alice V. Minugh , on oath state that I am 29 years of age and a citizen by blood , of the Creek Nation; that I am the lawful wife of C.E. Minugh , who is a citizen, by ----- of the U.S. Nation; that a male child was born to me on 25 day of Aug , 1902 , that said child has been named Jesse L. Minugh , and is now living.

Alice V Minugh

Witnesses To Mark:
{

Applications for Enrollment of Creek Newborn
Act of 1905   Volume IX

Subscribed and sworn to before me this 31 day of March, 1905.

Edw C Griesel
Notary Public.

BIRTH AFFIDAVIT.
DEPARTMENT OF THE INTERIOR.
COMMISSION TO THE FIVE CIVILIZED TRIBES.

IN RE APPLICATION FOR ENROLLMENT, as a citizen of the Muskogee Nation, of Myrtice A Robinson, born on the 10 day of Nov, 1904

Name of Father: Will R. Robinson   a citizen of the US.   Nation.
                                nee Wright
Name of Mother: Maysie A Robinson   a citizen of the Muskogee   Nation.

Postoffice   Catoosa Ind. T.

AFFIDAVIT OF MOTHER.

UNITED STATES OF AMERICA, Indian Territory,
    Western   DISTRICT.

I, Maysie A Robinson nee Wright, on oath state that I am 25 years of age and a citizen by blood, of the Muskogee Nation; that I am the lawful wife of Will R Robinson, who is a citizen, by *(blank)* of the U.S. Nation; that a female child was born to me on 10 day of Nov, 1904, that said child has been named Myrtice A Robinson, and is now living.

Maysie A. Robinson

Witnesses To Mark:

Subscribed and sworn to before me 28 day of March, 1905.

WW Whitman
My Commission Expires Nov. 5 1907   Notary Public.

Applications for Enrollment of Creek Newborn
Act of 1905 Volume IX

AFFIDAVIT OF ATTENDING PHYSICIAN OR MID-WIFE.

UNITED STATES OF AMERICA, Indian Territory, ⎫
Western Jud   DISTRICT.   ⎬

I, Dr J C Smith , a M D , on oath state that I attended on Mrs. Maysie A Robinson , wife of Will R Robinson on the 10 day of Nov , 1904 ; that there was born to her on said date a female child; that said child is now living and is said to have been named Myrtice A Robinson

J C Smith MD

Witnesses To Mark:

{

Subscribed and sworn to before me 28 day of March , 1905.

WW Whitman
My Commission Expires Nov. 5 1907   Notary Public.

C 711

DEPARTMENT OF THE INTERIOR,
COMMISSION TO THE FIVE CIVILIZED TRIBES.
Holdenville, Indian Territory I. T., March 29, 1905.

In the matter of the application for the enrollment of Winey Harjo as a citizen of the Creek Nation.

RHODA HARJO, being duly sworn, testified as follows:

Through Alex Posey Official Interpreter:

BY COMMISSION:
Q What is your name? A Rhoda Harjo.
Q How old are you? A About 22.
Q What is your post office address? A Yeager.
Q Are you a citizen of the Creek Nation? A Yes, sir.
Q To what town do you belong? A Tuckabatche.
Q Do you make application for the enrollment of your minor child, Winey Harjo, as a citizen by blood of the Creek Nation blood of the Creek Nation? A Yes, sir.
Q What is the name of the child's father? A Lily Harjo.
Q Is he your lawful husband? A Yes, sir.

Applications for Enrollment of Creek Newborn
Act of 1905   Volume IX

Q Is he a citizen of the Creek Nation? A Yes, sir.
Q To what town does he belong? A Tuckabatche.
Q When was your child Winey born? A March 2, this year.
Q On what day was the child born? A Saturday.
Q You stated in your affidavit that the child was born on the 2" day of March, that would have been on Thursday? The child was born on Saturday.
Q How old is the child? A The child is over two weeks old.
Q Is it three weeks old? A Going on three weeks old.
Q How many Sundays have passed since the child was born? A Two Sundays.
Q Who attended on you at the birth of the child? A Lindy Harjo.
Q Are you positive that the child was born on the 2 day of March, this year? A Yes, sir.
Q Was there any record made of the birth of the child? A My husband made a record.
Q Where is that record? A It was left at home.

LILY HARJO, being duly sworn, testified as follows:

Through Alex Posey Official Interpreter:

BY COMMISSION:
Q What is your name? A Lily Harjo
Q How old are you? A About twenty-four.
Q What is your post office address? A Yeager.
Q Are you a citizen of the Creek Nation? A Yes, sir.
Q To what town do you belong? A Tuckabatche.
Q Do you know Rhoda Harjo? A Yes, sir.
Q Is she your wife? A Yes, sir.
Q Are you the father of her child, Winey Harjo? A Yes, sir.
Q Do you know when that child was born? A March 2.
Q What year? A This year.
Q On what day of the week was she born? A Tuesday night.
Q Was there any record made as to when the child was born? A I made a record and have it at home.
Q What kind of a book did you make that record in? A On a piece of paper.
Q Is it written with a pencil or with ink? A Pencil.
Q When did you make the record? A Wednesday.
Q How old is the child? A I think the child is about three weeks old.
Q When did you learn that Creek Citizens could make application for the enrollment of New-born children? A I do not know. Probably about a month ago.
Q Was the child born at that time? A The child was not born.
Q How long after you heard about it was the child born? A I do not know.
Q Who was present when the child was born? A Lindy Harjo.
Q Was there any one else? A No, sir.
Q Would any of your immediate neighbors know when the child was born? A Probably so.
Q Who are some of your immediate neighbors? A Lawyer Deere, Jackson Yahola and Conuccee Lowe.

Applications for Enrollment of Creek Newborn
Act of 1905 Volume IX

LINDY HARJO, being duly sworn, testified as follows:

Through Alex Posey Official Interpreter:

BY COMMISSION:
Q What is your name? A Lindy Harjo.
Q How old are you? A I do not know.

Witness appears to be about forty.
Q What is your post office address? A Yeager.
Q Are you a citizen of the Creek Nation? A Yes sir.
Q To what town do you belong? A Tuckabatche.
Q Are you acquainted with Lily and Rhoda Harjo? A Yes, sir.
Q Do you know a child of theirs named Winey Harjo? A Yes, sir.
Q Do you know when that child was born? A March 2.
Q What year? A This year.
Q What day of the week was the child born? A I think the child was born on Saturday.
Q Did you attend on Rhoda Harjo as mid-wife at the birth of the child? A Yes, sir.
Q Was the next day af[sic] the birth of the child Sunday? A Yes, sir.
Q If the child was born on Saturday it could not have ben born on the 2nd day of March?
A I am positive the child was born on Saturday, but I do not know what date.
Q How old is the child? A The child, I think, is not quite three weeks old.
Q Will the child be three weeks old next Saturday? A I think so.
Q Are you positive that the child is not three weeks old? A The child will not be three weeks old until next Saturday.

CANUGGEE LAWE[sic], being duly sworn, testified as follows:

Through Alex Posey Official Interpreter:

BY COMMISSION:
Q What is your name? A Canuggee Lowe
Q How old are you? A Twenty-nine.
Q What is your post office address? A Holdenville.
Q Are you a citizen of the Creek Nation? A Yes, sir.
Q To what town do you belong? A Tuckabatche.
Q Are you acquainted with Lily and Rhoda Harjo? A Yes, sir.
Q Do you know a child of theirs named Winey Harjo? A Yes, sir.
Q Do you know when that child was born? A March 2, 1905.
Q How far do you live from them? A About a half mile.
Q Were you present when the child was born? A No, sir, but I heard of the birth of the child the next day.
Q On what day of the week was the child born? A I heard the child was born about nine o'clock on Thursday night.
Q On what day did you her of the child's birth? A On Friday morning.
Q How old is the child? A About three weeks old.

Applications for Enrollment of Creek Newborn
Act of 1905   Volume IX

Q Do you know whether or not is over three weeks old? A I cannot say as to that.
Q What relation is the child to you? A I am the child's uncle.
Q Are you positive that the child was born March 2, 1905? A Yes, sir.

JACKSON YAHOLA, being duly sworn, testified as follows:

Through Alex Posey Official Interpreter:

BY COMMISSION:
Q What is your name? A Jackson Yahola.
Q How old are you? A About thirty-four.
Q What is your post office address? A Holdenville.
Q Are you a citizen of the Creek Nation? A Yes, sir.
Q To what town do you belong? A Tuckabatche.
Q Do you know Lily and Rhoda Harjo? A Yes, sir.
Q Do you k now a child of theirs named Winey Harjo? A Yes, sir.
Q Do you know when that child was born? A On the second day of this month, this year.
Q How do you know it was born then? A I am a near neighbor of theirs.
Q Were you present when the child was born? A No, sir.
Q When was the first time you saw the child? A I saw the child on Friday.
Q On what day of the week was the child born? A Thursday.
Q How old is the child? A About three weeks old, I think.
Q Was that child born in the day time or at night? A At night.
Q Is the child any relation to you? A No, sir.
Q Are you positive the child was born on the second day of March in this year? A Yes, sir.

---oooOOOooo---

I, D. C. Skaggs, on oath state that the above and foregoing is a full and true transcript of my stenographic notes as taken in said cause on said date.

DC Skaggs

Subscribed and sworn to before me this 20" day of July, 1905.

Edw C Griesel
Notary Public

Applications for Enrollment of Creek Newborn
Act of 1905   Volume IX

N.C. 711.
DEPARTMENT OF THE INTERIOR,
COMMISSIONER TO THE FIVE CIVILIZED TRIBES.
Holdenville, I. T., May 23, 1906.

In the matter of the application for the enrollment of Winey Harjo as a citizen by blood of the Creek Nation.

LILA HARJO, being duly sworn, testified as follows:

Through Alex Posey Official Interpreter:

BY THE COMMISSIONER:
Q What is your name? A Lila Harjo.
Q How old are you? A About twenty-five.
Q What is your post office address? A Yeager.
Q Are you a citizen of the Creek Nation? A Yes, sir.
Q To what town do you belong? A Tuckabatche.
Q You desire to introduce additional evidence, do you, in the matter of the application for the enrollment of your minor child, Winey Harjo? A Yes, sir.
Q Have you succeeded in fixing the exact date of the birth of your child, Winey? A The child was born on Thursday, March 2, 1905.
Q How do you fix the date of the birth? A By a record which my brother has.
Q Who made the record: A My brother, Sandy Harjo.
Q When did he make that record? A He made a record on the door facing of his house shortly after the child was born. I don't know just how long after. He is present and has a transcript of the record.
Q Did you ask him to make a record of the birth of the child after you had made application for its enrollment or before? A He made the record before I made application for the child's enrollment.
Q Is the child living? A No, sir, it is dead.
Q When did it die? A It was either on the 2nd or 3rd of September, 1905.
Q Was there a record made of the child's death? A Yes, sir, my brother also has a record which he made of the child's death.
Q Other witnesses have been examined in this case and they testify that the child was born at a later date than you give. How do you explain that? A I have no explanation to make, except that they did not know the date of the child's birth. My brother does and I desire to introduce his evidence.

Witness is identified opposite Creek Indian Roll No. 5918.

SANDY HARJO, being duly sworn, testified as follows:

Through Alex Posey Official Interpreter:

Applications for Enrollment of Creek Newborn
Act of 1905   Volume IX

BY THE COMMISSIONER:
Q What is your name? A Sandy Harjo?
Q How old are you? A About twenty-two.
Q What is your post office address? A Yeager.
Q Are you acquainted with Lila Harjo and his wife, Rhoda Harjo? A Yes, sir.
Q What relation are they to you? A Lila is my brother.
Q Did you know a child of theirs named Winey Harjo? A Yes, sir.
Q Do you know the date of the birth of that child? A The child was born on the evening of March 2, last year.
Q What circumstance fixes it in your mind that the child was born on that date? A My brother informed me the next day after the child was born that he had a new baby at his house and I made a record of it.
Q Did he ask you to make that record? A No, sir.
Q What reason did you have for making the record? A When he told me of the birth of the child I got a piece of chalk and wrote down the date on the wall of my house and had no special reason for making the record.
Q How does that record read (witness is handed a piece of paper and requested to write what he wrote on the wall of his house, and writes the following, in Creek)? A "It is born on the evening of March 2."
Q Have you a transcript of that record with you? A Yes, sir.

Witness presents a piece of paper upon which appears the following record, written in Creek: "Child born the night of March 2."
On the same piece of paper appears another record as follows: "September 3, 1905."

Q Does this record refer to the birth of Winey Harjo? A Yes, sir.
Q What does "September 3, 1905" refer to? A The date of her death.
Q Do you remember on what day of the week the child was born? A On Thursday evening.
Q Are you positive the child was born on the date you give? A Yes, sir, the child was born on Thursday evening, March 2.
Q You had already made your record, had you, at the time Lila appeared before the Commission and made application for the enrollment of this child? A Yes, sir.
Q Is the original writing still to be seen? A Yes, sir.
Q Was there any one present when you wrote the record on the wall of your house? A There was no one present. I did not know, at the time I made the record, that it would ever be needed. When my brother came to Holdenville and made application for the child he had some difficulty in fixing the date of the birth of the child and I told him I had a record of its birth at home.
Q You swear positively do you that you made that record the day after the birth of the child? A Yes, sir.

Applications for Enrollment of Creek Newborn
Act of 1905 Volume IX

JOHNSON REED, being duly sworn, testified as follows:

Through Alex Posey Official Interpreter:

BY THE COMMISSIONER:
Q What is your name? A Johnson Reed.
Q How old are you? A Thirty-six.
Q What is your post office address? A Yeager.
Q Are you a citizen of the Creek Nation? A Yes, sir.
Q Do you know Lila Harjo and his wife, Rhoda Harjo? A Yes, sir. I live about a mile from them.
Q Did you know a child of theirs named Winey Harjo? A Yes, sir.
Q When was the child born? A On the 2nd of March.
Q In what year? A 1905.
Q How do you fix the date? A I just know the date of the child's birth.
Q Has any one told you that the child was born on that date? A I heard of the birth of the child the next day after it was born. I think the father told me.
Q What day was the next day? A Friday.
Q Has Lila Harjo asked you to be a witness in this case? A Yes, sir, he asked me to testify as to the birth and death of the child.
Q Did you already know the date of the child's birth and death when he asked you to be a witness? A Yes, sir.
Q How long after the child's birth before you saw it? A I think I saw the child on Saturday, the 4th.
Q Do you know of your own personal knowledge, and swear positively that the child was born March 2, 1905? A Yes, sir.
Q Do you know it is a grave offence to swear falsely? A I am fully aware of that.

LILA HARJO recalled:

BY THE COMMISSIONER:
Q Did you know at the time you made application for this child, that your brother, Sandy Harjo, had a record of the birth of the child? A No, sir, I did not know that he had such a record until after I had made application for the child.
Q When was the first time you knew he had such a record? A It has not bee[sic] a great while ago. I appeared before the Commission at Muskogee and was referred to the Field Party here, and upon my return I talked to my brother about the case and he told me he had a record of the child's birth.
Q Do you desire to introduce further evidence in this case? A Yes, sir, I desire to introduce the testimony of Tom Culler.

TOM CULLER?[sic] being duly sworn, testified as follows:

Through Alex Posey Official Interpreter:

Applications for Enrollment of Creek Newborn
Act of 1905 Volume IX

BY THE COMMISSIONER:
Q What is your name? A Tom Culler.
Q How old are you? A Fifty-four.
Q What is your post office address? A Yeager.
Q Do you know Lila and Rhoda Harjo? A Very well.
Q Did you know a child of theirs named Winey Harjo? A Yes, sir.
Q Do you know when that child was born? A I do not know the exact date of the birth of the child but it was born sometime before the Commission was at Holdenville last year.
Q Do you know in what month it was born? A No, sir, I do not.

---oooOOOooo---

I, D. C. Skaggs, on oath state that the above and foregoing is a full and true transcript of my stenographic notes as taken in said cause on said date.

DC Skaggs

Subscribed and sworn to before me this 14th day of June, 1906.

Alex Posey
Notary Public.

BIRTH AFFIDAVIT.
DEPARTMENT OF THE INTERIOR,
COMMISSIONER TO THE FIVE CIVILIZED TRIBES.

ENROLLMENT OF MINORS. ACT OF CONGRESS, APPROVED APRIL 26, 1906.

IN RE APPLICATION FOR ENROLLMENT, as a citizen of the Creek Nation, of Winey Harjo, born on the 2nd day of March, 1905

Name of Father: Lilla Harjo   a citizen of the Creek Nation.
Name of Mother: Rhoda Harjo   a citizen of the Creek Nation.

Tribal enrollment of father   Creek   Tribal enrollment of mother   Creek

Postoffice   Yeager Indian Terr.

Applications for Enrollment of Creek Newborn
Act of 1905 Volume IX

AFFIDAVIT OF MOTHER.

UNITED STATES OF AMERICA, Indian Territory, ⎫
Western   District. ⎭

    I, Rhoda Harjo , on oath state that I am 23 years of age and a citizen by blood , of the Creek Nation; that I am the lawful wife of Lilla Harjo , who is a citizen, by blood of the Creek Nation; that a female child was born to me on 2nd day of March , 1905, that said child has been named Winey Harjo , and was living March 4, 1906.

                                                her
                                    Rhoda x Harjo
WITNESSES TO MARK: mark
⎰ James Smith
⎱ Sunday Harjo

Subscribed and sworn to before me this sixth day of July , 1906.

My Com Ex Apr 16th   *(Illegible)* D Clawson
             1910   Notary Public.

AFFIDAVIT OF ATTENDING PHYSICIAN OR MID-WIFE.

UNITED STATES OF AMERICA, Indian Territory, ⎫
Western   District. ⎭

    I, Linda Harjo , a midwife , on oath state that I attended on Rhoda Harjo , wife of Lilla Harjo on the 2nd day of March , 1905 ; that there was born to her on said date a female child; that said child was living March 4, 1906, and is said to have been named Winey Harjo
                                              her
                                  Linda x Harjo
WITNESSES TO MARK: mark
⎰ James Smith
⎱ Sunday Harjo

Subscribed and sworn to before me this sixth day of July , 1906.

My Com Ex Apr 16th 1910   *(Illegible)* D Clawson
                                             Notary Public.

Applications for Enrollment of Creek Newborn
Act of 1905 Volume IX

BIRTH AFFIDAVIT.

Supplemental testimony taken

DEPARTMENT OF THE INTERIOR.
COMMISSION TO THE FIVE CIVILIZED TRIBES.

IN RE APPLICATION FOR ENROLLMENT, as a citizen of the Creek Nation, of Winey Harjo, born on the 2 day of March, 1905

Name of Father: Lily Harjo   a citizen of the   Creek   Nation.
Tuckabatche Town
Name of Mother: Rhoda Harjo (nee Fixico)   a citizen of the   Creek   Nation.
Tuckabatche Town
                      Postoffice   Yeager, Ind. Ter.

AFFIDAVIT OF MOTHER.

UNITED STATES OF AMERICA, Indian Territory, }
     Western   DISTRICT.   Child is present

     I, Rhoda Harjo, on oath state that I am about 22 years of age and a citizen by blood, of the Creek Nation; that I am the lawful wife of Lily Harjo, who is a citizen, by blood of the Creek Nation; that a female child was born to me on 2 day of March, 1905, that said child has been named Winey Harjo, and was living March 4, 1905.
                                             her
                               Rhoda x Harjo
Witnesses To Mark: mark
{ Alex Posey
{ DC Skaggs

     Subscribed and sworn to before me this 29 day of March, 1905.

                                      Drennan C Skaggs
                                        Notary Public.

AFFIDAVIT OF ATTENDING PHYSICIAN OR MID-WIFE.

UNITED STATES OF AMERICA, Indian Territory, }
     Western   DISTRICT. }

     I, Lindy Harjo, a midwife, on oath state that I attended on Mrs. Rhoda Harjo, wife of Lily Harjo on the 2 day of March, 1905 ; that there was born to her on said date a female child; that said child was living March 4, 1905, and is said to have been named Winey Harjo

Applications for Enrollment of Creek Newborn
Act of 1905 Volume IX

Witnesses To Mark:
{ Alex Posey
{ DC Skaggs

                her
Lindy x Harjo
                mark

Subscribed and sworn to before me this 29 day of March , 1905.

                Drennan C Skaggs
                Notary Public.

BIRTH AFFIDAVIT.
DEPARTMENT OF THE INTERIOR.
COMMISSION TO THE FIVE CIVILIZED TRIBES.

IN RE APPLICATION FOR ENROLLMENT, as a citizen of the Creek Nation, of Nancy Harjo , born on the 22 day of March , 1903

Name of Father: Lily Harjo   a citizen of the   Creek   Nation.
Tuckabatche Town
Name of Mother: Rhoda Harjo (nee Fixico)   a citizen of the   Creek   Nation.
Tuckabatche Town
                Postoffice   Yeager, Ind. Ter.

AFFIDAVIT OF MOTHER.

UNITED STATES OF AMERICA, Indian Territory, }   Child is present
    Western   **DISTRICT.**

     I, Rhoda Harjo , on oath state that I am about 22 years of age and a citizen by blood , of the Creek   Nation; that I am the lawful wife of Lily Harjo , who is a citizen, by blood of the Creek   Nation; that a female   child was born to me on 22 day of March , 1903 , that said child has been named Nancy Harjo , and was living March 4, 1905.
                her
              Rhoda x Harjo
Witnesses To Mark: mark
{ Alex Posey
{ DC Skaggs

Subscribed and sworn to before me this 29 day of March , 1905.

                Drennan C Skaggs
                Notary Public.

Applications for Enrollment of Creek Newborn
Act of 1905 Volume IX

AFFIDAVIT OF ATTENDING PHYSICIAN OR MID-WIFE.

UNITED STATES OF AMERICA, Indian Territory, }
Western DISTRICT. }

I, Lindy Harjo , a midwife , on oath state that I attended on Mrs. Rhoda Harjo , wife of Lily Harjo on the 22 day of March , 1903 ; that there was born to her on said date a female child; that said child was living March 4, 1905, and is said to have been named Nancy Harjo
                                        her
                                Lindy x Harjo
Witnesses To Mark: mark
{ Alex Posey
{ DC Skaggs

Subscribed and sworn to before me this 29 day of March , 1905.

                                Drennan C Skaggs
                                Notary Public.

BIRTH AFFIDAVIT.

DEPARTMENT OF THE INTERIOR.
COMMISSION TO THE FIVE CIVILIZED TRIBES.

IN RE APPLICATION FOR ENROLLMENT, as a citizen of the Creek Nation, of Alfred Harjo , born on the 10 day of July , 1901

Name of Father: Lily Harjo   a citizen of the   Creek   Nation.
Tuckabatche Town
Name of Mother: Rhoda Harjo (nee Fixico)   a citizen of the   Creek   Nation.
Tuckabatche
                      Postoffice   Yeager, Ind. Ter.

AFFIDAVIT OF MOTHER.

UNITED STATES OF AMERICA, Indian Territory, }   <u>Child</u> is <u>present</u>
Western DISTRICT. }

I, Rhoda Harjo , on oath state that I am about 22 years of age and a citizen by blood , of the Creek Nation; that I am the lawful wife of Lily Harjo , who is a citizen, by blood of the Creek Nation; that a male child was born to me on 10 day of July , 1901 , that said child has been named Alfred Harjo , and was living March 4, 1905.

Applications for Enrollment of Creek Newborn
Act of 1905 Volume IX

Witnesses To Mark:
{ Alex Posey
{ DC Skaggs

             her
Rhoda x Harjo
           mark

Subscribed and sworn to before me this 29 day of March, 1905.

                  Drennan C Skaggs
                  Notary Public.

AFFIDAVIT OF ATTENDING PHYSICIAN OR MID-WIFE.

UNITED STATES OF AMERICA, Indian Territory, }
   Western   DISTRICT.

I, Lindy Harjo, a midwife, on oath state that I attended on Mrs. Rhoda Harjo, wife of Lily Harjo on the 10 day of July, 1901; that there was born to her on said date a male child; that said child was living March 4, 1905, and is said to have been named Alfred Harjo

Witnesses To Mark:
{ Alex Posey
{ DC Skaggs

             her
Lindy x Harjo
           mark

Subscribed and sworn to before me this 29 day of March, 1905.

                  Drennan C Skaggs
                  Notary Public.

C 712
DEPARTMENT OF THE INTERIOR,
COMMISSION TO THE FIVE CIVILIZED TRIBES.
Holdenville, I. T., March 29, 1905.

In the matter of the application for the enrollment of Martha and Flora Charlesey as citizens by blood of the Creek Nation.

ELLEN CHARLESEY, being duly sworn, testified as follows:

BY COMMISSION:
Q What is your name? A Ellen Charlesey.

Applications for Enrollment of Creek Newborn
Act of 1905 Volume IX

Q What is your age? A Twenty-six.
Q What is your post_office address? A Sasakwa.
Q Are you a citizen of the Creek Nation? A Yes, sir.
Q To what town do you belong? A Nuyaka.
Q Do you make application for the enrollment of your two children, Martha and Flora Charlesey as citizens of the Creek Nation? A Yes, sir.
Q What is the name of the father of those two children? A Charlesey.
Q Has he any other name? A No, sir.
Q Is he living? A He is dead.
Q Is he a citizen of the Creek Nation? A He is a Seminole.
Q Is he your lawful husband? A He was my husband according to Indian custom. By my father's consent.
Q If it should be found that your two children, Martha and Flora Charlesey, are entitled to enrollment in either the Creek or Seminole Nations in which nation do you desire to have them enrolled? A In the Creek Nation.

---oooOOOooo---

I, D. C. Skaggs, on oath state that the above and foregoing is a full and true transcript of my stenographic notes as taken in said cause on said date.

DC Skaggs

Subscribed and sworn to before me this 19" day of July, 1905.

Edw C Griesel
Notary Public.

BIRTH AFFIDAVIT.
DEPARTMENT OF THE INTERIOR.
COMMISSION TO THE FIVE CIVILIZED TRIBES.

IN RE APPLICATION FOR ENROLLMENT, as a citizen of the Creek Nation, of Martha Charlesey, born on the 5 day of October, 1904

Name of Father: Charlesey   a citizen of the Seminole   Nation.
Name of Mother: Ellen Charlesey   a citizen of the Creek   Nation.
Nuyaka Town
                 Postoffice   Sasakwa, I.T.

Applications for Enrollment of Creek Newborn
Act of 1905   Volume IX

AFFIDAVIT OF MOTHER. Child present
Testimony 3/29/05

UNITED STATES OF AMERICA, Indian Territory, }
Western   DISTRICT.

I, Ellen Charlesey , on oath state that I am 26 years of age and a citizen by blood , of the Creek   Nation; that I am not the lawful wife of Charlesey , who is a citizen, by blood of the Seminole   Nation; that a female   child was born to me on 5 day of October, 1904 , that said child has been named Martha Charlesey , and was living March 4, 1905.

Ellen Charlesey

Witnesses To Mark:
{

Subscribed and sworn to before me this 29 day of March , 1905.

Drennan C Skaggs
Notary Public.

---

relative
AFFIDAVIT OF ~~ATTENDING PHYSICIAN OR MID-WIFE.~~

UNITED STATES OF AMERICA, Indian Territory, }
Western   DISTRICT.

I, Bessie Cully , a *(blank)* , on oath state that I attended on Mrs. Ellen Charlesey , wife according to Indian custom of Charlesey on the 5 day of October , 1904 ; that there was born to her on said date a female child; that said child was living March 4, 1905, and is said to have been named Martha Charlesey

Bessie Cully

Witnesses To Mark:
{

Subscribed and sworn to before me this 29 day of March , 1905.

Drennan C Skaggs
Notary Public.

Applications for Enrollment of Creek Newborn
Act of 1905 Volume IX

NC. 712.

Muskogee, Indian Territory, July 15, 1905.

Chief Clerk,
    Seminole Enrollment Division,
        Muskogee, Indian Territory.

Dear Sir:

    March 31, 1905, application was made to the Commission to the Five Civilized Tribes for the enrollment of Flora Charlesey, born October 5, 1904, and Martha Charlesey, born October 5, 1904, as citizens by blood of the Creek Nation. It is stated in said application that the father of said children is Charlesey, a citizen of the Seminole Nation, and that the mother is Ellen Charlesey, a citizen of the Creek Nation.

    You are requested to inform the Creek Enrollment Division as to whether application has been made for the enrollment of said children as citizens of the Seminole Nation, and if so, what disposition has been made of the same.

                        Respectfully,

                                        Commissioner.

DEPARTMENT OF THE INTERIOR.
COMMISSION TO THE FIVE CIVILIZED TRIBES.

Muskogee, Indian Territory, July 19, 1905.

Chief Clerk,
    Creek Enrollment Division.

Dear Sir:

    Receipt is acknowledged of your letter of July 15, 1905 (NC-712) stating that application was made to the Commission to the Five Civilized Tribes for the enrollment of Flora Charlesey, born October 5, 1904, and Martha Charlesey, born October 5, 1904, children of Charlesey, a citizen of the Seminole Nation, and Ellen Charlesey, a citizen of the Creek Nation, as citizens by blood of the Creek Nation and requesting to be informed as to whether application has been made for the enrollment of said children as citizens of the Seminole Nation.

    In reply to your letter you are advised that it does not appear from an examination of the records of this office that any application was made to the Commission to the Five Civilized Tribes for the enrollment of said Flora Charlesey and Martha Charlesey as citizens of the Seminole Nation.

Applications for Enrollment of Creek Newborn
Act of 1905   Volume IX

Respectfully,
Tams Bixby Commissioner.

BIRTH AFFIDAVIT.
DEPARTMENT OF THE INTERIOR.
COMMISSION TO THE FIVE CIVILIZED TRIBES.

IN RE APPLICATION FOR ENROLLMENT, as a citizen of the Creek Nation, of Flora Charlesey, born on the 5 day of October, 1904

Name of Father: Charlesey   a citizen of the Seminole   Nation.
Name of Mother: Ellen Charlesey   a citizen of the   Creek   Nation.
Nuyaka Town
                Postoffice   Sasakwa, I.T.

AFFIDAVIT OF MOTHER.   Child present
Testimony 3/29/05
UNITED STATES OF AMERICA, Indian Territory,
    Western   **DISTRICT.**

    I, Ellen Charlesey, on oath state that I am 26 years of age and a citizen by blood, of the Creek Nation; that I am not the lawful wife of Charlesey, who is a citizen, by blood of the Seminole Nation; that a female child was born to me on 5 day of October, 1904, that said child has been named Flora Charlesey, and was living March 4, 1905.

                                Ellen Charlesey

Witnesses To Mark:

    Subscribed and sworn to before me this 29 day of March, 1905.

                                Drennan C Skaggs
                                Notary Public.

                      relative
AFFIDAVIT OF ~~ATTENDING PHYSICIAN OR MID-WIFE~~.

UNITED STATES OF AMERICA, Indian Territory,
    Western   **DISTRICT.**

                                          am a sister of
    I, Bessie Cully, a *(blank)*, on oath state that I ~~attended on~~ Mrs. Ellen Charlesey, wife according to Indian custom of Charlesey, that on the 5 day of October, 1904 ; that there was born to her on said date a female child; that said child was living March 4, 1905, and is said to have been named Flora Charlesey

Applications for Enrollment of Creek Newborn
Act of 1905 Volume IX

Witnesses To Mark:
Bessie Cully

{

Subscribed and sworn to before me this 29 day of March, 1905.

Drennan C Skaggs
Notary Public.

NC 712

Muskogee, Indian Territory, November 13, 1906

Chief Clerk,
    Seminole Enrollment Division,
        General Office.

Dear Sir:

    You are hereby advised that the names of Flora and Martha Charlesey, children of Charlesey, an alleged citizen of the Seminole Nation and Ellen Charlesey, a citizen by blood of the Creek Nation, are contained in schedule of minor citizens by blood of the Creek Nation, approved by the Secretary of the Interior, September 27, 1905, opposite Roll numbers 665 and 666.

Respectfully,
Commissioner.

BIRTH AFFIDAVIT.
DEPARTMENT OF THE INTERIOR.
COMMISSION TO THE FIVE CIVILIZED TRIBES.

IN RE APPLICATION FOR ENROLLMENT, as a citizen of the Creek Nation, of Russell H. Pitts, born on the 5th day of November, 1904

Name of Father: Frank Fields Pitts	a citizen of the -----	Nation.
Name of Mother: Emma Pitts	a citizen of the Creek	Nation.

Postoffice   Wagoner Ind. Ter.

Applications for Enrollment of Creek Newborn
Act of 1905 Volume IX

Child Present APR 5 1905 Gr

AFFIDAVIT OF MOTHER.

UNITED STATES OF AMERICA, Indian Territory,
Western Judicial DISTRICT.

    I, Emma Pitts , on oath state that I am Thirty (30) years of age and a citizen by blood , of the Creek Nation; that I am the lawful wife of Frank Fields Pitts , who is a citizen, by birth only of the Creek Nation; that a male child was born to me on day 5th of November , 1904 , that said child has been named Russell H. Pitts , and is now living.

Emma Pitts

Witnesses To Mark:
{ J D Hinton
{ GW Strawn

    Subscribed and sworn to before me this 29th day of March , 1905.

B.V. Leonard
Notary Public.

AFFIDAVIT OF ATTENDING PHYSICIAN OR MID-WIFE.

UNITED STATES OF AMERICA, Indian Territory,
Western Judicial DISTRICT.

    I, Ida Hallford , a married lady , on oath state that I attended on Mrs. Emma Pitts , wife of Frank Fields Pitts on the 5th day of November , 1904 ; that there was born to her on said date a male child; that said child is now living and is said to have been named Russell H. Pitts

Mrs Ida Hallford

Witnesses To Mark:
{ J D Hinton
{ GW Strawn

    Subscribed and sworn to before me this 29th day of March , 1905.

B.V. Leonard
Notary Public.

Applications for Enrollment of Creek Newborn
Act of 1905 Volume IX

BIRTH AFFIDAVIT.
DEPARTMENT OF THE INTERIOR.
COMMISSION TO THE FIVE CIVILIZED TRIBES.

IN RE APPLICATION FOR ENROLLMENT, as a citizen of the Creek Nation, of Drannan Pitts, born on the 21St day of March, 1903

Name of Father: Frank Fields Pitts   a citizen of the   *(Illegible)*   Nation.
Name of Mother: Emma Pitts   a citizen of the   Creek   Nation.

Postoffice   Wagoner Ind. Ter.

Child Present APR 5 1905 Gr

AFFIDAVIT OF MOTHER.

UNITED STATES OF AMERICA, Indian Territory,
Western Judicial   DISTRICT.

    I, Emma Pitts, on oath state that I am Thirty (30) years of age and a citizen by blood, of the Creek Nation; that I am the lawful wife of Frank Fields Pitts, who is a citizen, by birth only of the Creek Nation; that a male child was born to me on day 21st of March, 1903, that said child has been named Drannan Pitts, and is now living.

Emma Pitts

Witnesses To Mark:
  { GW Strawn
    J D Hinton

    Subscribed and sworn to before me this 29th day of March, 1905.

B.V. Leonard
Notary Public.

AFFIDAVIT OF ATTENDING PHYSICIAN OR MID-WIFE.

UNITED STATES OF AMERICA, Indian Territory,
Western Judicial   DISTRICT.

    I, George R. Gordon, a practicing physician, on oath state that I attended on Mrs. Emma Pitts, wife of Frank Fields Pitts on the 21st day of March, 1903; that there was born to her on said date a female child; that said child is now living and is said to have been named Drannan Pitts

G R Gordon

Applications for Enrollment of Creek Newborn
Act of 1905   Volume IX

Witnesses To Mark:
{ G.A. Posey
  B.V. Leonard

Subscribed and sworn to before me this 29th day of March, 1905.

B.V. Leonard
Notary Public.

BIRTH AFFIDAVIT.
DEPARTMENT OF THE INTERIOR.
COMMISSION TO THE FIVE CIVILIZED TRIBES.

IN RE APPLICATION FOR ENROLLMENT, as a citizen of the Creek Nation, of Mamie Grayson, born on the 8th day of September, 1903

Name of Father: Joseph Grayson   a citizen of the United States Nation.
Name of Mother: Alice Grayson   a citizen of the Creek Nation.

Postoffice   Checotah, Ind. Terr.

AFFIDAVIT OF MOTHER.

UNITED STATES OF AMERICA, Indian Territory,
Western   DISTRICT.

I, Alice Grayson, on oath state that I am 24 years of age and a citizen by blood, of the Creek Nation; that I am the lawful wife of Joseph Grayson, who is a citizen, by *(blank)* of the United States ~~Nation~~; that a female child was born to me on 8th day of September, 1903, that said child has been named Mamie Grayson, and was living March 4, 1905.

Alice Grayson

Witnesses To Mark:
{

Subscribed and sworn to before me this 21st day of March, 1905.

My commission expires July 3rd 1906.   Charles Buford
Notary Public.

Applications for Enrollment of Creek Newborn
Act of 1905 Volume IX

Cr Ba-1276-B

Muskogee, Indian Territory, May 31, 1905.

Alice Grayson,
    Checotah, Indian Territory.

Dear Madam:

    There is on file with the Commission an affidavit, executed by you, in the matter of the application for the enrollment of your minor child, Mamie Grayson, as a citizen of the Creek Nation.

    The Commission is unable to identify you on its rolls as a citizen of the Creek Nation. You are advised to furnish the Commission with your maiden name, the names of your parents, the Creek Indian Town to which you claim to belong, and, if possible, the number which appears on your deeds to land in said Nation, which will help to identify you as a citizen of said Nation.

Respectfully,

Chairman.

(NC 714)

NC-714.

(Copy)

Henryetta, Ind. Ter. June 26th 1905.

Hon. Tams Bixby, Chairman,
    Muskogee, I. T.

Dear Sir:

    Answering your letter May 31st 1905, refering to enrollment of my minor child, Mamie Grayson, wish to say that my name has always been Grayson. My file No. or Roll No. is 3302.

Yours very truly,

(signed)   ALICE (her x mark) GRAYSON.

Witnesses:
    J. W. Sullins, Henryetta, I.T.
    W. L. Sullins, Henryetta, I.T.

Applications for Enrollment of Creek Newborn
Act of 1905 Volume IX

NC. 714.

J. MONROE VANDERPOOL, M.D.　　　　　　　　　　Office Hours:
Physician and Surgeon.　　　　　　　　　　　8 to 12 A.M.: 1 to 6 P.M.
Central Dist.
　　　　　　　　　　　　　　　　Kiowa, I.T., July 8" /05.

To the Hon. Com. to the Five Civilized Tribes
　　　Muskogee, I.T.

Dear Sir:

　　　Mrs. Allice Grayson is the wife of Mr. Joe Grayson, and a sister of Mrs. Albert W. Arnett of Checotah. Her mother I cannot call to mind her name just now but she lives near the Indian High School Building in Eufaula.

　　　I just sent your letter to Mr. Chas. Buford Mr. Joe Grayson attorney with the request that he have Mr. and Mrs. Grayson furnish you with the desired information.

　　　　　　　　　　　Very resp.

　　　　　　　　　　　(Signed) J. Monroe Vanderpool, M.D.

　　　　　　　　　　　COPY.

Charles Buford
Attorney-at-Law
　　　　　　　　　　Checotah, I.T. August 7th 1905

Hon. Commission to the Five Civilized Tribes,
　　　Muskogee, I T

Gentlemen:
　　　　　　　　　　　N.C.714
　　　In reply to your communication of the 7th of July 1905, addressed to James M. Vanderpool, M.D. which letter was forwarded to me by Vanderpool for answer, I would say that the present post office address of Alice Grayson is now Henryetta, I.T. to which place she moved about two months ago. The maiden name of Mrs. Alice Grayson was Alice Marshall, her parents are Tip Marshall, father, her mother is Delphine Marshall; they reside at Eufaula, I.T. Mrs. Grayson belongs to the Creek Town of Coweta.

　　　Mrs. Alice Grayson is present at this writing and signs this letter for identification. She is unable to give the number on her allotment deeds, as these deeds are at her home near Henryetta, I.T.

Applications for Enrollment of Creek Newborn
Act of 1905   Volume IX

Yours very respectfully,

Signed   Charles Buford

Signed- Alice Grayson.

United States of America,)
Indian Territory,   : ss.
............District.   )

James M. Vanderpool, being first duly sworn, on his oath deposes and says: My name is James M. Vanderpool, my age is 45; my Post Office is Kiowa, Choctaw Nation, Indian Territory. I am a practicing physician and surgeon and am engaged at the present time in the active practice of my profession. During the year 1903 and part of the year 1904 and for a number of years prior to the year 1903 I resided at Checotah, Creek Nation, Indian Territory, where I was engaged in the practice of medicine. I was the family physician for the family of Joseph Grayson, whose wife, Alice Grayson, is a citizen of the Creek Nation. I attended Mrs. Alice Grayson in the capacity of her physician during the month of September, 1903. On the 8th day of September, 1903 she, Alice Grayson, gave birth to a female child, which child was given the name of Mamie Grayson, I was present at the birth and attended mother and child for some time after the birth of this child: This child Mamie Grayson was living at the time I left Checotah, I.T. and is to my best knowledge and belief living at the present time. I have known Joseph Grayson and Alice Grayson, the parents of this child, for 5 years.

James M. Vanderpool, M.D.

Subscribed and sworn to before me this 18th day of March 1905.

My commission expires Feby. 28th 1907

(Name Illegible)
Notary Public.

NC 714.

Alice Grayson,
     Henryetta, Indian Territory.

Dear Madam:

Receipt is acknowledged of your letter of June 26, 1905, in which you state that your roll number is 3302.

You are requested to advise this office as to your maiden name, the names of your parents, your age and the Creek Indian Town to which you belong.

Applications for Enrollment of Creek Newborn
Act of 1905   Volume IX

Respectfully,
Commissioner.

NC 714.

Muskogee, Indian Territory, July 1, 1905.

Alice Grayson,
Henryetta, Indian Territory.

Dear Madam:

The Commission is in receipt of your letter of June 26, 1905, in which you state that your roll number is 3302.

You are again requested to advise the Commission as to your maiden name, the names of your parents, your age and the Creek Indian Town to which you belong.

Respectfully,
Commissioner.

N.C. 714

Muskogee, Indian Territory, July 7, 1905.

James M. Vanderpool, M.D.,
Checotah, Indian Territory.

Dear Sir:

There is on file at this office an affidavit executed by you relative to the birth of Mamie Grayson, a minor child of Alice Grayson, whom post office is given as Checotah.

A letter written to her at said post office has been returned "unclaimed".

You are requested to furnish this office with the present post office of said Alice Grayson. If you are unable to furnish present address, you are advised that this office desires to be furnished with the maiden name of the said Alice Grayson, the names of her parents, the Creek Indian town to which she belongs, and, if possible, the number which appears on her deeds to land in the Creek Nation.

Without this information, it is impossible to identify said Alice Grayson as a citizen of the Creek Nation.

Respectfully,
Commissioner

Applications for Enrollment of Creek Newborn
Act of 1905   Volume IX

REFER IN REPLY TO THE FOLLOWING:

DEPARTMENT OF THE INTERIOR, N.C.714.
COMMISSIONER TO THE FIVE CIVILIZED TRIBES.

Muskogee, Indian Territory, July 19, 1905.

Alice Grayson,
    Eufaula, Indian Territory.

Dear Madam:

    There is on file at this office an affidavit executed by you in the matter of the application for the enrollment of your minor child, Mamie Grayson, as a citizen of the Creek Nation.

    Without further information it is impossible to identify you as a citizen of the Creek Nation.

    You are requested to state your maiden name, the names of your parents, the Creek Indian Town to which you belong and any other information that will help to identify you as a citizen of the Creek Nation.

                  Respectfully,

                            Tams Bixby   Commissioner.

                    Henryetta I.T.
                    Aug 2, 1905
Hon. Dawes Commission

    I was informed that you wanted to know what my maiden name was and what town that I belong to It is the Coweta town and ny name was Alice Marshall I am the mother of Vinnie Ree Grayson and Clearance[sic] Grayson and my baby name is Mamie she is two years old the 8 of September

                    Yours truly
                    Alice Grayson
                  Henryetta I T

My father name is Tip Marshall that lives to Eufaula I T
the daughter of T B Marshall
the sister of Arthur Marshall
      Nettie Marshall
      Nora Marshall

Applications for Enrollment of Creek Newborn
Act of 1905 Volume IX

NC 714

Muskogee, Indian Territory, August 4, 1906.

Alice Grayson,
   Henryetta, Indian Territory.

Dear Madam:

   Replying to your letter of August 1, 1906, you are advised that the name of your minor child, Mamie Grayson, is contained in a partial list of creek[sic] citizens approved by the Secretary of the Interior, January 4, 1906, opposite new born Creek Indian roll no. 669, and that a selection of land in the Creek Nation may now be made for said child at the Creek Land Office in Muskogee, Indian Territory.

   Respectfully,
   Commissioner.

C715
DEPARTMENT OF THE INTERIOR,
COMMISSION TO THE FIVE CIVILIZED TRIBES.
Holdenville, I. T., March 27, 1905.

   In the matter of the application for the enrollment of Winey and Jeffy Fixico as a citizens by blood of the Creek Nation.

   FANNIE FIXICO, being duly sworn, testified as follows:

   Through Alex Posey Official Interpreter:

   BY COMMISSION:
Q What is your name? A Fannie Fixico.
Q How old are you? A Twenty-three.
Q What is your post office address? A Sasakwa.
Q Are you a citizen of the Creek Nation? A Yes, sir.
Q To what town do you belong? A Little River Tulsa.
Q Do you make application for the enrollment of your children, Winey and Jeffy Fixico, as citizens of the Creek Nation? A Yes, sir.
Q Who is the father of these children? A Watty Fixico.
Q Is he a citizen of the Creek Nation. A He is a Seminole.

150

Applications for Enrollment of Creek Newborn
Act of 1905   Volume IX

Q If it should be found that your two minor children Winey and Jeffy Fixico, are entitled to be enrolled in either the Creek or Seminole Nations, in which nation do you desire to have them enrolled? A In the Creek Nation.

---oooOOOooo---

I, D. C. Skaggs, on oath state that the above and foregoing is a full and true transcript of my stenographic notes as taken in said cause on said date.

DC Skaggs

Subscribed and sworn to before me this 17" day of July, 1905.

J McDermott
Notary Public.

NC-715

Muskogee, Indian Territory, August 14, 1905.

Fanny Fixico,
    Care of Watty Fixico,
        Sasakwa, Indian Territory.

Dear Madam:

    In the matter of the application for the enrollment of your minor children, Winey Fixico, born June 15, 1901, and Jeffy Fixico, born March 13, 1903, as citizens by blood of the Creek Nation, it will be necessary for you to furnish this Office with the affidavits of two disinterested persons as to the birth of said children. Said affidavits must set forth the names of said children, the dates of their birth, the names of their parents, and whether or not they were living on March 4, 1905.

    This Office is unable to identify you upon the final roll of citizens by blood of the Creek Nation. It is necessary that you be so identified before the rights of your said children can be finally determined. You are therefore requested to imimediately[sic] inform this Office as to the name under which you are finally enrolled, the names of your parents and other members of your family, the Creek Indian Town to which you belong, and if possible, your roll number as the same appears on your allotment certificate and deeds.

Respectfully,
Acting Commissioner.

Applications for Enrollment of Creek Newborn
Act of 1905 Volume IX

W.F.

REFER IN REPLY TO THE FOLLOWING:

DEPARTMENT OF THE INTERIOR,
COMMISSIONER TO THE FIVE CIVILIZED TRIBES.

Muskogee, Indian Territory, August 14, 1905.

Clerk in Charge,
    Creek Enrollment Division.

Dear Sir:

    In reply to your verbal inquiry of this date as to whether or not application was ever made to the Commission to the Five Civilized Tribes for the enrollment of Winey Fixico, born June 15, 1901, and Jeffy Fixico, born March 13, 1903, children of Watty Fixico, a citizen of the Seminole Nation, and Fanny Fixico, a citizen of the Creek Nation, as citizens of the Seminole Nation, you are advised that it does not appear from an examination of the records of this office that application has been made for the enrollment of said children as citizens of the Seminole Nation.

                Respectfully,
                        Wm. O. Beall
                        Acting Commissioner.

NC 715

Muskogee, Indian Territory, November 13, 1906

Chief Clerk,
    Seminole Enrollment Division,
        General Office.

Dear Sir:

    You are hereby advised that the names of Winey and Jeffy Fixico, children of Watty Fixico, an alleged citizen of the Seminole Nation, and Fanny Fixico a citizen by blood of the Creek Nation, are contained in schedule of minor citizens by blood of the Creek Nation, approved by the Secretary of the Interior, November 27, 1905, opposite Roll numbers 741 and 742.

                Respectfully,
                        Commissioner.

Applications for Enrollment of Creek Newborn
Act of 1905 Volume IX

United States of America

)

Indian Territory   ) ss

)

Western Judicial District   )

       Lesly Tiger being first duly sworn on oath, deposes and says that he is a citizen of the Creek Nation, Indian Territory, and ___ years of age, that he is acquainted with Fanny Factor, Now Fanny Fixico, and that their[sic] was born to her on the 15th day of June, 1901 a female child who was name Winey Fixico, and is now liveing[sic], And on the 13th day of March 1903 their[sic] was born to the said Fanny Fixico (Nee Factor) a male child who was named Jeffy Fixico and the name of the mother is Fanny Fixico, and the above said children ane[sic] now liveing[sic], her Fathers[sic] name Was Joe Factor and her mothers[sic] name was Youthlechee Factor.

I have no interest in this claim and make this statement as a disinterested party.
Witness to mark   his
A Z *(Illegible)*   Lesly Tiger x
Frank Jacobs   mark

Signed and sworn to this the 9th day of September 1905

                                                                             Chas Rider
                                                                             Notary Public.
My Commission expires July 11th, 1906

United States of America

)

Indian Territory   ) ss

)

Western Judicial District   )

       (blank) being first duly sworn on oath, deposes and says that he is a citizen of the Creek Nation, Indian Territory, and ___ years of age, that he is acquainted with Fanny Factor, Now Fanny Fixico, and that their[sic] was born to her on the 15th day of June, 1901 a female child who was name Winey Fixico, and is now liveing[sic], And on the 13th day of March 1903 their[sic] was born to the said Fanny Fixico (Nee Factor) a male child who was named Jeffy Fixico and the name of the mother is Fanny Fixico, and the above said children ane[sic] now liveing[sic], her Fathers[sic] name Was Joe Factor and her mothers[sic] name was Youthlechee Factor.

I have no interest in this claim and make this statement as a disinterested party.

                                                                         Frank Jacobs

Applications for Enrollment of Creek Newborn
Act of 1905   Volume IX

Signed and sworn to this the 9th day of September 1905

                                              Chas Rider
                                              Notary Public.
My Commission expires July 11th, 1906

BIRTH AFFIDAVIT.

                          Supplemental testimony taken
DEPARTMENT OF THE INTERIOR.
COMMISSION TO THE FIVE CIVILIZED TRIBES.

IN RE APPLICATION FOR ENROLLMENT, as a citizen of the Creek Nation, of Jeffy Fixico, born on the 13 day of March, 1903

Name of Father: Watty Fixico   a citizen of the Seminole   Nation.
Name of Mother: Fanny Fixico   a citizen of the   Creek   Nation.
Tulsa Little River Town
                        Postoffice   Sasakawa[sic], Ind. Ter.

AFFIDAVIT OF MOTHER.

UNITED STATES OF AMERICA, Indian Territory,
    Western   **DISTRICT.**   Child is present

    I, Fanny Fixico, on oath state that I am 23 years of age and a citizen by blood, of the Creek Nation; that I am the lawful wife of Watty Fixico, who is a citizen, by blood of the Creek[sic] Nation; that a male child was born to me on 13 day of March, 1903, that said child has been named Jeffy Fixico, and was living March 4, 1905. That no one attended on me as midwife or physician at the birth of the child except my husband   her
                                                Fanny x Fixico
Witnesses To Mark: mark
  { Alex Posey
    DC Skaggs

    Subscribed and sworn to before me this 27 day of March, 1905.

                                        Drennan C Skaggs
                                             Notary Public.

Applications for Enrollment of Creek Newborn
Act of 1905 Volume IX

AFFIDAVIT OF ATTENDING PHYSICIAN OR MID-WIFE.

UNITED STATES OF AMERICA, Indian Territory,
Western DISTRICT.

my wife
I, Watty Fixico , a ~~(blank)~~ , on oath state that I attended on ^ Mrs. Fanny Fixico, ~~wife of~~ *(blank)* on the 13 day of March , 1903 ; that there was born to her on said date a male child; that said child was living March 4, 1905, and is said to have been named Jeffy Fixico

              his
            Watty x Fixico
Witnesses To Mark: mark
{ Alex Posey
{ DC Skaggs

  Subscribed and sworn to before me 27 day of March, 1905.

            Drennan C Skaggs
              Notary Public.

BIRTH AFFIDAVIT.

       Supplemental testimony taken

DEPARTMENT OF THE INTERIOR.
COMMISSION TO THE FIVE CIVILIZED TRIBES.

IN RE APPLICATION FOR ENROLLMENT, as a citizen of the Creek Nation, of Winey Fixico , born on the 15 day of June , 1901

Name of Father: Watty Fixico   a citizen of the Seminole Nation.
Name of Mother: Fanny Fixico   a citizen of the Creek Nation.
Tulsa Little River Town
         Postoffice Sasakawa[sic], Ind. Ter.

AFFIDAVIT OF MOTHER.

UNITED STATES OF AMERICA, Indian Territory,
Western   DISTRICT.   <u>Child is present</u>

  I, Fanny Fixico , on oath state that I am 23 years of age and a citizen by blood , of the Creek Nation; that I am the lawful wife of Watty Fixico , who is a citizen, by blood of the Seminole Nation; that a female child was born to me on 15 day of June , 1901 , that said child has been named Winey Fixico , and was living March 4, 1905. That no one attended on me as midwife or physician at the birth of the child except my husband

Applications for Enrollment of Creek Newborn
Act of 1905   Volume IX

Witnesses To Mark:
{ Alex Posey
  DC Skaggs

her
Fanny x Fixico
mark

Subscribed and sworn to before me this 27 day of March, 1905.

Drennan C Skaggs
Notary Public.

AFFIDAVIT OF ATTENDING PHYSICIAN OR MID-WIFE.

UNITED STATES OF AMERICA, Indian Territory, }
  Western   DISTRICT.

my wife
I, Watty Fixico , a ~~(blank)~~ , on oath state that I attended on ^ Mrs. Fanny Fixico, ~~wife of~~ (blank) on the 15 day of June , 1901 ; that there was born to her on said date a female child; that said child was living March 4, 1905, and is said to have been named Winey Fixico

Witnesses To Mark:
{ Alex Posey
  DC Skaggs

his
Watty x Fixico
mark

Subscribed and sworn to before me 27 day of March, 1905.

Drennan C Skaggs
Notary Public.

C 716

DEPARTMENT OF THE INTERIOR,
COMMISSION TO THE FIVE CIVILIZED TRIBES.
Holdenville, I. T., March 29, 1905.

In the matter of the application for the enrollment of Arthur and Nellie Stebbin as citizens by blood of the Creek Nation.

NICEY STEBBIN, being duly sworn, testified as follows:

Through Alex Posey Official Interpreter:

Applications for Enrollment of Creek Newborn
Act of 1905   Volume IX

BY COMMISSION:
Q What is your name? A Nicey Stebbin.
Q How old are you? A Twenty-eight.
Q What is your post office address? A Sasakwa.
Q Are you a citizen of the Creek Nation? A Yes, sir.
Q To what town do you belong? A Thlewathle.
Q Do you make application for the enrollment of your children, Arthur and Nellie Stebbin, as citizens by blood of the Creek Nation blood of the Creek Nation? A Yes, sir.
Q What is the name of the father of these children? A Stebbin M Martin.
Q Is he living? A He is dead?
Q Was he your lawful husband? A Yes, sir.
Q Was he a citizen of the Creek Nation? A He was a Seminole.
Q If it should be found that your two children, Arthur and Nellie Stebbin, are entitled to be enrolled in either the Creek or Seminole Nations in which nation do you desire to have them enrolled? A In the Creek Nation.

---oooOOOooo---

I, D. C. Skaggs, on oath state that the above and foregoing is a full and true transcript of my stenographic notes as taken in said cause on said date.

DC Skaggs

Subscribed and sworn to before me this 20" day of July, 1905.

Edw C Griesel
Notary Public.

NC-716
DEPARTMENT OF THE INTERIOR,
COMMISSIONER TO THE FIVE CIVILIZED TRIBES.

Muskogee, Indian Territory, August 14, 1905

In the matter of the application for the enrollment of Arthur and Nellie Tebe as citizens by blood of the Creek Nation.

Alex Posey, being duly sworn, testified as follows:

EXAMINATION BY THE COMMISSIONER:
Q What is your name? A Alex Posey.
Q Mr. Posey, you are a citizen by blood of the Creek Nation? A Yes sir.
Q You are well acquainted among the full-blood citizens? A Yes sir.
Q Creek and Seminole Nations? A Yes sr.
Q You are familiar with their customs? A Yes sir.

Applications for Enrollment of Creek Newborn
Act of 1905   Volume IX

Q You speak the Creek language, do you? A Yes sir.
Q Mr. Posey, there is on file with the records of this office an application for the enrollment of Arthur and Nellie Stebbin. In that application the mother's name is given as Wisey Stebbin and the father's name is given as Stebin Martin. The mother of these children is identified on the final Creek roll as Wisey Tebe, and the father of the children is identified on the Seminole Roll as Steppe. What is your opinion as to whether or not the name Stebbin Tebe and Steppe are one and the same name? A I think the name means--it is an Indian way of pronouncing "Stephen." Frequently they call Stephen, Stebe or Tebe.
Q Call it Stebe? A Yes, or Tebe. It is very difficult for fullbloods to pronounce English names correctly and they get them mixed.
Q And it is your opinion that when the mother of these children gave the name in as Stebbin, she intended to give the surname the same as she was enrolled herself under, and you think undoubtedly they are one and the same name? A Yes sir.
Q You don't think this is any question as to the identification of the mother of these children, Wisey Stebbin--Wisey Tebe being correct, do you? A No sir.

INDIAN TERRITORY, Western District.
    I, J. Y. Miller, a stenographer to the Commissioner to the Five Civilized Tribes, do hereby certify that the above and foregoing is a true and complete translation of my notes as same appear in my stenographic report of this case.

                                        JY Miller

Sworn to and subscribed before
  me this the 15th day of
  August, 1905.   JB Campbell
                                            Notary Public.

BIRTH AFFIDAVIT.   Supplemental testimony taken
                        DEPARTMENT OF THE INTERIOR.
              COMMISSION TO THE FIVE CIVILIZED TRIBES.

   IN RE APPLICATION FOR ENROLLMENT, as a citizen of the Creek Nation, of Nellie Stebbin, born on the 2 day of August , 1904

Name of Father: Stebbin Martin, deceased   a citizen of the Seminole   Nation.
Name of Mother: Wisey Stebbin (nee Harjo   a citizen of the   Creek   Nation.
Thlewathle Town
                        Postoffice   Sasakwa, Ind. Ter.

Applications for Enrollment of Creek Newborn
Act of 1905   Volume IX

AFFIDAVIT OF MOTHER.

UNITED STATES OF AMERICA, Indian Territory,
Western   DISTRICT.   } Child is present

I, Wisey Stebbin , on oath state that I am about 28 years of age and a citizen by blood , of the Creek Nation; that I am the lawful wife of Stebbin Martin, deceased , who is a citizen, by blood of the Seminole Nation; that a female child was born to me on 2 day of August , 1904 , that said child has been named Nellie Stebbin , and was living March 4, 1905.

            her
Witnesses To Mark: Wisey x Stebbin
 { Alex Posey   mark
   DC Skaggs

Subscribed and sworn to before me this 29 day of March , 1905.

           Drennan C Skaggs
           Notary Public.

AFFIDAVIT OF ATTENDING PHYSICIAN OR MID-WIFE.

UNITED STATES OF AMERICA, Indian Territory,
Western   DISTRICT.   }

I, Melinda Harjo , a midwife , on oath state that I attended on Mrs. Wisey Stebbin , wife of Stebbin Martin on the 2 day of August , 1904 ; that there was born to her on said date a female child; that said child was living March 4, 1905, and is said to have been named Nellie Stebbin

            her
Witnesses To Mark: Melinda x Harjo
 { Alex Posey   mark
   DC Skaggs

Subscribed and sworn to before me this 29 day of March , 1905.

           Drennan C Skaggs
           Notary Public.

Applications for Enrollment of Creek Newborn
Act of 1905   Volume IX

BIRTH AFFIDAVIT.
DEPARTMENT OF THE INTERIOR.
COMMISSION TO THE FIVE CIVILIZED TRIBES.

IN RE APPLICATION FOR ENROLLMENT, as a citizen of the Creek Nation, of Nellie Tebe, born on the 2nd day of August, 1904

Name of Father: Stebbin Martin, (or Stephens)   a citizen of the   Seminole   Nation.
Name of Mother: Wisey Tebe   a citizen of the   Creek   Nation.

                Postoffice   Sasakwa, Ind. Ter.

AFFIDAVIT OF MOTHER.

UNITED STATES OF AMERICA, Indian Territory, }
    Western   DISTRICT.

    I, Wisey Tebe, on oath state that I am about 28 years of age and a citizen by blood, of the Creek Nation; that I am the lawful wife of Stebbin Martin, deceased, who is was a citizen, by blood of the Seminole Nation; that a female child was born to me on 2nd day of August, 1904, that said child has been named Nellie Tebe, and was living March 4, 1905.

                                              her
                                    Wisey Tebe x
Witnesses To Mark: mark
  { AG Goat
    John K Goat

    Subscribed and sworn to before me this 4th day of November, 1905.

                                    Chas Rider
                                    Notary Public.
My commission expires July 11th 1906

AFFIDAVIT OF ATTENDING PHYSICIAN OR MID-WIFE.

UNITED STATES OF AMERICA, Indian Territory, }
    Western   DISTRICT.

    I, Melinda Harjo, a mid-wife, on oath state that I attended on Mrs. Wisey Tebe, wife of Stebbin Martin on the 2nd day of August, 1904; that there was born to her on said date a female child; that said child was living March 4, 1905, and is said to have been named Nellie Tebe
                                        her
                                  Melinda x Harjo
                                      mark

Applications for Enrollment of Creek Newborn
Act of 1905 Volume IX

Witnesses To Mark:
{ AG Goat
{ John K Goat

Subscribed and sworn to before me this 4th day of November, 1905.

Chas Rider
Notary Public.
My commission expires July 11th 1906

BIRTH AFFIDAVIT.
DEPARTMENT OF THE INTERIOR.
COMMISSION TO THE FIVE CIVILIZED TRIBES.

IN RE APPLICATION FOR ENROLLMENT, as a citizen of the Creek Nation, of Arthur Tebe, born on the 31st day of August, 1902

Name of Father: Stebbin Martin, (or Stephens)   a citizen of the Seminole Nation.
Name of Mother: Wisey Tebe   a citizen of the Creek Nation.

Postoffice   Sasakwa, Ind. Ter.

AFFIDAVIT OF MOTHER.

UNITED STATES OF AMERICA, Indian Territory, }
   Western   DISTRICT.   }

I, Wisey Tebe, on oath state that I am about 28 years of age and a citizen by blood, of the Creek Nation; that I am the lawful wife of Stebbin Martin, deceased, who ~~is~~ was a citizen, by blood of the Seminole Nation; that a male child was born to me on 31st day of August, 1902, that said child has been named Arthur Tebe, and was living March 4, 1905.   her

Witnesses To Mark: Wisey Tebe x
{ AG Goat   mark
{ John K Goat

Subscribed and sworn to before me this 4th day of November, 1905.

Chas Rider
Notary Public.
My commission expires July 11th 1906

Applications for Enrollment of Creek Newborn
Act of 1905 Volume IX

AFFIDAVIT OF ATTENDING PHYSICIAN OR MID-WIFE.

UNITED STATES OF AMERICA, Indian Territory, }
Western   DISTRICT.

I, Melinda Harjo , a mid-wife , on oath state that I attended on Mrs. Wisey Tebe , wife of Stebbin Martin on the 31st day of August , 1902 ; that there was born to her on said date a male child; that said child was living March 4, 1905, and is said to have been named Arthur Tebe
               her
           Melinda Harjo x
Witnesses To Mark: mark
{ AG Goat
{ John K Goat

Subscribed and sworn to before me this 4th day of November , 1905.

          Chas Rider
           Notary Public.

BIRTH AFFIDAVIT.   Sup. test. taken
DEPARTMENT OF THE INTERIOR.
COMMISSION TO THE FIVE CIVILIZED TRIBES.

  IN RE APPLICATION FOR ENROLLMENT, as a citizen of the Creek Nation, of Arthur Stebbin, born on the 31 day of August , 1902

Name of Father: Stebbin Martin, deceased a citizen of the Seminole Nation.
Name of Mother: Wisey Stebbin (nee Harjo) a citizen of the Creek   Nation.
Thlewathle Town
        Postoffice Sasakwa, Ind. Ter.

AFFIDAVIT OF MOTHER.

UNITED STATES OF AMERICA, Indian Territory, }
Western   DISTRICT.   Child is present

 I, Wisey Stebbin , on oath state that I am about 28 years of age and a citizen by blood , of the Creek Nation; that I am the lawful wife of Stebbin Martin, deceased , who is a citizen, by blood of the Seminole Nation; that a male child was born to me on 31 day of August , 1902 , that said child has been named Arthur Stebbin , and was living March 4, 1905.   her
          Wisey x Stebbin
           mark

Applications for Enrollment of Creek Newborn
Act of 1905 Volume IX

Witnesses To Mark:
{ Alex Posey
{ DC Skaggs

Subscribed and sworn to before me this 29 day of March, 1905.

Drennan C Skaggs
Notary Public.

AFFIDAVIT OF ATTENDING PHYSICIAN OR MID-WIFE.

UNITED STATES OF AMERICA, Indian Territory,
Western DISTRICT.

I, Melinda Harjo, a midwife, on oath state that I attended on Mrs. Wisey Stebbin, wife of Stebbin Martin on the 31 day of August, 1902; that there was born to her on said date a male child; that said child was living March 4, 1905, and is said to have been named Arthur Stebbin

                              her
                      Melinda x Harjo

Witnesses To Mark: mark
{ Alex Posey
{ DC Skaggs

Subscribed and sworn to before me this 29 day of March, 1905.

Drennan C Skaggs
Notary Public.

NC. 716.

Muskogee, Indian Territory, July 15, 1905.

Chief Clerk,
    Seminole Enrollment Division,
        Muskogee, Indian Territory.

Dear Sir:

        March 31, 1905, application was made to the Commission to the Five Civilized Tribes for the enrollment of Arthur Stebbin, born August 31, 1902, and Nellie Stebbin, born August 2, 1904, as citizens by blood of the Creek Nation. It is stated in said application that the father of said children is Stebbin Martin, deceased, a citizen of the Seminole Nation, and that the mother is Wisey Stebbin, identified as Wisey Tebe, a citizen of the Creek Nation.

Applications for Enrollment of Creek Newborn
Act of 1905 Volume IX

You are requested to inform the Creek Enrollment Division as to whether application has been made for the enrollment of said children as citizens of the Seminole Nation, and if so, what disposition has been made of the same.

Respectfully,
Commissioner.

W.F.
DEPARTMENT OF THE INTERIOR.
COMMISSION TO THE FIVE CIVILIZED TRIBES.

Muskogee, Indian Territory, July 19, 1905.

Chief Clerk,
Creek Enrollment Division.

Dear Sir:

Receipt is acknowledged of your letter of July 15, 1905 (NC-716) stating that application was made to the Commission to the Five Civilized Tribes for the enrollment of Arthur Stebbin, born August 31, 1902, and Nellie Stebbin, born August 2, 1904, children of Stebbin Martin, deceased, a citizen of the Seminole Nation, and Wisey Stebbin, identified as Wisey Tebe, a citizen of the Creek Nation, as citizens by blood of the Creek Nation and requesting to be informed as to whether application was made for the enrollment of said children as citizens of the Seminole Nation.

In reply to your letter your[sic] are advised that it does not appear from an examination of the records of this office that any application was ever made for the enrollment of said Arthur Stebbin and Nellie Stebbin as citizens of the Seminole Nation.

Respectfully,
Tams Bixby   Commissioner.

NC-716
Muskogee, Indian Territory, August 15, 1905.
Wisey Tebe (or Stephen)
Sasakwa, Indian Territory.

Dear Madam:

In the matter of the application for the enrollment of your minor children, Arthur Tebe and Nellie Tebe, as citizens by blood of the Creek Nation blood of the Creek Nation, it will be necessary for you to furnish this Office with proper proof of the birth of these children on the two blanks which have been filled out and are enclosed herewith.

Applications for Enrollment of Creek Newborn
Act of 1905   Volume IX

The affidavits of the birth of said children now on file give the surname Stebbin, while you are identified on the Creek Roll as Wisey Tebe.

Be careful to see that the notary public before whom the affidavits are sworn to, attaches his name and seal to each affidavit. In case any signature is by mark the same must be witnesses by two persons.

Respectfully,
CTD-48   Acting Commissioner.
Env

DEPARTMENT OF THE INTERIOR,
COMMISSIONER TO THE FIVE CIVILIZED TRIBES.

REFER IN REPLY TO THE FOLLOWING:
C-670

Muskogee, Indian Territory, October 6, 1905.

Wisey Stebbin, (Tebe)
   Sasakwa, Indian Territory

Dear Madam:

You are hereby advised that on **September 27, 1905**, the Secretary of the Interior approved the enrollment of your minor child, **Arthur Tebe**, as a citizen by blood of the **Creek** Nation, and that the name of said child appears upon the roll of new born citizens of the **Creek** Nation as Number   670 .

The child is now entitled to an allotment, and application therefor should be made without delay at the Land Office for the Nation in which the prospective allotment is located.

An entire allotment for said child must be selected at the time of the original application.

Respectively,

Tams Bixby
Commissioner.

165

Applications for Enrollment of Creek Newborn
Act of 1905   Volume IX

NC 716

Muskogee, Indian Territory, November 13, 1906.

Chief Clerk,
    Seminole Enrollment Division,
        General Office,

Dear Sir:

    You are hereby advised that the names of Arthur and Nellie Tebe, children of Steppe, deceased, Seminole Care number 200 and Wisey Stebbin, a citizen by blood of the Creek Nation, are contained in schedule of minor citizens by blood of the Creek Nation, approved by the Secretary of the Interior September 27, 1905, opposite Roll numbers 670 and 671.

                              Respectfully,
                                                  Commissioner.

NC 717
DEPARTMENT OF THE INTERIOR,
COMMISSIONER TO THE FIVE CIVILIZED TRIBES.

Muskogee, Indian Territory, October 14, 1905

    In the matter of the application for the enrollment of Willie E., Robert N. and George Nubbie, Jr. as citizens by blood of the Creek Nation.

    George W. Nubbie, being duly sworn, testified as follows:

EXAMINATION BY THE COMMISSION:
Q What is your name? A George W. Nubbie.
Q How old are you? A I am 28.
Q What is your postoffice? A Stidham.
Q You are a citizen of the Creek Nation, are you not? A Yes sir.

    The witness is identified as a Creek Indian, on "I" Card, field No. 1365, and his name is contained in the partial list of citizens by blood of the Creek Nation approved by the Department March 13, 1902, opposite No. 4354.

Q You have previously made application for the enrollment of your three minor children, Willie E., Robert and George Nubbie, Jr., have you not? A Yes sir.
Q Who is the mother of George Nubbie, Jr.? A Sophia Nubbie.
Q Is she living? A No, she is dead.

Applications for Enrollment of Creek Newborn
Act of 1905   Volume IX

Q When did she die? A She died the 17th day of January, 1901.
Q Was she your lawful wife? A Yes sr.
Q Is George, Jr. living? A Yes sr.
Q When was George born? A 16th day of November, 1900.
Q Was Sophia, your wife and the mother of George, a citizen of the Creek Nation? A No sir.
Q Was she a citizen of any Nation in Indian Territory? A No sir.
Q George is living now, is he? A Yes sir.
Q When was Robert born? A The 10th day of December, 1904. It was about two o'clock in the morning.
Q Is Robert living now? A Yes sir.
Q Who is the mother of Robert? A Harley Barnett.
Q Is she your lawful wife? A Yes sir.

Harley Barnett is identified on Creek Indian card, field No. 1804, and her name is contained in the partial list of citizens by blood of the Creek Nation approved by the Department March 28, 1902, opposite No. 5725.

Q When was Willie E. Nubbie born? A Born on the 6th day of July, 1902.
Q Is Willie living now? A No, he is dead.
Q When did he die? A The 9th of December, 1904.
Q Who is the mother of Willie E.? A Harley Barnett.
Q Were you lawfully married to Harley Barnett? A Yes sir.
Q Have you ever made application for George prior to the one that you made in April?
A I didn't made[sic] application for George in April--I did made[sic] in April.
Q Had you ever made application? A No, never had.

I, J. Y. Miller, a stenographer to the Commissioner to the Five Civilized Tribes, do hereby certify that the above and foregoing is a true and complete translation of my notes as same appear in my stenographic report of this case.   JY Miller
       Sworn to and subscribed before me this
14th day of October, 1905.   Edw C Griesel   NOTARY PUBLIC

N.C. 717.
DEPARTMENT OF THE INTERIOR,
COMMISSIONER TO THE FIVE CIVILIZED TRIBES.
Beggs, Indian Territory, September 13, 1906.

In the matter of the application for the enrollment of George Nubbie Jr as a citizen by blood of the Creek Nation.
       LEWIS ADAMS, being duly sworn, testified as follows:

Applications for Enrollment of Creek Newborn
Act of 1905   Volume IX

BY COMMISSIONER:

Q What is your name? A Lewis Adams.
Q What is your age? A I am 34.
Q What is your postoffice address? A Beggs, I.T.
Q Are you a citizen of the Creek Nation? A Yes sir.
Q Do you know George Nubbie? A Yes sir.
Q Do you know his wife Sophia Nubbie? A Yes sir.
Q Is Sophia living? A No sir.
Q When did she die? A I don't know for sure.
Q Did Sophia have a child by George Nubbie Sr? A Yes sir.
Q What is the name of the child? A George.
Q When was little George born? A I have forgot.

There is an affidavit on file at the office of the Commissioner to the Five Civilized Tribes signed by you on November 17, 1905, stating that George Nubbie Jr was born November 17, 1901. There is also another affidavit on file at the office of the Commissioner to the Five Civilized Tribes signed by Sarah Chamblen, the midwife, on January 6, 1903, stating that George Nubbie Jr was born November 10, 1901.

Q Now, who do you say has given the correct date about the birth of the child? A Why, the midwife has it right.
Q So you were mistaken when you stated that George Nubbie was born November 17, 1901, were you? A Yes sir.

There is another affidavit on file signed by you on January 6, 1906, before Fred Comstock, a notary public, stating that Sophia Nubbie died January 17, 1902.

Q Do you recollect signing such affidavits? A Yes, George and Fred Comstock came up here together with some papers and asked us to sign them and we did so.
Q Did the Notary read over and explain the contents of the affidavit to you? A No, he just said it was about the death of Sophia.
Q You don't know when she died do you? A Not for sure.

George Nubbie Sr testified on October 14, 1905, that Sophia Nubbie died January 17, 1901.

Q Do you [sic] whether or not he was correct? A No, I don't.
Q Where is Sarah Chamblen now? A She[sic] down about Sallisaw.
Q This George Nubbie Jr is living is he not? A Yes, he's living.

(Statement by the witness).
Sarah Chamblen could tell you all about when this child was born and all about the[sic] when the mother died because right there is where she was when the child was born and when its mother died.

Applications for Enrollment of Creek Newborn
Act of 1905   Volume IX

ANNA ADAMS, being duly sworn testified as follows:

BY COMMISSIONER:

Q What is your name? A Anna Adams.
Q What is your age? A I am *(illegible and marked over)*
Q What is your postoffice address? A Beggs.
Q Are you a citizen of the Creek Nation? A No sir.
Q Do you know George Nubbie? A Yes sir.
Q Do you know his wife? A His first wife I do, she was my sister.
Q What is her name? A Sophia Nubbie.
Q Is she living? A No sir.
Q When did she die? A I don't know just when it was.
Q Did Sophia have a child by George Nubbie? A Yes sir.
Q What is the name of the child? A George Nubbie.

There is an affidavit on file signed by you on November 7, 1905, stating that George Nubbie Jr was born November 17, 1901. There is another one on file signed by Sarah Chamblen on January 6, 1906, stating that the child was born November 10, 1901.

Q Now, who has given the correct date, you or the midwife? A The midwife has it right ' cause she was right there when the child was born.
Q You were mistaken when you signed an affidavit saying that the George Nubbie Jr was born November 17, 1901, were you not? A Yes sir.

There is another affidavit signed by you on January 6, 1906, in which you state that Sophia Nubbie died January 17, 1902.

Q Do you remember signing such affidavit? A Yes, Comstock and George came right here and Comstock asked me if that was my sister's child (pointing to a small boy) and I told him yes. Well, allright he says then asked me to sign some papers that they had with them. I asked them what it was for and they said that it was about the death of Sophia. So I signed it for them.
Q Did the Notary read the papers over to you before you signed them? A No sir, the only things he said was that the papers were about the death of Sophia.
Q Do you actually know when Sophia died? A No, I don't.
Q Is George Nubbie Jr living? A Yes, he is at my sister Maggie's right now.
Q Were Sophia and George lawfully married when this child was born? A Yes, I suppose they were.

I, Jesse McDermott, on oath state that the above and foregoing is a full and true transcript of my notes as taken in said cause on said date.

Jesse McDermott

Applications for Enrollment of Creek Newborn
Act of 1905 Volume IX

Subscribed and sworn to before me this 15th day of November 1906.

My Commission exp 1/31/09

Dan Upton
Notary Public.

NC 717

DEPARTMENT OF THE INTERIOR,
COMMISSIONER TO THE FIVE CIVILIZED TRIBES.
Muskogee, Indian Territory, November 19, 1906.

In the matter of the application for the enrollment of GEORGE NUBBIE, JR., as a citizen by blood of the Creek Nation.

SARAH CHAMBLEN, being first duly sworn by Edward Merrick, a Notary Public, testified as follows:

BY THE COMMISSIONER:

Q Your name is Sarah Chamblen? A Sarah Chamblen.
Q How old are you? A 61 years old.
Q What is your postoffice address? A Okmulgee.
Q Are you a citizen of the Creek Nation? A No sir, I am a citizen of the Cherokee Nation.
Q Are you the identical Sarah Chamblen who made affidavit before one Fred Comstock, a notary[sic] Public, on January 6th of this year, as to the date of birth of one George Nubbie? A Yes sir.
Q The date of the birth of this child is stated by his father, George Nubbie as one date; you give another date; how many years ago was this child born? A He was born 1901.
Q Born in 1901? A Yes sir, be five years old the 17th of this month.
Q Is this child living? A Yes sir, it is living.
Q What is he name of his mother? A Her name was Sophy.
Q Sophia, S-o-p-h-i-a Nubbie? A Yes sir.
Q Did she ever go by the name of Sophia Nubbie? A Yes sir.
Q For how long did she go by that name? A Till she was married to Ed Morgan.
Q Is Sophia a citizen of the Creek Nation? A No sir, she belonged to the Cherokee side.
Q Did she get an allotment as a Cherokee? A No sir they never got an allotment.
Q In fact she is not a citizen of any of the five tribes? A No sir.
Q How many times was Sophia married? A Three times.
Q What was the name of her first husband? A Ben Perryman.
Q Did he die, or was she separated from him? A No sir, he died.
Q When did he die? A He died 1898.
Q 1898? A Yes sir.

Applications for Enrollment of Creek Newborn
Act of 1905   Volume IX

Q Who was the second man she lived with? A Georg Nubbie.
Q When did she take up with George Nubbie? A Took up with him 1900, in the winter of 1900.
Q How long did she live with George Nubbie? A She lived with him about six months.
Q How long did she live in the same house with him? A Four months.
Q Was she ever married to him? A We have their word for it, that is all we know about it.
Q Did you see that marriage ceremony performed? A No sir.
Q Did they ever tell you they had one performed? A No sir, didn't tell us; said they were married, that is all we know about it.
Q How long after she left George Nubbie was this child born? A He left her in October and the child was born in November.
Q Was the father of this child a citizen of any nation? A Citizen of the Creek.
Q Were you the midwife in attendance at the birth of this child? A Yes sir.
Q Did you make any record of the date of the birth? A No sir.
Q Any record in the bible, any other? A No sir.
Q No written record? A No sir.
Q How do you happen to remember that is was on this date that you gave that the child was born? A I just remembered it, that is al.
Q Who is the child living with at the present time? A Staying with its mother's sister, Maggie Derisaw.
Q D-e-r-i-s-a-w? A Yes sir.
Q Is Sophia Nubbie living? A No sir, she's dead.
Q Is George Nubbie living? A No sir, he's dead; he died last May.
Q When did Sophia die? A She's dead, soon be three years, going on three years.
Q Do you remember of signing a joint affidavit with Annie Adams in regard to the birth of this child? A I dont[sic] remember of ever signing one that way; I dont[sic] think I was there when that was got up.
Q But you are now positively sure that this child was born on November 17, 1901?
A Yes sir.
Q In the affidavit previously referred to you stated that this child was born on November 10, 1901? A No sir, I didnt[sic] have that; I got nothing to do with that.
Q Then the affidavit that is before us and I will show it to you, is this your signature?
A I guess it is my signature; I never signed it.
Q Then you now state that the date that is given in that affidavit is incorrect if it says November 10, 1901? A Yes sir.
Q And you are now positive it is November 17? A Yes sir, you see it right there.

WITNESS EXCUSED.

Applications for Enrollment of Creek Newborn
Act of 1905   Volume IX

LEWIS ADAMS, being first duly sworn by Edward Merrick, a Notary Public, testified as follows:

BY THE COMMISSIONER:

Q What is your name? A Lewis Adams.
Q How old are you? A 34.
Q What is your postoffice address? A Beggs.
Q You a citizen of the Creek Nation? A Yes sir.
Q Are you, or were you ever acquainted with any one by the name of George Nubbie? A Yes sir.
Q Were you acquainted with his wife? A Yes sir.
Q What was the name of his wife? A Sophia, called her Sophia.
Q Do you know whether he was married to her? A Except what they both tells me.
Q Did he have a child by her? A Yes sir.
Q What is the name of that child? A George Nubbie.
Q George Nubbie, Jr.? A Yes sir.
Q Is that child living? A Yes sir.
Q How old is that child; dont[sic] want the date, want to know how old it is? A dont[sic] want the date?
Q How old is that child, about how old? A I think he must be about five.
Q Do you live near, or did you live near George Nubbie and Sophia Nubbie? A At that time?
A At the time of the birth of that child? A Yes sir.
Q How far did you live from there? A About a quarter or half mile, something like that.
Q You are not related to them are you? A No sir, except by marriage.
Q You have previously filed certain affidavits, made certain affidavit as to the date of birth of this child, have you not? A Why yes I think I did.
Q Do you know the exact date this child was born? A Why not exactly, but I think it was on the 17th of November.
Q How do you happen to remember that date? A Why I dont[sic] know exactly, but it is in November, must be about that time, I got a child about the same age, both nearly one age.
Q You have a child about the same age? A Yes sir, I think so; I think his'n is a little bit older than mine, I think.
Q How much older? A I dont[sic] know the exact date of neither one of my children, unless I go to the record.
Q You swore to an affidavit, together with your wife, to the affidavit that George Nubbie, Jr. was born on the 17th day of November, 1901; were you positive when you made that affidavit as to the date of birth, as to the date of it? A Yes sir.

WITNESS EXCUSED.

Cora Moore, being first duly sworn, states that as stenographer to the Commissioner to the Five Civilized Tribes she reported the proceedings had in the above

Applications for Enrollment of Creek Newborn
Act of 1905 Volume IX

entitled cause on November 19, 1906, and that the above and foregoing is a true and correct transcript of her stenographic notes taken in said cause on said date.

Cora Moore

Subscribed and sworn to before me this November 19, 1906.

Chas E Webster
Notary Public.

NC 717.   F.H.W.
DEPARTMENT OF THE INTERIOR,
COMMISSIONER TO THE FIVE CIVILIZED TRIBES.

In the matter of the application for the enrollment of George Nubbie, as a citizen by blood of the Creek Nation.

DECISION.

The record in this case shows that on May 2, 1905, application was made, in affidavit form, for the enrollment of George Nubbie, as a citizen by blood of the Creek Nation. Supplemental affidavits as to the birth of said applicant, executed April 3, and November 7, 1905, and January 6, 1906, are attached to and made a part of the record herein. Further proceedings at Beggs, Indian Territory, before a Creek enrollment field party, were had September 13, 1905, and before the Commissioner to the Five Civilized Tribes, at Muskogee, Indian Territory, on November 19, 1906.

The evidence shows that the said George Nubbie, the son of Sophia Nubbie, a non citizen, and George W. Nubbie, whose name appears on a partial schedule of Citizens by blood of the Creek Nation, approved by the Secretary of the Interior March 13, 1902, opposite number 4354.

There is a discrepancy in the affidavits as to the date of birth of said applicant, one showing the date to be November 10, 1901, another November 17, 1901, but a preponderance of the testimony established the fact that the said George Nubbie was born November 17, 1901. It further appears that the said George Nubbie was living on the date of the last proceedings herein.

The Act of Congress approved March 3rd, 1905, (33 Stat. 10480, provides in part as follows:

"That the Commission to the Five Civilized Tribes is authorized for sixty days after the date of the approval of this Act to receive and consider applications for enrollments of children born subsequent to May twenty five, nineteen hundred and one, and prior to March fourth, nineteen hundred and five, and living on said latter date, to citizens of the Creek tribe of Indians whose enrollment has been approved by the Secretary of the Interior prior to the approval of this act; and to enroll and make allotments to such children."

Applications for Enrollment of Creek Newborn
Act of 1905 Volume IX

It is therefore ordered and adjudged that the said George Nubbie is entitled to enrollment as a citizen by blood of the Creek Nation, in accordance with the provisions of the Act of Congress above quoted and the application for his enrollment as such is accordingly granted.

Tams Bixby COMMISSIONER.

Muskogee, Indian Territory.

_____.

BIRTH AFFIDAVIT.
DEPARTMENT OF THE INTERIOR.
COMMISSION TO THE FIVE CIVILIZED TRIBES.

IN RE APPLICATION FOR ENROLLMENT, as a citizen of the Creek Nation, of Willie E. Nubbie, born on the 6 day of July, 1902 and died September 10, 1904

Name of Father: George W. Nubbie   a citizen of the   Creek   Nation.
Ketchopatcky Town
Name of Mother: Harlie Nubbie (nee Barnett)   a citizen of the   Creek   Nation.
Quasarte No. 1 Town
                      Postoffice   Stidham Ind. Ter.

AFFIDAVIT OF MOTHER.

UNITED STATES OF AMERICA, Indian Territory,
     Western   DISTRICT.

I, Harlie Nubbie, on oath state that I am 27 years of age and a citizen by blood, of the Creek Nation; that I am the lawful wife of George W. Nubbie, who is a citizen, by blood of the Creek Nation; that a male child was born to me on 6 day of July, 1902, that said child has been named Willie E. Nubbie, and ~~was living March 4, 1905~~. died September 10, 1904.
                                            her
                                 Harlie x Nubbie
Witnesses To Mark: mark
   { Alex Posey
   { DC Skaggs

Subscribed and sworn to before me this 5 day of April, 1905.

                                   Drennan C Skaggs
                                   Notary Public.

Applications for Enrollment of Creek Newborn
Act of 1905   Volume IX

Father
AFFIDAVIT OF ~~ATTENDING PHYSICIAN OR MID-WIFE~~.

UNITED STATES OF AMERICA, Indian Territory, }
Western   DISTRICT.

my wife
I, George W. Nubbie , ~~a (blank)~~ , on oath state that I attended on ^ Mrs. Harlie Nubbie , ~~wife of~~ (blank) on the 6 day of July , 1902 ; that there was born to her on said date a   male   child; that said child ~~was living March 4, 1905~~, died September 10, 1904 and is said to have been named Willie E. Nubbie

George W. Nubbie

Witnesses To Mark:
{

Subscribed and sworn to before me this 5 day of April , 1905.

Drennan C Skaggs
Notary Public.

NC 717   JLD
DEPARTMENT OF THE INTERIOR,
COMMISSIONER TO THE FIVE CIVILIZED TRIBES.
. . . .

In the matter of the application for the enrollment of Willie E. Nubbie, deceased, as a citizen by blood of the Creek Nation.
. . . .

STATEMENT AND ORDER.

The record in this case shows that on April 10, 1905, application was made, in affidavit form, supplemented by sworn testimony taken October 14, 1905, for the enrollment of Willie E. Nubbie, deceased, as a citizen by blood of the Creek Nation, under the provisions of the act of Congress approved March 3, 1905.

It appears from the evidence filed in this matter that said Willie E. Nubbie, deceased, was born July 6, 1902, and it also appears from the weight of evidence that he died September 10, 1904.

The Act of Congress approved March 3, 1905, (33 Stats., 1048), provides:
"That the Commission to the Five Civilized Tribes is authorized for sixty days after the date of the approval of this act to receive and consider applications for enrollment, of children, <u>born subsequent to May twenty-fifth, nineteen hundred and one, and prior to March fourth, nineteen hundred and five, and living on said latter date,</u> to citizens of the Creek tribe of Indians whose enrollment has been

175

Applications for Enrollment of Creek Newborn
Act of 1905   Volume IX

approved by the Secretary of the Interior prior to the approval of this act; and to enroll and make allotments to such children."
It is, therefore, ordered that the application for the enrollment of said Willie E. Nubbie, deceased, as a citizen by blood of the Creek Nation, be, and the same is hereby dismissed.

Muskogee, Indian Territory.
JAN 15 1907

Tams Bixby Commissioner.

NC-717

Muskogee, Indian Territory, August 15, 1905.

George W. Nubby,
    Stidham, Indian Territory.

Dear Sir:

    In the matter of the application for the enrollment of your minor children, Robert Nubby, born December 9, 1904, and George Nubby, Jr., born November 10, 1901, as citizens by blood of the Creek Nation blood of the Creek Nation, it will be necessary for you to file with this Office the affidavits of two disinterested persons as to the birth of these children. Said affidavits must set forth said children's names, the dates of their birth, the names of their parents, and whether or not they were living on March 4, 1905.
    This Office is unable to identify Sophia Nubby, the mother of George Nubby Jr., upon the final rolls of the citizens by blood of the Creek Nation. You are therefore requested to immediately inform this Office as to the name under which the said Sophie Nubby was finally enrolled, the names of her parents and other members of her family, the Creek Indian Town to which she belongs, and if possible, her final roll number as the same appears upon your allotment certificate and deeds.

                    Respectfully,
                      Acting Commissioner.

NC717

Muskogee, Indian Territory, October 20, 1905.
George W. Nubbie
    Stidham I.T.

Dear Sir:

    Receipt is acknowledged of your letter of October 18, 1905, in which you state that you have examined the family record relative to the birth of your minor child George Nubbie Jr. you ask what to do in regard to his enrollment.

Applications for Enrollment of Creek Newborn
Act of 1905 Volume IX

In reply you are advised that you will be allowed twenty days from date hereof within which to appear before this office with the above mentioned record for the purpose of being examined under oath.

         Respectfully,
           Commissioner

NC 717

         Muskogee, Indian Territory, December 14, 1905

Take Testimony as requested herein

George W. Nubbie,
  Stidham, Indian Territory

Dear Sir:

  In the matter of the application for the enrollment of your minor child, George Nubbie, Jr. as a citizen by blood of the Creek Nation, there is on file at this office an affidavit executed by Sarah Chamblen, relative to the birth of said child, in which she states that said George Nubbie Jr. was born November 10, 1901. There is also on file affidavits, executed by Lewis and Annie Adams relative to the birth of said child; stating that said George Nubbie Jr. was born November 17, 1901. These affidavits conflict with your testimony of October 14, 1905, in which you state that said George Nubbie Jr was born November 16, 1900. In an affidavit executed by you April 3, 1905, you state that Sophia Nubbie, the mother of said child, died January 17, 1902; in your testimony of October 14, 1905, you say that said Sophia Nubbie died January 17, 1901.

  In order that these discrepancies may be corrected and that this office may be enabled to ascertain the exact date of the birth of said child, George Nubbie Jr. there is herewith enclosed a blank form of birth affidavit, which you are requested to execute giving the correct date of the birth of said George Nubbie Jr. There is also enclosed a blank form of death affidavit, which you are requested to execute giving the correct date of the death of said Sophia Nubbie the mother of said Geo Nubbie Jr When you have executed said affidavits you will return same to this office in the inclosed envelope. This matter should receive your immediate attention.

         Respectfully,

            Commissioner.

Applications for Enrollment of Creek Newborn
Act of 1905   Volume IX

(The letter below typed as given)

Beggs I T   June 2 1906

Com to the Five Civ Tribes
    Muskogee I T

Dear Sir

    Was Geo Nubbie Jr minor of Geo W Nubbie of Kechepakee town was his affidavit approve or not the child mother was Sophia Nubbie a non citizen of the Creek Nation

    Geo W Nubbie Sr is dead and I wants to not said application was approved or not Let me here from by return mail and oblige

        Yours
        Lewis Adams

N.C. 717

    Muskogee, I.T. June 30, 1906

Lewis Adams
    Beggs, I.T.

Dear Sir:

    Receipt is acknowledged of your letter dated June 2, 1906, requesting information as to the status of the application for the enrollment of George Nubbie Jr. as a citizen by blood of the Creek Nation. You state that George W. Nubbie, the father of said applicant is dead.

    In reply you are advised that the matter of the application for the enrollment of said George Nubbie Jr as a citizen of the Creek Natioj[sic]; is now pending in this office and that when final action is had in same, you or the guardian of said child, if such guardian is appointed will be duly notified.

    In order that the death of George W. Nubbie may be made a matter of record there is enclosed herewith a blank form of proof of death which you are requested to have properly executed and return to this office at an early date.

        Respectfully,
                Commissioner.

Applications for Enrollment of Creek Newborn
Act of 1905   Volume IX

C 717

Muskogee I T July 5, 1906

Lewis Adams
        Beggs I T

Dear Sir:

    It appears from the records of this office that on November 8, 1905, the joint affidavit of yourself and Annie Adams was filed in the matter of the application for the enrollment of Geo Nubbie Jr. as a citizen by blood of the Creek Nation. The date of birth of said applicant, as shown in said affidavit is different from that given in the affidavit of Sarah Chamblen the midwife in attendance at the birth of said child, and also differs from the date of birth as shown in the testimony of Geo W Nubbie, the father of said child, taken October 14, 1905.

    You are advised that before final action can be had in this matter it is required that you and said Sarah Chamblen appear in person before this office for the purpose of testifying as o the correct date of birth of said applicant.

                        Respectfully,
                                              Commissioner.

(The letter below typed as given)

                        Beggs I T July 10 1906

Commission to the Five Civilized Tribes,
        Muskogee, I T

Gents:

    Your letter is at hand relating to the enrollment of Geo Nubbie Jr requesting I and Sarah Chamblen to appear at your office in order that a final record can be made of said child. Now will say that the said Sarah Chamblen cannot walk she is cripple she go about on a chair but she is a grate midwife she go far and near but she has a verry poor way of getting out on a trip of that kind a person would have to carry her up to your office by hand, she cannot make a step without her chair and she is not very well now You said that the George Nubbie Sr the father of said child and I & Annie Adams & Sarah Chamblen affadavitts are all conflict with one an other Now I will tell you how this come about when I an Annie Adams made out our affadavitts the said Sarah Chamblenwere not here and for fearing that said office would be close before she get here we made out one we did not wants to see said child loose its land when we know he was entitle to it. We must have made a mistake in the dat of its birth I will say that Mrs Sarah Chamblen affidavits are correct for Sophie Nubbie the mother of said child is the

Applications for Enrollment of Creek Newborn
Act of 1905 Volume IX

daughter of Mrs Sarah Chamblen the midwife and the said Sarah Chamblen were living with her daughter Mrs Nubbie when said child were born and everybody in the country no this to be a fact I will also say that the affidavit given by Geo Nubbie the father of said child is not correct for he was away and he had been away for about three months when said child were born for further information I will be gladly to offer let me no and if she must come I will write her to come to Beggs I T and she and I will go down but you will have to take her testimony at the hotel for it is inconvents for her to get about she has been in bad health for about 3 or 4 weeks she is a poor widow woman

       Hoping to hear from you soon
        Yours Lewis Adams
         Beggs I T

HGH

REFER IN REPLY TO THE FOLLOWING:

DEPARTMENT OF THE INTERIOR,
COMMISSIONER TO THE FIVE CIVILIZED TRIBES.

Muskogee, Indian Territory, November 12, 1906.

Lewis Adams
  Beggs, Indian Territory.

Dear Sir:

  Replying to your communication of November 6, 1906 you are advised that you should appear at this office at an early date together with Sarah Chamblen to be examined under oath.

      Respectfully,
        Tams Bixby Commissioner.

NC 717.

       Muskogee, Indian Territory, January 15, 1907.
Harlie Nubbie,
  c/o George W. Nubbie,
    Stidham, Indian Territory.

Dear Madam:

  There is herewith enclosed one copy of the Statement and Order of the Commissioner to the Five Civilized Tribes, dated January 15, 1907, dismissing the application made by you for the enrollment of your minor children, Willie E. and George Nubbie, Jr., as citizens by blood of the Creek Nation.

Applications for Enrollment of Creek Newborn
Act of 1905   Volume IX

LM-66.

Respectfully,

Commissioner.

N C 717.

Muskogee, Indian Territory, March 7, 1907.

Lewis Adams,
   Beggs, Indian Territory.

Dear Sir:

You are hereby advised that on March 2, 1907 the Secretary of the Interior approved the enrollment of George Nubbie, minor child of George W. Nubbie and Sophia Nubbie, as a citizen by blood of the Creek Nation, and that the name of said child appears upon the roll of new born citizens by blood of the Creek Nation enrolled under the Act of Congress approved March 3, 1905, as number 1235.

This child is now entitled to an allotment and application therefor should be made without delay at the Creek Land Office, Muskogee, Indian Territory.

Commissioner.

N C 717.

Muskogee, Indian Territory, March 7, 1907.

George W. Nubbie,
   Stidham, Indian Territory.

Dear Sir:

You are hereby advised that on March 2, 1907 the Secretary of the Interior approved the enrollment of your minor child George Nubbie as a citizen by blood of the Creek Nation, and that the name of said child appears upon the roll of new born citizens by blood of the Creek Nation enrolled under the Act of Congress approved March 3, 1905, as number 1235.

This child is now entitled to allotment and application therefor should be made without delay at the Creek Land Office, Muskogee, Indian Territory.

Respectfully,

Commissioner.

Applications for Enrollment of Creek Newborn
Act of 1905   Volume IX

BIRTH AFFIDAVIT.

DEPARTMENT OF THE INTERIOR.
COMMISSION TO THE FIVE CIVILIZED TRIBES.

IN RE APPLICATION FOR ENROLLMENT, as a citizen of the Creek Nation, of George Nubbie, born on the 10th day of November, 1901

Name of Father: George W Nubbie   a citizen of the   Creek   Nation.
Name of Mother: Sophia Nubbie   a citizen of the   *(blank)*   Nation.

Postoffice   Stidham Ind. Ter.

AFFIDAVIT OF ATTENDING PHYSICIAN OR MID-WIFE.

UNITED STATES OF AMERICA, Indian Territory,
    Western   DISTRICT.

I, Sarah Chamblen, a Mid Wife, on oath state that I attended on Mrs. Sophia Nubbie, wife of George W Nubbie on the 10th day of November, 1901 ; that there was born to her on said date a male child; that said child was living March 4, 1905, and is said to have been named George Nubbie

                                  Sarah Chamblen

Witnesses To Mark:

Subscribed and sworn to before me 2nd day of April, 1905.

                        Richard J Hill
                               Notary Public.
My commission expires March 25th 1907

(The above Birth Affidavit given again without the Notary's signature)

BIRTH AFFIDAVIT.
DEPARTMENT OF THE INTERIOR.
COMMISSION TO THE FIVE CIVILIZED TRIBES.

IN RE APPLICATION FOR ENROLLMENT, as a citizen of the Creek Nation, of George Nubbie Jr, born on the 10 day of November, 1901

Name of Father: George W Nubbie   a citizen of the   Creek   Nation.
Name of Mother: Sophia Nubbie   a citizen of the   *(blank)*   Nation.

Applications for Enrollment of Creek Newborn
Act of 1905   Volume IX

Postoffice   Stidham Ind. Ter.

AFFIDAVIT OF ATTENDING PHYSICIAN OR MID-WIFE.

UNITED STATES OF AMERICA, Indian Territory, ⎫
  Western   DISTRICT.   ⎬
                                    ⎭

I, Sarah Chamblen, a Mid Wife, on oath state that I attended on Mrs. Sophia Nubbie, wife of George W Nubbie on the 10th day of November, 1901; that there was born to her on said date a male child; that said child was living March 4, 1905, and is said to have been named George Nubbie

Sarah Chamblen

Witnesses To Mark:
{

Subscribed and sworn to before me 2nd day of April, 1905.

Richard J Hill
Notary Public.

My commission expires March 25th 1907

BIRTH AFFIDAVIT.

DEPARTMENT OF THE INTERIOR.
COMMISSION TO THE FIVE CIVILIZED TRIBES.

IN RE APPLICATION FOR ENROLLMENT, as a citizen of the Creek Nation, of George Nubbie Jr, born on the 10 day of November, 1901

Name of Father: George W Nubbie   a citizen of the   Creek   Nation.
Name of Mother: Sophia Nubbie   not a citizen of the *(blank)*   Nation.

Postoffice   Stidham I.T.

AFFIDAVIT OF ATTENDING PHYSICIAN OR MID-WIFE.

UNITED STATES OF AMERICA, Indian Territory, ⎫
  Western   DISTRICT.   ⎬
                                    ⎭

I, Sarah Chamblen, a Mid-wife, on oath state that I attended on Mrs. Sophia Nubbie, wife of George W Nubbie on the 10th day of November, 1901; that there was born to her on said date a Male child; that said child was living March 4, 1905, and is said to have been named George Nubbie

Applications for Enrollment of Creek Newborn
Act of 1905 Volume IX

Witnesses To Mark: Sarah Chamblen

{

Subscribed and sworn to before me 6 day of January, 1906.

Fred Comstock
Notary Public.

My Com Exp 7/2/06

Birth Affidavit

Department of the Interior
Commission to the Five Civilized Tribes

    I George W Nubbie on oath states[sic] that I am ~~the~~ 28 years of age, a citizen of Creek Nation by blood, That I am the father of the minor child George Nubbie Jr named in the attached application, That the mother of said child, George Nubbie, is dead and has been since Jan 17th 1902 That the mother of said child Sophia Nubbie was my lawful wife

George W. Nubbie

Subscribed and sworn to before me this 3rd day of April 1905

Richard H Hill
Notary Public

My commission expires Mar 25th 1909

BIRTH AFFIDAVIT.

DEPARTMENT OF THE INTERIOR.
COMMISSION TO THE FIVE CIVILIZED TRIBES.

    IN RE APPLICATION FOR ENROLLMENT, as a citizen of the Creek Nation, of Robert Nubbie, born on the 9 day of Dec., 1904

Name of Father: George W. Nubbie   a citizen of the   Creek   Nation.
Ketchopatcky Town
Name of Mother: Harlie Nubbie (nee Barnett)   a citizen of the   Creek   Nation.
Quasarte No. 1

                   Postoffice   Stidham, Ind. Ter.

Applications for Enrollment of Creek Newborn
Act of 1905   Volume IX

AFFIDAVIT OF MOTHER.

UNITED STATES OF AMERICA, Indian Territory, ⎫
   Western   DISTRICT.   ⎭   Child is present

    I, Harlie Nubbie , on oath state that I am 27 years of age and a citizen by blood , of the Creek Nation; that I am the lawful wife of George W. Nubbie , who is a citizen, by blood of the Creek Nation; that a male child was born to me on 9 day of December , 1904 , that said child has been named Robert Nubbie , and was living March 4, 1905.

her
Harlie x Nubbie
mark

Witnesses To Mark:
{ Alex Posey
  DC Skaggs

    Subscribed and sworn to before me this 5 day of April , 1905.

Drennan C Skaggs
Notary Public.

Father
AFFIDAVIT OF <s>ATTENDING PHYSICIAN OR MID-WIFE</s>.

UNITED STATES OF AMERICA, Indian Territory, ⎫
   Western   DISTRICT.   ⎭

my wife

    I, George W. Nubbie , <s>a (blank)</s> , on oath state that I attended on ^ Mrs. Harlie Nubbie , <s>wife of</s> *(blank)* on the 9 day of December , 1904 ; that there was born to her on said date a male child; that said child was living March 4, 1905, and is said to have been named Robert Nubbie

George W. Nubbie

Witnesses To Mark:
{

    Subscribed and sworn to before me this 5 day of April, 1905.

Drennan C Skaggs
Notary Public.

Applications for Enrollment of Creek Newborn
Act of 1905   Volume IX

BIRTH AFFIDAVIT.

DEPARTMENT OF THE INTERIOR,
COMMISSION TO THE FIVE CIVILIZED TRIBES.

In Re Application for Enrollment, as a citizen of the Creek Nation, of George Nubbie Jr , born on the   10" day of November , 1901

Name of Father: George W. Nubbie   a citizen of the   Creek   Nation.
Name of Father: Sophia Nubbie   not a citizen of the   Creek   Nation.

Post-office   Stidham IT

AFFIDAVIT OF ATTENDING PHYSICIAN OR MID-WIFE.

UNITED STATES OF AMERICA,
INDIAN TERRITORY,
Western   District.

I, Sarah Chamblen , a Midwife , on oath state that I attended on Mrs. Sophia Nubbie , wife of George W. Nubbie on the 10" day of November , 1901 ; that there was born to her on said date a male child; that said child is now living March 4, 1905 and is said to have been named George Nubbie

(signed) Sarah Chamblen

WITNESSES TO MARK:

Subscribed and sworn to before me this 6 day of   January , 1906.

Fred Comstock
NOTARY PUBLIC.

My Com Exp 7/2/06

DEPARTMENT OF THE INTERIOR.
COMMISSION TO THE FIVE CIVILIZED TRIBES.

In the matter of the death of   Sophia Nubbie   Not   a citizen of the Creek Nation, who formerly resided at or near   Stidham   , Ind. Ter., and died on the 17" day of   January , 1902

Applications for Enrollment of Creek Newborn
Act of 1905 Volume IX

AFFIDAVIT OF RELATIVE.

UNITED STATES OF AMERICA, Indian Territory,
    Western   DISTRICT.

                                                                                     not

I, Anna Adams, on oath state that I am 29 years of age and ^ a citizen by birth, of the Creek Nation; that my postoffice address is Beggs, Ind. Ter.; that I am sister of Sophia Nubbie who was Not a citizen, by birth, of the Creek Nation and that said Sophia Nubbie died on the 17" day of January, 1902

                               (Signed) Anna Adams

Witnesses To Mark:
{

    Subscribed and sworn to before me this 6" day of January, 1906.

                                    Fred Comstock
                                      Notary Public.

My Com Exp 7/2/06

                              Copy
AFFIDAVIT OF ACQUAINTANCE.

UNITED STATES OF AMERICA, Indian Territory,
    Western   DISTRICT.

I, Lewis Adams, on oath state that I am 34 years of age, and a citizen by Blood of the Creek Nation; that my postoffice address is Beggs, Ind. Ter.; that I was personally acquainted with Sophia Nubbie who was not a citizen, by Blood, of the Creek Nation; and that said Sophia Nubbie died on the 17 day of January, 1902

                                      Lewis Adams

Witnesses To Mark:
{

    Subscribed and sworn to before me this 6" day of January, 1906.

                                    Fred Comstock
                                      Notary Public.

My Com Exp 7/2/06

(The above Death Affidavit given again)

Applications for Enrollment of Creek Newborn
Act of 1905   Volume IX

United States of America   I
Indian Territory   I ss
Western Judicial District   I

We the undersigned   Lewis Adams   and   Annie Adams   upon oath state that we know it to be a fact that a male child was born to George W. Nubbie and Sophie Nubbie on the 17th., day of November 1901; that the child is now living and is named George Nubbie.

Witness our hands and seals this 7th day of Nov 1905.

Lewis Adams

Annie Adams

Subscribed and sworn to before me this 7th day of November 1905.

Wm F A *(Illegible)*
Notary Public.
My Commission expires 6-29-1908

Birth Affidavit
Department of the Interior
Commission to the Five Civilized Tribes

I George W Nubbie on oath states that I am 28 years of age, a citizen of Creek Nation by blood that I am the father of the minor child George Nubbie Jr named in the attached application that the mother of said child George Nubbie is dead and has been since Jan 17 1902 that the mother of said child Sophia Nubbie was my lawful wife

George W Nubbie

Subscribed and sworn to before me this 3rd day of April 1905

Richard J. Hill
Notary Public

My commission expires Mar 25, 1909
Seal

Applications for Enrollment of Creek Newborn
Act of 1905 Volume IX

United States of America I
   Indian Territory I ss
Western Judicial District I

    We the undersigned Lewis Adams and Annie Adams upon oath state that we know it to be a fact that a Male child was born to George W. Nubbie and Harley Barnett Nubbie (nee Harley Barnett) on the 9th day of December 1904; That the child is now living and is named Robert Nubbie.

    Witness our hands and seals this Seventh day of November 1905.

                        Lewis Adams

                         Annie Adams

    Subscribed and sworn to before me this Seventh day of November 1905.

                        Wm F A *(Illegible)*
                        Notary Public.
                        My Commission expires 6-29-1908

C 718

DEPARTMENT OF THE INTERIOR,
COMMISSION TO THE FIVE CIVILIZED TRIBES.
Eufaula, I. T., April 5, 1905.

    In the matter of the application for the enrollment of Etta May Backbun as a citizen by blood of the Creek Nation.

    NEECIE BACKBUN, being duly sworn, testified as follows:

BY COMMISSION:
Q What is your name? A Neecie Backbun/[sic]
Q How old are you? A Twenty-seven.
Q What is your post office address? A Cathay.
Q Are you a citizen of the Creek Nation? A Yes, sir.
Q To what town do you belong? A Broken Arrow.
Q Do you make application for the enrollment of your minor child, Etta May Backbun, as a citizen of the Creek Nation? A Yes, sir.
Q What is the name of the father of the child? A Cal Backbun.
Q Is he a citizen of the Creek Nation? A No, sir, he is a Cherokee

Applications for Enrollment of Creek Newborn
Act of 1905   Volume IX

Q Is he your lawful husband? A Yes, sir.
Q When was the child born? A The first of March.
Q What year? A 1905.
Q How do you fix the date? A Why, I always keep up with the day of the month.
Q On what day of the week was the child born? A Wednesday
Q Was it born at night or during the day time? A Just before day.
Q On the morning of the 1st of March? A Yes, sir.
Q Was there any record made of the child's birth? a No, sir.
Q Who attended on you at the time the child was born? A Jane Tiger and my husband and my sister, Ada Runnelle.
Q How old is the child now? A It is about a month old. It was a month old the first of this month.
Q You are positive are you that the child was born on that date? A Yes, sir.

CAL BACKBUN, being duly sworn, testified as follows:

BY COMMISSION:
Q What is your name? A Ca/[sic] Backbun.
Q How old are you? A Twenty-seven.
Q What is your post office address? A Cathay.
Q Are you a citizen of the Creek Nation? A No, sir, I am a Cherokee
Q Have you a child named Etta May Backbun? A Yes, sir.
Q What is the name of her mother? A Neecie Backbun.
Q Is she your lawful wife? A Yes, sir.
Q Is she a citizen of the Cherokee Nation? A No, sir, she is a citizen of the Creek Nation.
Q When was your child, Etta May Backbun, born? A The first of March.
Q How do you fix the date of the child's birth? A Because I paid close attention.
Q Was there any record made of the birth of the child? A No, sir.
Q What day of the week was that? A On Wednesday morning.
Q You are positive are you that the child was born on that day? A Yes, sir.
Q You made no record in the Bible or any book? A No, sir.
Q Who was present when the child was born? A Jane Tiger, Ada Runnels and myself.
Q Does any one else know when the child was born? A Yes, sir, I guess they do, them that lives around me.
Q Name some of your neighbors? A Turner's family and Murray's folks.

I, D. C. Skaggs, on oath state that the above and foregoing is a full and true transcript of my stenographic notes as taken in said cause on said date.

DC Skaggs

Subscribed and sworn to before me this 22 day of July, 1905.

J McDermott
Notary Public.

Applications for Enrollment of Creek Newborn
Act of 1905 Volume IX

N.C. 718   DEPARTMENT OF THE INTERIOR,
COMMISSIONER TO THE FIVE CIVILIZED TRIBES.
Eufaula, I. T., May 9, 1906.

In the matter of the application for the enrollment of Etta May Backbun as a citizen by blood of the Creek Nation.

ARNECIE BACKBUN, being duly sworn, testified as follows:

BY THE COMMISSIONER:
Q What is your name? A Arnecie Backbun.
Q How old are you? A 28.
Q What is your post office address? A Cathay.
Q Are you a citizen of the Creek Nation? A Yes, sir.
Q To what town do you belong? A Broken Arrow.
Q Have you a child named Etta May Backbun, for whom you have made application? A Yes, sir.
Q Who is the father of the child? A Calvin Backbun.
Q Is he a citizen of the Creek Nation? A He is a citizen of the Cherokee Nation.
Q When was that child born? A March 1, 1905.
Q If it should be found that your child, Etta May Backbun, is entitled to enrollment in either the Creek or Cherokee Nation in which nation do you elect to have her enrolled? A In the Creek Nation.

---oooOOOooo---

I, D. C. Skaggs, on oath state that the above and foregoing is a full and true transcript of my stenographic notes as taken in said cause on said date.

DC Skaggs

Subscribed and sworn to before me this 9th day of May, 1906.

Alex Posey
Notary Public.

Applications for Enrollment of Creek Newborn
Act of 1905   Volume IX

BIRTH AFFIDAVIT.

DEPARTMENT OF THE INTERIOR.
COMMISSION TO THE FIVE CIVILIZED TRIBES.

IN RE APPLICATION FOR ENROLLMENT, as a citizen of the Creek Nation, of Etta May Backbun, born on the 1 day of March, 1905

Name of Father: Cal Backman[sic]   a citizen of the Cherokee   Nation.
                           (nee Ansiel)
Name of Mother: Necie Backman[sic]   a citizen of the   Creek   Nation.
Broken Arrow Town
                         Postoffice   Cathay Ind Ter

AFFIDAVIT OF MOTHER.

UNITED STATES OF AMERICA, Indian Territory,
     Western   DISTRICT.   Child is present

     I, Necie Backman, on oath state that I am 27 years of age and a citizen by blood, of the Creek Nation; that I am the lawful wife of Cal Backman, who is a citizen, by *(blank)* of the United States ~~Nation~~; that a female child was born to me on 1 day of March, 1905, that said child has been named Etta May Backman, and was living March 4, 1905.

                               Necie Backbun
Witnesses To Mark:

     Subscribed and sworn to before me this 5 day of April, 1905.

                               Drennan C Skaggs
                               Notary Public.

N.C. 718
BIRTH AFFIDAVIT.

DEPARTMENT OF THE INTERIOR,
COMMISSIONER TO THE FIVE CIVILIZED TRIBES.

ENROLLMENT OF MINORS.   ACT OF CONGRESS, APPROVED APRIL 26, 1906.

     IN RE APPLICATION FOR ENROLLMENT, as a citizen of the Creek Nation, of Etta May Backbun, born on the 1 day of March, 1905

Name of Father: Calvin Backbun   a citizen of the   Cherokee   Nation.
Name of Mother: Arnecie Backbun   a citizen of the   Creek   Nation.

Applications for Enrollment of Creek Newborn
Act of 1905 Volume IX

Tribal enrollment of father   -----   Tribal enrollment of mother   Broken Arrow

Postoffice   Cathay Indian Territory

AFFIDAVIT OF MOTHER.   Child Present

UNITED STATES OF AMERICA, Indian Territory, ⎱
Western   District. ⎰

I, Arnecie Backbun , on oath state that I am 28 years of age and a citizen by blood , of the Creek   Nation; that I am the lawful wife of Calvin Backbun , who is a citizen, by blood of the Cherokee   Nation; that a female   child was born to me on 1st day of March , 1905 , that said child has been named Etta May Backbun , and was living March 4, 1906.

Arnecie BackBun

WITNESSES TO MARK:
{

Subscribed and sworn to before me this 9"   day of May , 1906.

Drennan C Skaggs
Notary Public.

AFFIDAVIT OF ATTENDING PHYSICIAN OR MID-WIFE.

UNITED STATES OF AMERICA, Indian Territory, ⎱
Western   District. ⎰

I, Jennie Tiger , a mid-wife , on oath state that I attended on Arnecie Backbun , wife of Calvin Backbun on the 1st day of March , 1905 ; that there was born to her on said date a   female   child; that said child was living March 4, 1906, and is said to have been named Etta May Backbun

Jennie Tiger

WITNESSES TO MARK:
{

Subscribed and sworn to before me this 9"   day of May , 1906.

Drennan C Skaggs
Notary Public.

193

Applications for Enrollment of Creek Newborn
Act of 1905 Volume IX

NC. 718.

Muskogee, Indian Territory, July 15, 1905.

Chief Clerk,
    Cherokee Enrollment Division,
        Muskogee, Indian Territory.

Dear Sir:

    April 10, 1905, application was made to the Commission to the Five Civilized Tribes for the enrollment of Etta May Blackbun[sic], born March 1, 1905, as a citizen by blood of the Creek Nation. It is stated in said application that the father of said child is Cal Backbun, a citizen of the Cherokee Nation, and that the mother is Necie Blackbun, a citizen of the Creek Nation.

    You are requested to inform the Creek Enrollment Division as to whether application has been made for the enrollment of said Etta May Blackbun, as a citizen of the Cherokee Nation, and if so, what disposition has been made of the same.

        Respectfully,

                Commissioner.

REFER IN REPLY TO THE FOLLOWING:

DEPARTMENT OF THE INTERIOR,
COMMISSIONER TO THE FIVE CIVILIZED TRIBES.

Muskogee, Indian Territory, July 18, 1905.

Chief Clerk,
    Creek Enrollment Division,
        Muskogee, Indian Territory.

Dear Sir:

    Replying to your letter of July 15, 1905, (NC. 718) asking to be advised whether or not any application has ever been made for the enrollment, as a citizen of the Cherokee Nation, of Etta May Blackbun, a child of Cal Blackbun, a citizen of the Cherokee Nation, and Necie Blackbun, a citizen of the Creek Nation, you are advised that from an examination of the records of the Cherokee Enrollment Division it does not appear that any application has ever been made for the enrollment of said child as a citizen of that nation.

        Respectfully,
              Tams Bixby   Commissioner.

GHL

Applications for Enrollment of Creek Newborn
Act of 1905   Volume IX

NC-718

Muskogee, Indian Territory, August 15, 1905.

Necie Backbun,
    Care of Cal Backbun,
        Cathay, Indian Territory.

Dear Madam:

    In the matter of the application for the enrollment of your minor daughter Ella May Backbun, as a citizen by blood of the Creek Nation, it will be necessary for you to furnish this Office with the affidavit of the attending physician or midwife at the birth of said child, and a blank for that purpose is enclosed herewith.

    You are also requested to furnish this Office with the affidavits of two disinterested persons as to the birth of said child. Said affidavits must set forth said child's name, the date of her birth, the names of her parents, and whether or not she was living on March 4, 1905.

                     Respectfully,
                                     Acting Commissioner.

1 B C
Env

NC-718

Muskogee, Indian Territory, October 18, 1905.

Necie Backbun,
    c/o Cal Backbun,
        Cathay, Indian Territory.

Dear Madam:

    In the matter of the application for the enrollment of your minor daughter Ella May Backbun, born March 1, 1905, as a citizen by blood of the Creek Nation it will be necessary for you to furnish this office with the affidavit of the attending physician or midwife at the birth of said child, and a blank for that purpose is inclosed herewith.

    You are also requested to furnish this office with the affidavits of two disinterested persons relative to the birth of said child. Said affidavits must set forth said child's name, the date of her birth, the names of her parents, and whether or not she was living on March 4, 1905.

                     Respectfully,
                                     Commissioner.

B C
Env

Applications for Enrollment of Creek Newborn
Act of 1905   Volume IX

NC-718

Muskogee, Indian Territory, December 14, 1905.

Arnecie Backbun,
    Care of Cal Backbun,
        Cathay, Indian Territory.

Dear Madam:

    In the matter of the application for the enrollment of your minor daughter Etta May Backbun, as a citizen by blood of the Creek Nation, it will be necessary for you to furnish this Office with the affidavit of the attending physician or midwife at the birth of said child, and a blank for that purpose is herewith enclosed.

    You are also requested to furnish this Office with the affidavits of two disinterested witnesses relative to said child's birth. A blank for that purpose is herewith enclosed.

    You are advised that your affidavit relative to the birth of said child is defective, inasmuch as your name, the name of said child and the name of your husband is spelled in the body of the affidavit as Backman, and your name is singed thereto "Lecie Backbun."

    You are identified on the final roll of citizens by blood of the Creek Nation as Arnecie Ansiel, and it necessarily follows that if the name of your husband is Backman, your name and the name of your asid[sic] child, should be spelled "Backman:" if, however, the correct name of your husband is Backbun, and your correct name is Arnecie Backbun, the correct name of said child is Etta May Backbun.

    It will be necessary for you to execute new affidavits, giving your correct name, the correct name of said child and of its father, and return said affidavits in enclosed envelope.

                        Respectfully,

                                          Commissioner.

1 B A
Dis

Applications for Enrollment of Creek Newborn
Act of 1905   Volume IX

BIRTH AFFIDAVIT.

Department of the Interior,
COMMISSION TO THE FIVE CIVILIZED TRIBES.

IN RE APPLICATION FOR ENROLLMENT, as a citizen of the Creek Nation, of Alex Brown, born on the 12 day of Nov, 1903

Name of Father: Dave Brown   a citizen of the   not citizen   Nation.
Name of Mother: Mariah Brown (nee Tobler)   a citizen of the   Creek   Nation.
Thlewathlee[sic] Town
                              Post-Office: Huttin Ville I.T.

AFFIDAVIT OF MOTHER.

UNITED STATES OF AMERICA,
   INDIAN TERRITORY,
   Western   District.

I, Maria[sic] Brown, on oath state that I am 29 years of age and a citizen by blood, of the Creek Nation; that I am the lawful wife of Dave Brown, who is a citizen, ~~by~~ not a citizen of the Creek Nation; that a male child was born to me on 12 day of Nov, 1903, that said child has been named Alex Brown, and is now living.

Maria Brown

WITNESSES TO MARK:
{

Subscribed and sworn to before me this 14 day of March, 1905.

L.G. McIntosh
Notary Public.

AFFIDAVIT OF ATTENDING PHYSICIAN OR MID-WIFE.

UNITED STATES OF AMERICA,
   INDIAN TERRITORY,
   Western   District.
                      mid-wife
I, Judy Grayson, a ~~citizen of Creek~~, on oath state that I attended on Mrs. Maria Brown, wife of Dave Brown on the 12 day of Nov, 1903 ; that there was born to her on said date a male child; that said child is now living and is said to have been named Alex Brown

Judy Grayson her x m[sic]

WITNESSES TO MARK:
{ Sam E Haynes
  Alice Haynes

Applications for Enrollment of Creek Newborn
Act of 1905 Volume IX

Subscribed and sworn to before me this 14 day of March, 1905.

L.G. McIntosh
Notary Public.

NC-720

Muskogee, Indian Territory, August 15, 1905.

Nora McCalvey,
    Care of Everett McCalvey,
        Eufaula, Indian Territory.

Dear Madam:

    In the matter of the application for the enrollment of your minor son, Emmit McCalvey, as a citizen by blood of the Creek Nation, it will be necessary for you to furnish this Office with the evidence of your marriage to Everett McCalvey, the father of said child, which evidence of marriage may consist of either the original or a certified copy of the marriage license and certificate.

        Respectfully,

                Acting Commissioner.

N.C. 720

Muskogee, Indian Territory, October 17, 1905.

Nora McCalvey,
    Care of Everett McCalvey,
        Eufaula, Indian Territory.

Dear Madam:

    In the matter of the application for the enrollment of your minor child, Emmit McCalvey, as a citizen by blood of the Creek Nation, you are advised that the copy of your marriage license filed with this office is not sufficient proof of said marriage because said copy is not certified to.

    You are again requested to furnish this office with either the original or a certified copy of the marriage license and certificate.

        Respectfully,

                Commissioner.

Applications for Enrollment of Creek Newborn
Act of 1905 Volume IX

N.C. 720

Muskogee, Indian Territory, October 26, 1905.

Nora McCalvey,
    Care Everett McCalvey,
        Eufaula, Indian Territory.

Dear Madam:

There is herewith returned to you original license and certificate of your marriage to Everett McCalvey.

You are advised that a certified copy of same has been made and filed in this office in the matter of the application for the enrollment of your minor child, Emmit McCalvey, as a citizen by blood of the Creek Nation.

It does not appear at this time that any further evidence is necessary in said case.

Respectfully,

AG-17   Commissioner.

BIRTH AFFIDAVIT.

DEPARTMENT OF THE INTERIOR.
COMMISSION TO THE FIVE CIVILIZED TRIBES.

IN RE APPLICATION FOR ENROLLMENT, as a citizen of the Creek Nation, of Emmit McCalvey, born on the 28th day of Oct, 1903

Name of Father: Everett McCalvey   a citizen of the   Creek   Nation.
Big *(Illegible)* Town
Name of Mother: Nora McCalvey   a citizen of the   U.S.   Nation.

Postoffice   Eufaula I.T.

AFFIDAVIT OF MOTHER.

UNITED STATES OF AMERICA, Indian Territory, ⎫
        Western   DISTRICT.   ⎬

I, Nora McCalvey, on oath state that I am 20 years of age and a citizen by marriage, of the Creek Nation; that I am the lawful wife of Everett McCalvey, who

Applications for Enrollment of Creek Newborn
Act of 1905 Volume IX

is a citizen, by blood of the Creek Nation; that a male child was born to me on 28th day of Oct , 1903 , that said child has been named Emmit McCalvey , and was living March 4, 1905.

Nora McCalvey

Witnesses To Mark:

{ Aug 1-1906

Subscribed and sworn to before me this 5 day of April , 1905.

Thos. F. (Illegible)
Notary Public.

AFFIDAVIT OF ATTENDING PHYSICIAN OR MID-WIFE.

UNITED STATES OF AMERICA, Indian Territory,
    Western   DISTRICT.

I, W.A. Tolleson , a Physician , on oath state that I attended on Mrs. Nora McCalvey , wife of Everett McCalvey on the 28th day of Oct , 1903 ; that there was born to her on said date a male child; that said child was living March 4, 1905, and is said to have been named Emmit McCalvey

W.A. Tolleson

Witnesses To Mark:

{

Subscribed and sworn to before me 4 day of April, 1905.

W.T. (Illegible)
Notary Public.

CERTIFICATE OF RECORD.

United States of America
Indian Territory
Western District

I, Robert P. Harrison, Clerk of the United States Court in the Western District Indian Territory do hereby certify that the instrument hereto attached was filed for record in my office the 17 day of Feb. 1903 at 3 P.M. and duly recorded in Book O Marriage record, page 158.

Witness my hand and seal of said court at Muskogee in said Territory this 17 day of Feb. A.D. 1903

R.P. Harrison, Clerk

Applications for Enrollment of Creek Newborn
Act of 1905   Volume IX

By R.A. Bayne, deputy.

I, Anna Garrigues, state on oath that the above and foregoing is a true and correct copy of the original.

Anna Garrigues

Subscribed and sworn to before me this 26 day of October 1905

J McDermott
Notary Public.

MARRIAGE LICENSE

United States of America
Indian Territory   SS.   No. 82
Western District.

To any person authorized by law to solemnize marriage-Greeting

You are hereby commanded to solemnize the rite and publish the Banns of matrimony between Mr. Everett McCalvey of Eufaula in the Indian Territory, aged 24 years, and Miss Nora Barnes of Eufaula in the Indian Territory, aged 17 years, according to law, and do you officially sign and return this License to the parties therein named.

Witness my hand and official seal at Eufaula Indian Territory this 3 day of January A D 1903.

R.P. Harrison
Clerk of the U.S. Court.

By C.E. Wilcox   Deputy

CERTIFICATE OF MARRIAGE.

United States of America
Indian Territory
Western District

I, B.F. McElvain, a minister of the gospel do hereby certify that on the 4 day of February A.D. 1903 did duly and according to law as commanded in the foregoing license solemnize the rite and publish the banns of matrimony between the parties therein named.

Witness my hand this 4 day of February A.D. 1903

My credentials are recorded in the office of the Clerk of the United States Court, Indian Territory, Western District, Book C page 150

Applications for Enrollment of Creek Newborn
Act of 1905   Volume IX

B.F. McElvain
A Minister of the Gospel.

Note. This license and certificate must be returned to the office of the Clerk of the United States Court in the Western District Indian Territory from whence it was issued within sixty days from the date thereof or the party to whom the license was issued will be liable in the amount of one hundred dollars ($100.00).

BA-1781 & 1782

DEPARTMENT OF THE INTERIOR,
COMMISSION TO THE FIVE CIVILIZED TRIBES.
MUSKOGEE, INDIAN TERRITORY, APRIL 21, 1905.

-ooOoo-

In the matter of the application for the enrollment of Sam and Pleas Chissoe as citizens of the Creek Nation by blood.

SAM CHISSOE, being duly sworn, testified as follows, testified as follows:

EXAMINATION BY THE COMMISSION:
Q What is your name? A Sam Chissoe.
Q How old are you? A Right at twenty-eight, I expect.
Q What is your postoffice address? A Wagoner.
Q Are you a citizen of the Creek Nation? A Yes.
Q Are you the father of Sam Chissoe and Pleas Chissoe? A Yes.
Q Do you know when Sam Chissoe was born? A No, I do not know what year it was, but it was 1901, I think----1902.
Q I am asking about Sam, he is the younger of the two is he not? A Yes, and he is about twenty or twenty-one months old.
Q He was born in 1903, was he? A Let me see---I do not know when Pleas was born.
Q But I an not asking about Pleas I am asking you about Sam-- do you know when Sam was born? A Let me see--No, I do not know.
Q Well, do you know when Pleas was born? A Yes.
Q What year was he born in? A In 1901, I think.
Q What month? A The 29th of March.
Q How many years ago was Pleas born? A He is somewhere around about three years old or may be over three; I put it down in a family bible.
Q Were these affidavits that you have signed and filed with the Commission based on the record that is in that family bible? A Yes.
Q Is the mid-wife living that attended the mother of these children? A No.
Q Are the children living? A Yes.

Applications for Enrollment of Creek Newborn
Act of 1905   Volume IX

Q How long has the mid-wife been dead? A Pretty near a month; she died on the 13th of April.

Q What was her name? A Susan D. McIntosh.

Q Then the reason that you have not secured her evidence is because she is dead, is that correct? A Yes.

      Zera Ellen Parrish, being sworn on her oath states that as stenographer to the Commission to the Five Civilized Tribes she reported the above case and that this is a full, true and correct transcript of her stenographic notes in same.

                                  Zera Ellen Parrish

Subscribed and sworn
to before me this 6th day of
May, 1905.
                                  Edw C Griesel
                                          Notary Public.

NC-721

                                Muskogee, Indian Territory, August 15, 1905.

Sam Chissoe,
      Wagoner, Indian Territory..

Dear Sir:

      In the matter of the application for the enrollment of your minor son, Sam Chissoe, Jr., born August 3, 1903, as a citizen by blood of the Creek, it will be necessary for you to furnish this Office with the affidavit of the attending physician or midwife as to the birth of said child; or, in case you are unable to obtain the affidavit of the attending physician or midwife, it will be necessary for you to furnish this Office, in lieu thereof, the affidavits of two disinterested persons as to the birth of said child. Said affidavits must set forth said child's name, the date of his birth, the names of his parents, and whether or not he was living on March 4, 1905.

      Please give this matter your immediate attention.

                            Respectfully,

                                          Acting Commissioner.

1 B C
Env

Applications for Enrollment of Creek Newborn
Act of 1905   Volume IX

BIRTH AFFIDAVIT.

DEPARTMENT OF THE INTERIOR,
COMMISSION TO THE FIVE CIVILIZED TRIBES.

In Re Application for Enrollment, as a citizen of the Creek Nation, of Please[sic] S. Chissoe, born on the 29 day of March, 1902

Name of Father:	Samuel W. Chissoe	a citizen of the Creek	Nation.
Name of Father:	Lena E. Chissoe	a citizen of the Creek	Nation.

Post-office   Wagoner, I. T.

AFFIDAVIT OF MOTHER.

UNITED STATES OF AMERICA,
  INDIAN TERRITORY,
  (blank)   District.

I, Lena E. Chissoe, on oath state that I am 22 years of age and a citizen by blood, of the Creek Nation; that I am the lawful wife of Samuel W Chissoe, who is a citizen, by blood of the Creek Nation; that a male child was born to me on 29" day of March, 1902, that said child has been named Please S Chissoe, and is now living.

Lena E. Chissoe

WITNESSES TO MARK:

Subscribed and sworn to before me this 19 day of May, 1902.

William T Martin
NOTARY PUBLIC.

AFFIDAVIT OF ATTENDING PHYSICIAN OR MID-WIFE.

UNITED STATES OF AMERICA,
  INDIAN TERRITORY,
  (blank)   District.

I, Susan D McIntosh, a midwife, on oath state that I attended on Mrs. Lena E Chissoe, wife of Samuel W Chissoe on the 29" day of March, 1902; that there was born to her on said date a male child; that said child is now living and is said to have been named Please S. Chissoe

Susan D x McIntosh
her mark

Applications for Enrollment of Creek Newborn
Act of 1905 Volume IX

WITNESSES TO MARK:
{ Oliver C Hinkle
{ Wm T Martin

Subscribed and sworn to before me this 29 day of May , 1902.

                         William T Martin
                               NOTARY PUBLIC.

BIRTH AFFIDAVIT.

DEPARTMENT OF THE INTERIOR.
COMMISSION TO THE FIVE CIVILIZED TRIBES.

(Child present)
    IN RE APPLICATION FOR ENROLLMENT, as a citizen of the CREEK Nation, of Please E. Chissoe, born on the 29 day of March, 1902

Name of Father: Sam Chissoe   a citizen of the   Creek   Nation.
Name of Mother: Lena   "   a citizen of the   Creek   Nation.

                 Postoffice   Wagoner, I.T.

AFFIDAVIT OF MOTHER.

UNITED STATES OF AMERICA, Indian Territory, }
    WESTERN   DISTRICT. }

    I, Lena Chissoe , on oath state that I am 24 years of age and a citizen by blood , of the Creek Nation; that I am the lawful wife of Sam Chissoe , who is a citizen, by blood of the Creek Nation; that a male child was born to me on 29 day of Mar. , 1902 , that said child has been named Please E. Chissoe , and is now living.

                       Lena E. Chissoe

Witnesses To Mark:
{

Subscribed and sworn to before me this 7" day of April , 1903.

                       J McDermott
                           Notary Public.

Applications for Enrollment of Creek Newborn
Act of 1905   Volume IX

BIRTH AFFIDAVIT.

DEPARTMENT OF THE INTERIOR.
COMMISSION TO THE FIVE CIVILIZED TRIBES.

(Child present)

IN RE APPLICATION FOR ENROLLMENT, as a citizen of the CREEK Nation, of Sam Chissoe Jr. , born on the 3 day of Aug, 1903

Name of Father: Sam Chissoe	a citizen of the Creek	Nation.
Name of Mother: Lena "	a citizen of the Creek	Nation.

Postoffice   Wagoner, I.T.

AFFIDAVIT OF MOTHER.

UNITED STATES OF AMERICA, Indian Territory, }
    WESTERN   DISTRICT.

    I, Lena Chissoe , on oath state that I am 24 years of age and a citizen by blood , of the Creek Nation; that I am the lawful wife of Sam Chissoe , who is a citizen, by blood of the Creek Nation; that a male child was born to me on 3" day of August , 1903 , that said child has been named Sam Chissoe Jr , and is now living.

                                                  Lena E. Chissoe

Witnesses To Mark:
{

    Subscribed and sworn to before me this 7" day of April , 1903.

                                          J McDermott
                                               Notary Public.

BIRTH AFFIDAVIT.

DEPARTMENT OF THE INTERIOR.
COMMISSION TO THE FIVE CIVILIZED TRIBES.

IN RE APPLICATION FOR ENROLLMENT, as a citizen of the Creek Nation, of Sam Chissoe Jr. , born on the 3 day of August, 1903

Name of Father: Sam Chissoe	a citizen of the Creek	Nation.
Name of Mother: Lena Chissoe	a citizen of the Creek	Nation.

Postoffice   Wagoner I.T.

Applications for Enrollment of Creek Newborn
Act of 1905   Volume IX

AFFIDAVIT OF ATTENDING PHYSICIAN OR MID-WIFE.

UNITED STATES OF AMERICA, Indian Territory,
Western   DISTRICT.

was acquainted with

I, T.T. Weaver , a *(blank)* , on oath state that I ~~attended on~~ Mrs. Lena Chissoe , wife of Sam Chissoe on the 3 day of August , 1903 ; that there was born to her on said date a male child; that said child was living March 4, 1905, and is said to have been named Sam Chissoe Jr. I further state that I am not related to said Lena or Sam Chissoe and that I have no interest in this case.

T. T. Weaver

Witnesses To Mark:
{

Subscribed and sworn to before me 5" day of Sept, 1905.

Henry G. Hains
Notary Public.

BIRTH AFFIDAVIT.

DEPARTMENT OF THE INTERIOR.
COMMISSION TO THE FIVE CIVILIZED TRIBES.

IN RE APPLICATION FOR ENROLLMENT, as a citizen of the Creek Nation, of Sam Chissoe Jr. , born on the 3 day of August, 1903

Name of Father: Sam Chissoe	a citizen of the Creek	Nation.
Name of Mother: Lena Chissoe	a citizen of the Creek	Nation.

Postoffice   Wagoner

AFFIDAVIT OF ATTENDING PHYSICIAN OR MID-WIFE.

UNITED STATES OF AMERICA, Indian Territory,
Western   DISTRICT.

was acquainted with

I, Emma Weaver , ~~a~~ *(blank)* , on oath state that I ~~attended on~~ Mrs. Lena Chissoe , wife of Sam Chissoe on the 3 day of August , 1903 ; that there was born to her on said date a male child; that said child was living March 4, 1905, and is said to have been named Sam Chissoe Jr. I further state that I am not related to said Lena or Sam Chissoe and that I have no interest in this case.

Emma Weaver

Applications for Enrollment of Creek Newborn
Act of 1905   Volume IX

Witnesses To Mark:

{ Subscribed and sworn to before me 5" day of Sept, 1905.

                                         Henry G. Hains
                                         Notary Public.

NC 723.

                             Muskogee, Indian Territory, August 15, 1905.

Lewis Deer[sic],
       Lenna, Indian Territory.

Dear Sir:

       In the matter of the application for the enrollment of your minor son, Turner Bear, born September 9, 1904, as a citizen by blood of the Creek Nation, it will be necessary for you to furnish this office with the affidavits of two disinterested persons as to the birth of said child. Said affidavits must set forth said child's name, the date of his birth, the names of his parents, and whether or not he was living on March 4, 1905.

                             Respectfully,
                                       Commissioner.

NC 723.

                             Muskogee, Indian Territory, October 17, 1905.

Lewis Bear,
       Lenna, Indian Territory.

Dear Sir:

       In the matter of the application for the enrollment of your minor child, Turner Bear, born September 9, 1904, as a citizen by blood of the Creek Nation, you are again advised that it will be necessary for you to furnish this office with the affidavits of two disinterested witnesses as to the birth of said child; said affidavits must set forth said child's name, the date of his birth, the names of his parents and whether or not he was living March 4, 1905.

                             Respectfully,
                                       Commissioner.

Applications for Enrollment of Creek Newborn
Act of 1905   Volume IX

N C 723   JWH

Muskogee, Indian Territory, March 1, 1907.

Annie Bear,
    c/o Lewis Bear,
        Lenna, Indian Territory.

Dear Madam :--

    You are hereby advised that on February 15, 1907, the Secretary of the Interior approved the enrollment of your minor child, Turner Bear, as a citizen by blood of the Creek Nation, and that the name of said child appears upon the roll of New Born citizens by blood of the Creek Nation, enrolled under the Act of Congress approved March 3, 1905, as number 1165.

    This child is now entitled to allotment and application therefor should be made without delay at the Creek Land Office, Muskogee, Indian Territory.

                      Respectfully,

                                        Commissioner.

Copy

BIRTH AFFIDAVIT.

DEPARTMENT OF THE INTERIOR.
COMMISSION TO THE FIVE CIVILIZED TRIBES.

    IN RE APPLICATION FOR ENROLLMENT, as a citizen of the Creek Nation, of Turner Bear, born on the 9 day of Sept, 1904

Name of Father: Lewis Bear   a citizen of the   Creek   Nation.
A.N.F.T.
Name of Mother: Annie Bear (nee Jones)   a citizen of the   Creek   Nation.
Weogufkey
                        Postoffice   Lenna, Ind. Ter.

AFFIDAVIT OF MOTHER.

UNITED STATES OF AMERICA, Indian Territory, ⎫
       Western   DISTRICT. ⎭   Child is present

    I, Annie Bear , on oath state that I am about 22 years of age and a citizen by blood , of the Creek Nation; that I am the lawful wife of Lewis Bear , who is a citizen, by blood of the Creek Nation; that a male child was born to me on 9 day of

Applications for Enrollment of Creek Newborn
Act of 1905   Volume IX

September, 1904 , that said child has been named   Turner Bear   , and was living March 4, 1905.

                                                        her

Witnesses To Mark: Annie x Bear
{ Alex Posey   mark
{ DC Skaggs

Subscribed and sworn to before me this 5" day of April, 1905.

                                        Drennan C Skaggs
                                        Notary Public.

                            Father
AFFIDAVIT OF ~~ATTENDING PHYSICIAN OR MID-WIFE~~.

UNITED STATES OF AMERICA, Indian Territory, }
    Western   DISTRICT.

                                                             my wife
    I, Lewis Bear   , a ~~(blank)~~ , on oath state that I attended on ^ Mrs. Annie Bear , ~~wife of~~ (blank) on the 9" day of September , 1904 ; that there was born to her on said date a   male   child; that said child was living March 4, 1905, and ~~is said to have~~ has been named   Turner Bear

                                               Lewis his
Witnesses To Mark: ~~Annie~~ x Bear
{ Alex Posey   mark
{ DC Skaggs

Subscribed and sworn to before me this 5" day of April, 1905.

                                        Drennan C Skaggs
                                          Notary Public.

                  AFFIDAVIT OF DISINTERESTED WITNESS.

UNITED STATES OF AMERICA,
Western DISTRICT,   SS
INDIAN TERRITORY.

    We, the undersigned, on oath state that we are personally acquainted with Annie Bear (nee Jones)   wife of   Lewis Bear   ; that there was born to her a male   child on or about the   4th   day of   Sept   1904; that the said child has been named   Turner Bear   ; and was living March 4, 1905.

    We further state that we have no interest in this case.

Applications for Enrollment of Creek Newborn
Act of 1905   Volume IX

T.E. Moore

Witnesses: _____

I V Moore

_____

Subscribed and sworn to before me this this   19"   day of Sept,   1906.

My Com.
Ex. July 25" 1907

J McDermott
Notary Public.

_____

BIRTH AFFIDAVIT.

DEPARTMENT OF THE INTERIOR.
COMMISSION TO THE FIVE CIVILIZED TRIBES.

_____

IN RE APPLICATION FOR ENROLLMENT, as a citizen of the Creek Nation, of   Turner Bear, born on the 9 day of Sept , 1904

Name of Father: Lewis Bear   a citizen of the   Creek   Nation.
(Illegible) North Fork Town
Name of Mother: Annie Bear (nee Jones)   a citizen of the   Creek   Nation.
Weogufkey[sic]
                        Postoffice   Lenna, Ind. Ter.

_____

AFFIDAVIT OF MOTHER.

UNITED STATES OF AMERICA, Indian Territory, ⎫
         Western   DISTRICT. ⎭   Child is present

I, Annie Bear , on oath state that I am about 22   years of age and a citizen by blood , of the Creek Nation; that I am the lawful wife of   Turner[sic] Lewis Bear , who is a citizen, by blood of the Creek   Nation; that a male   child was born to me on 9 day of   September, 1904 , that said child has been named Turner Bear   , and was living March 4, 1905.
                                                       her
                                            Annie x Bear
Witnesses To Mark: mark
  ⎰ Alex Posey
  ⎱ DC Skaggs

Subscribed and sworn to before me this 5 day of April, 1905.

Drennan C Skaggs
Notary Public.

_____

211

Applications for Enrollment of Creek Newborn
Act of 1905 Volume IX

Father
AFFIDAVIT OF ~~ATTENDING PHYSICIAN OR MID-WIFE~~.

UNITED STATES OF AMERICA, Indian Territory, }
Western DISTRICT.

                                                                my wife

I, Lewis Bear , a ~~(blank)~~ , on oath state that I attended on ^ Mrs. Annie Bear , ~~wife of~~ *(blank)* on the 9 day of September , 1904 ; that there was born to her on said date a male child; that said child was living March 4, 1905, and ~~is said to have~~ has been named Turner Bear

                                                  his

Witnesses To Mark: ~~Lewis~~ x Bear
{ Alex Posey   mark
{ DC Skaggs

Subscribed and sworn to before me this 5 day of April, 1905.

                                                       Drennan C Skaggs
                                                       Notary Public.

NC-724

                             Muskogee, Indian Territory, August 15, 1905.

Frank Corey,
       Eufaula, Indian Territory.

Dear Sir:

      In the matter of the application for the enrollment of your minor children, Tom Corey, born September 24, 1903, and Cordelia Corey, born December 25, 1904, as citizens by blood of the Creek Nation, it will be necessary for you to furnish this Office with the affidavits of the attending physicians or midwives at the birth of said children. For that purpose, there are herewith enclosed two blanks for proofs of birth, and you are requested to have same properly filled out, executed and returned to this Office in the enclosed envelope.

                                     Respectfully,

                                                                    Acting Commissioner.
2 B C
Env

Applications for Enrollment of Creek Newborn
Act of 1905 Volume IX

N.C. 724

Muskogee, Indian Territory, October 7, 1905.

Frank Corey,
    Eufaula, Indian Territory.

Dear Sir:

    Receipt is acknowledged of your communication of October 5, 1905, in which you state that you are unable to find the physician who attended on your wife at the birth of your minor child, Tom Corey. You ask what is now necessary for you to do in the matter.

    In reply you are advised that you should send to this office the affidavits of two disinterested witnesses who know when said Tom Carey was born and whether or not he was living on March 4, 1905.

                        Respectfully,

                                   Commisssion.

UNITED STATES OF AMERICA,
WESTERN DISTRICT OF THE
INDIAN TERRITORY.

Henry Martin, Being duly sworn states on his oath that he is acquainted with Josie Corey and Frank Corey, her husband and that he knows that there was born to the said Josie and Frank Corey, a mail[sic] child on or about the 24th. day of September, 1903, and that said child was named Tom, and that said child was living on the 4th. day of March, 1905, and is still living.

                                   Henry Martin

Subscribed and sworn to before me this 18th. day of November, 1905.

                                   Frank W. Rushing
                                      Notary Public.

UNITED STATES OF AMERICA,
WESTERN DISTRICT OF THE
INDIAN TERRITORY.

    F. B. Morris being duly sworn, states on his oath that he is acquainted with Josie Corey and Frank Corey, her husband, and that he has been about their place and that he knows that there was a male child born to the said Josie Corey on or about the 24th. day of September, 1903 and that said child was named Tom and that said child was living on the 4th. day of March, 1905, and is still living.

Applications for Enrollment of Creek Newborn
Act of 1905   Volume IX

F. B. Morris

Subscribed and sworn to before me this 18th. day of November, 1905.

Frank W. Rushing
Notary Public.

BIRTH AFFIDAVIT.

DEPARTMENT OF THE INTERIOR.
COMMISSION TO THE FIVE CIVILIZED TRIBES.

IN RE APPLICATION FOR ENROLLMENT, as a citizen of the Creek Nation, of Tom Corey, born on the 24 day of September, 1903

Name of Father: Frank Corey   a citizen of the   Greek[sic]   Nation.
~~Eufaula Town~~
Name of Mother: Josie Corey (Boone)   a citizen of the   Creek   Nation.
Hitchitee
                             Postoffice   Eufaula, Ind. Ter.

Child present.

AFFIDAVIT OF MOTHER.

UNITED STATES OF AMERICA, Indian Territory, ⎫
   Western   DISTRICT.   ⎬

I, Josie Corey, on oath state that I am 24 years of age and a citizen by blood, of the Creek Nation; that I am the lawful wife of Frank Corey, who is a citizen, by blood of the Greek Nation; that a male child was born to me on 24 day of September, 1903, that said child has been named Tom Corey, and was living March 4, 1905.

Josie Corey

Witnesses To Mark:
{

Subscribed and sworn to before me this 5 day of April, 1905.

Drennan C Skaggs
Notary Public.

Applications for Enrollment of Creek Newborn
Act of 1905 Volume IX

Father
AFFIDAVIT OF ~~ATTENDING PHYSICIAN OR MID-WIFE~~.

UNITED STATES OF AMERICA, Indian Territory,
Western   DISTRICT.

    I, Frank Corey, ~~a (blank)~~ , on oath state that I assisted the physician who attended on my wife Mrs. Josie Corey , ~~wife of (blank)~~ on the 24 day of September , 1903 ; that there was born to her on said date a male   child; that said child was living March 4, 1905, and is said to have Tom Corey

                                                    Frank Corey

Witnesses To Mark:

{

    Subscribed and sworn to before me this 5 day of April, 1905.

                                          Drennan C Skaggs
                                             Notary Public.

AFFIDAVIT OF ATTENDING PHYSICIAN OR MID-WIFE.

UNITED STATES OF AMERICA, Indian Territory,
Western   DISTRICT.

    I, F B Morris , a Physician , on oath state that I attended on Mrs. Jossie[sic] Corey , wife of Frank Corey on the 25 day of Dec , 1904 ; that there was born to her on said date a Female   child; that said child was living March 4, 1905, and is said to have been named   Cordelia

                                                    F B Morris

Witnesses To Mark:

{

    Subscribed and sworn to before me 26th day of Aug, 1905.

                                             E G Bailey
                                             Notary Public.

Applications for Enrollment of Creek Newborn
Act of 1905   Volume IX

BIRTH AFFIDAVIT.
DEPARTMENT OF THE INTERIOR.
COMMISSION TO THE FIVE CIVILIZED TRIBES.

IN RE APPLICATION FOR ENROLLMENT, as a citizen of the Creek Nation, of Cordelia Corey, born on the 25 day of December, 1904

Name of Father: Frank Corey   a citizen of the   Greace[sic]   Nation.
Name of Mother: Josie Corey   a citizen of the   Creek   Nation.

Postoffice   Eufaula, Ind. Terr.

Child present.
AFFIDAVIT OF MOTHER.

UNITED STATES OF AMERICA, Indian Territory,
 Western   DISTRICT.

I, Josie Corey, on oath state that I am 24 years of age and a citizen by blood, of the Creek Nation; that I am the lawful wife of Frank Corey, who is a citizen, by blood of ~~the~~ Greece ~~Nation~~; that a female child was born to me on 25 day of December, 1904, that said child has been named Cordelia Corey, and was living March 4, 1905.

                                        Josie Corey
Witnesses To Mark:
{

Subscribed and sworn to before me this 5 day of April, 1905.

                                        Drennan C Skaggs
                                        Notary Public.

AFFIDAVIT OF ATTENDING PHYSICIAN OR MID-WIFE.

UNITED STATES OF AMERICA, Indian Territory,
 Western   DISTRICT.

I, Frank Corey, ~~a (blank)~~, on oath state that I assisted the physician who attended on my wife Mrs. Josie Corey, ~~wife of (blank)~~ on the 25 day of December, 1904; that there was born to her on said date a female child; that said child was living March 4, 1905, and is said to have been named Cordelia Corey

                                        Frank Corey
Witnesses To Mark:
{

216

Applications for Enrollment of Creek Newborn
Act of 1905 Volume IX

Subscribed and sworn to before me 5 day of April, 1905.

                               Drennan C Skaggs
                               Notary Public.

BIRTH AFFIDAVIT.
                     DEPARTMENT OF THE INTERIOR.
                    COMMISSION TO THE FIVE CIVILIZED TRIBES.

IN RE APPLICATION FOR ENROLLMENT, as a citizen of the Creek Nation, of Tom Corey, born on the 24th. day of September, 1903

Name of Father: Frank Corey   a ~~citizen of the~~ non Citizen Nation.
Name of Mother: Josie Corey   a citizen of the Creek Nation.

                        Postoffice   EUfaula[sic] Creek Nation Ind. Tery.

                            AFFIDAVIT OF MOTHER.

UNITED STATES OF AMERICA, Indian Territory, ⎱
       Western   **DISTRICT.** ⎰

     I, Josie Corey, on oath state that I am 23 years of age and a citizen by Blood, of the Creek Nation; that I am the lawful wife of Frank Corey, who is a ~~citizen, by~~ noncitizen of the *(blank)* Nation; that a male child was born to me on the 24th. day of September, 1903, that said child has been named Tom Corey, and was living March 4, 1905.

                                 Josie Corey
Witnesses To Mark:
{

Subscribed and sworn to before me this 18th. day of November, 1905.

                              Frank W Rushing
     My Commission Expires Jan. 30, 1909   Notary Public.

            AFFIDAVIT OF ATTENDING PHYSICIAN OR MID-WIFE.

UNITED STATES OF AMERICA, Indian Territory, ⎱
       Western   **DISTRICT.** ⎰

     I, The Doctor who waited on my wife lived at Colgate I.T. Then But I am unable to locate him at this time. ....on the .... day of ...., 1.......; that there was

Applications for Enrollment of Creek Newborn
Act of 1905   Volume IX

born to her on said date a .... child; that said child is now living and is said to have been named ....

Witnesses To Mark:
{ ....
  .... }

    Subscribed and sworn to before me this .... day of ...., 190....

                                        Notary Public.

DEPARTMENT OF THE INTERIOR,
COMMISSION TO THE FIVE CIVILIZED TRIBES.
Eufaula, I. T., April 5, 1905.

    In the matter of the application for the enrollment of Sanford McGilbra as a citizen by blood of the Creek Nation.

    LEAH GREEN, being duly sworn, testified as follows:

    Through Alex Posey Official Interpreter:

    BY COMMISSION:
Q What is your name? A Leah Green.
Q How old are you? A About twenty-eight.
Q What is your post office address? A Eufaula.
Q Are you a citizen of the Creek Nation? A Yes, sir.
Q To what town do you belong? A Eufaula Canadian.
Q Do you make application for the enrollment of your minor child, Sanford McGilbra as a citizen of the Creek Nation? A Yes, sir.
Q What is the name of the child's father? A Lewis McGilbra.
Q Is he your lawful husband? A No, sir.
Q Were you ever married to him? A No, sir.
Q Does he recognize the child as his own? A Yes, sir.
Q Does he contribute to the support of the child? A Yes, sir.
Q Is Lewis McGilbra a citizen of the Creek Nation? A Yes, sir.
Q To what town does he belong? A Hickory Ground.

                ---oooOOOooo---

    I, D. C. Skaggs, on oath state that the above and foregoing is a full and true transcript of my stenographic notes as taken in said cause on said date.

Applications for Enrollment of Creek Newborn
Act of 1905 Volume IX

DC Skaggs

Subscribed and sworn to before me this 21 day of July, 1905.

J McDermott
Notary Public.

BIRTH AFFIDAVIT.

DEPARTMENT OF THE INTERIOR.
COMMISSION TO THE FIVE CIVILIZED TRIBES.

IN RE APPLICATION FOR ENROLLMENT, as a citizen of the Creek Nation, of Sanford McGilbra, born on the 25 day of March, 1903

Name of Father: Lewis McGilbra   a citizen of the   Creek   Nation.
Hickory Ground
Name of Mother: Leah Green   a citizen of the   CreekNation.
Eufaula Canadian
                        Postoffice   Eufaula, Ind. Ter.

AFFIDAVIT OF MOTHER.

UNITED STATES OF AMERICA, Indian Territory,
    Western   DISTRICT.   Child is present

I, Leah Green, on oath state that I am about 28 years of age and a citizen by blood, of the Creek Nation; that I am not the lawful wife of Lewis McGilbra, who is a citizen, by blood of the Creek Nation; that a male child was born to me on 25 day of March, 1903, that said child has been named Sanford McGilbra, and was living March 4, 1905.

Leah Green

Witnesses To Mark:
    Alex Posey

Subscribed and sworn to before me this 5 day of April, 1905.

Drennan C Skaggs
Notary Public.

Applications for Enrollment of Creek Newborn
Act of 1905   Volume IX

AFFIDAVIT OF ATTENDING PHYSICIAN OR MID-WIFE.

UNITED STATES OF AMERICA, Indian Territory,
Western   DISTRICT.

I, Martha Manley , a midwife , on oath state that I attended on Mrs. Leah Green, not the lawful wife of Lewis McGilbra on the 25 day of March , 1903 ; that there was born to her on said date a male child; that said child was living March 4, 1905, and is said to have been named Sanford McGilbra

             her
          Martha x Manley
Witnesses To Mark: mark
{ Alex Posey
{ DC Skaggs

Subscribed and sworn to before me 5 day of April, 1905.

         Drennan C Skaggs
         Notary Public.

        Territory of Oklahoma
        Payne County
        March 27th - 1905

To whom it may concern - I Vinita Burnett wife of E.H. Burnett - former name before marriage, Vinita Gorden[sic], do Solemly[sic] affirm and testify that on 27th of Jan 1903, I gave birth to male child - Joseph L. Burnett who is now living and whose father is E.H. Burnett. To the above named facts I solemng[sic] swear to be the truth and nothing but the truth, So Help Me God.

       Signed - Vinita Burnett
  (her mark) x

Ter of Okla. Payne Co. Paradise Township
Before me personally appeared Vinita Burnett who makes oath - (on this the 27th day of March - 1905, That the above is her own free act - and the same is sworn to and signed in my presence.
        Perry A Ballard
         Justice of the Peace
       For Paradise Township
       Payne Co. Ter. of Okla

Applications for Enrollment of Creek Newborn
Act of 1905   Volume IX

United States of America,)
)
Western District,) SS.
)
Indian Territory.)

  Elizabeth Gillis, being by me the undersigned authority, first duly sworn on oath says: That she is Seventy-one years of age; that she was present and waited upon Vinita Burnett when she gave birth to a male child, Joseph L. Burnett; That the said Joseph L. Burnett was bonr on the 27th day of January, 1903; That the said Joseph L. Burnett was born in the Indian Territory, six miles East of Tulsa therein.

  Affiant further says that the name of the said Vinita Burnett, the mother of said Joseph L. Burnett, before her marriage to E. H. Burnett, father of said Joseph L. Burnett, was Vinita Gordon.   her
             Elizabeth x Gillis
               mark

Subscribed and sworn to before me this 8th day of April, 1905.
Witness to mark
Ida Gilliss   Harwood Keaton
            NOTARY PUBLIC

My commission expires the 23rd day of April, 1908.

BIRTH AFFIDAVIT.
DEPARTMENT OF THE INTERIOR.
COMMISSION TO THE FIVE CIVILIZED TRIBES.

  IN RE APPLICATION FOR ENROLLMENT, as a citizen of the Creek Nation, of Joseph L. Burnett , born on the 27 day of January , 1903

Name of Father: E. H. Burnett   a citizen of the U. S. A. Nation.
Name of Mother: Vinita Burnett   a citizen of the Creek Nation.

       Postoffice Coyle, Okla Ter RFD #3

        AFFIDAVIT OF MOTHER.

UNITED STATES OF AMERICA, Indian Territory, ⎫
  (blank)   DISTRICT. ⎭

  I, Vinita Burnett , on oath state that I am Twenty Three years of age and a citizen by Birth , of the Creek Nation; that I am the lawful wife of E. H. Burnett ,

Applications for Enrollment of Creek Newborn
Act of 1905   Volume IX

who is a citizen, by Birth of the U. S. A. ~~Nation~~; that a   male   child was born to me on 27th   day of January , 1903 , that said child has been named Joseph L. Burnett , and is now living.

                                her
                            Vinita x Burnett

Witnesses To Mark: mark
{ W.S. Bentley
{ D. M. Barr

    Subscribed and sworn to before me this 18th day of April , 1905.

                            Perry A. Ballard
             (Seal)   ~~Notary Public~~.
                            Justice of the Peace
                            for Paradise Township
                                Payne Co. Okla Terr.

AFFIDAVIT OF ATTENDING PHYSICIAN OR MID-WIFE.

UNITED STATES OF AMERICA, Indian Territory, }
     Western   DISTRICT.   }

    I, Elizabeth Gilliss , a midwife , on oath state that I attended on Mrs. Vinita Burnett , wife of E. H. Burnett on the 27$^{\underline{th}}$ day of January , 1903 ; that there was born to her on said date a male child; that said child is now living and is said to have been named Joseph L. Burnett
                              her
                        Elizabeth x Gilliss
Witnesses To Mark: mark
{ Cecil Faubion
{ C O *(Illegible)*

    Subscribed and sworn to before me this 8th day of April, 1905.

                            Harwood Keaton
                            Notary Public.

Applications for Enrollment of Creek Newborn
Act of 1905 Volume IX

NC-727

Muskogee, Indian Territory, August 15, 1905.

John S. Wills,
    Mounds, Indian Territory.

Dear Sir:

    In the matter of the application for the enrollment of your minor son, Arthur Rex Wills, as a citizen by blood of the Creek Nation, it will be necessary for you to furnish this Office with either the original or a certified copy of the marriage license and certificate, showing marriage between you and Eunice May Wills, the non-citizen mother of said child.

    It is also advisable for you to furnish this Office with your affidavit as to the birth of the child, and a blank for proof of birth is enclosed herewith.

                      Respectfully,
                                        Acting Commissioner.

CTD-49
Env

CERTIFICATE OF TRUE COPY.

United States of America, ⎫
  Indian Territory,   ⎬ ss.
  Western District.   ⎭   *I, R. P. HARRISON,* Clerk of the United States Court in the Western District, Indian Territory, do hereby certify that the instrument hereto attached is a full, true and correct copy of a Marriage License as the same appears from the records of my office.

                WITNESS my hand and seal of said Court at   Muskogee
                in said Territory, this 31" day of Aug.   A. D. 1905

By   John Harlan   R. P. Harrison
           Deputy Clerk   *Clerk and Ex-Officio Recorder.*

                      Book   K at   Page 40.

Applications for Enrollment of Creek Newborn
Act of 1905 Volume IX

| ❋ | MARRIAGE LICENSE | ❋ |

UNITED STATES OF AMERICA ⎫
    Indian Territory   ⎬ ss.   No. 1172
Northern ~~Western~~ District ⎭

To Any Person Authorized by Law to Solemnize Marriage---Greeting:

You are Hereby Commanded to Solemnize the Rite and Publish the Banns of Matrimony between Mr. John Wills *of* Mounds *in the Indian Territory, aged* 28 *years and Miss* Eunice May Labaregh *of* Mounds *in the Indian Territory aged* 18 *years according to law, and do you officially sign and return this license to the parties therein named.*

    WITNESS my hand and official seal ~~at Muskogee Indian Territory~~ *this* 16" *day of* Jan *A.D.* 1901
    (Seal)   Chas A. Davidson
                                            Clerk of the U S Court.
By T. A. Chandler   Deputy.

| 🙵 🙵 | CERTIFICATE OF MARRIAGE | 🙶 🙶 |

UNITED STATES OF AMERICA ⎫
    Indian Territory   ⎬ ss.
Northern ~~Western~~ District ⎭

    I, Rev. P. Johnson *, a Minister of the Gospel, DO HEREBY CERTIFY that on the* 20 *day of* Jan *A. D.* 1901 *did duly and according to law as commanded in the foregoing License, solemnize the Rite and Publish the Banns of Matrimony between the parties therein named.*

    WITNESS my hand this 21 *day of* January *A. D.* 1901

    My credentials are recorded in the office of the Clerk of the United States Court, Indian Territory ~~Western~~ District Book B Page 126
Northern
                                            Rev. P. Johnson
                                        A Minister of the Gospel

Note This license and certificate of marriage must be returned to the office of the Clerk of the United States court in the Western District Indian Territory from whence it was issued within sixty days from the date thereof of the party to whom the license was issued will be liable in the amount of the one hundred dollars ($100.00).

Filed and duly recorded Feb. 6" 1901.
                                    Chas. A. Davidson Clerk U.S. Court

Applications for Enrollment of Creek Newborn
Act of 1905 Volume IX

BIRTH AFFIDAVIT.

DEPARTMENT OF THE INTERIOR.
COMMISSION TO THE FIVE CIVILIZED TRIBES.

IN RE APPLICATION FOR ENROLLMENT, as a citizen of the C R E E K - - - - - Nation, of Arthur Rex Wills - - - - - - - , born on the Fifth day of June - - - - - - - , 1904

Name of Father: John S. Wills - --- - - - - - - - - - - a citizen of the C R E E K Nation.

Name of Mother: Eunice May Wills - - - - - - - a^ non citizen of the C R E E K -Nation.

Postoffice   Mounds, I.T. - - - - - - - - - - - - - -

AFFIDAVIT OF MOTHER.

UNITED STATES OF AMERICA, Indian Territory, ⎱
  WESTERN   DISTRICT. ⎰

I, Eunice May Wills - - --- - - - - - - - - - , on oath state that I am twenty-three years of age and a non citizen ~~by (blank)~~ , of the C R E E K - - - - - - - - - - Nation; that I am the lawful wife of John S. Wills - - - - - - - - - - - - - - , who is a citizen, by Blood - - of the C R E E K - - - - - - - - Nation; that a male - - child was born to me on Fifth - -- day of June - - - - - - - - - - , 1904 , that said child has been named Arthur Rex Wills - - - - - - - - - , and was living March 4, 1905.

Mrs Eunice May Wills

Witnesses To Mark:
{

Subscribed and sworn to before me this 4th day of April - - - -, 1905.

(Name Illegible)
My Commission expires Feb. 21, 1907   Notary Public.

AFFIDAVIT OF ATTENDING PHYSICIAN OR MID-WIFE.

UNITED STATES OF AMERICA, Indian Territory, ⎱
  Western - - - - - - - - - - - DISTRICT. ⎰

I, M.D. Taylor - - - - - - - - - - - - - - , a Physician - - , on oath state that I attended on Mrs. Eunice May Wills - - - - , wife of John S. Wills - - - - - - - - on the fifth day of June - - - - - - , 1904 ; that there was born to her on said date a male - - - - child; that said child was living March 4, 1905, and is said to have been named Arthur Rex Wills

225

Applications for Enrollment of Creek Newborn
Act of 1905   Volume IX

Witnesses To Mark: M.D. Taylor, M.D.
{

Subscribed and sworn to before me this 4th day of April - - - -, 1905.

                                    (Name Illegible)
My Commission expires Feb. 21, 1907   Notary Public.

BIRTH AFFIDAVIT.

DEPARTMENT OF THE INTERIOR.
COMMISSION TO THE FIVE CIVILIZED TRIBES.

IN RE APPLICATION FOR ENROLLMENT, as a citizen of the Creek Nation, of Arthur Rex Wills, born on the 5th day of June, 1904

Name of Father: John S. Wills   a citizen of the   Creek   Nation.
Name of Mother: Eunice May Wills   a citizen of the United States Nation.

                    Postoffice   Mounds, I. T.

AFFIDAVIT OF MOTHER.

UNITED STATES OF AMERICA, Indian Territory, ⎱
      Western   DISTRICT.   ⎰

   I, John S. Wills, on oath state that I am *(blank)* years of age and a citizen by blood, of the Creek Nation; that I am the lawful ~~wife of~~ husband of Eunice May Wills, who is a citizen, ~~by~~ *(blank)* of the United States ~~Nation~~; that a male child was born to ~~me~~ us on 5th day of June, 1904, that said child has been named Arthur Rex Wills, and was living March 4, 1905.

                                    John S. Wills
Witnesses To Mark:
{

Subscribed and sworn to before me this 31st day of August, 1905.

                                    John G. Sieber
                                    Notary Public.

Applications for Enrollment of Creek Newborn
Act of 1905 Volume IX

N.C. 728.

DEPARTMENT OF THE INTERIOR,
COMMISSIONER TO THE FIVE CIVILIZED TRIBES.
Muskogee, I. T., August 2, 1905.

In the matter of the application for the enrollment of Lizzie Hancock as a citizen by blood of the Creek Nation.

HATTIE HANCOCK, being duly sworn, testified as follows:

BY COMMISSIONER:
Q What is your name? A Hattie Hancock.
Q Is your name Hattie or Hettie? A Hattie.
Q Were you enrolled as Hattie? A Yes, sir.
Q Do you know the name that is on the deed to your land? A Hattie.
Q We have it here as Hettie? A I guess they made a mistake.
Q Is Hattie the same as Hettie? A I guess so.
Q Do you say your name is Hattie Hancock? A Yes, sir.
Q What is the name of your father? A John Wilson.
Q Is he living? A Yes, sir.
Q Is he a citizen of the Creek Nation? A Yes, sir.
Q What is the name of your mother? A Lou Collins.
Q Is she living? A Dead.
Q Was she a citizen of the Creek Nation? A Yes, sir.
Q How many times have you been married? A Only once.
Q Have you had children by other men than your husband? A No, sir.
Q Give the names of your children? A This is the only one I have.
Q That the only child you ever had? A I had one which died unnamed.
Q It was not named? A No, sir.
Q Is that all the children you ever had? A Yes, sir.
Q Did you say your father was named John Wilson? A Yes, sir.
Q And your mother is named Lou Collins? A Yes, sir.
Q To what Creek Indian Town do you claim to belong? A I don't know.
Q You don't know? A No, sir.
Q Do you know whether or not you ever drew any money in the Creek Nation? A Yes, sir.
Q When did you draw money? A It has been about seven or eight or nine years ago.
Q How much money did you draw? A It was $21.00 I believe. I am not sure.
Q Where did you draw that money? A Muskogee, Indian Territory I think. My father drew the money for me.
Q Your father, John Wilson? A Yes, sir.
Q Do you know a man names J. P. Smith? A I don't know.
Q Do you know a man named R. B. Wilson? A No, sir.
Q Do you know a man named Roman Canard? A No, sir.
Q Do you know Verbena Wilson? A No, sir.
Q Do you know Washington Canard? A No, sir, but I have heard the name.

Applications for Enrollment of Creek Newborn
Act of 1905   Volume IX

Q Who was the Washington Canard you heard of? A I don't know.
Q What is your post office address? A Checotah.
Q Checotah now is it? A Yes, sir.
Q Where else have you lived? A I lived a while in Ireton, in the Chickasaw Nation.
Q Did you at that place execute an affidavit about a child named Lizzie Hancock?
A Yes, sir.
Q Who was the mid-wife when that child was born? A Mrs. Hendley.
Q Don't you know her full name? A Mamie Hendley, I think.
Q When was that child born? A The 26 of February.
Q What year? A 1905.
Q Are you positive of that date? A Yes, sir.
Q What fixes it in your mind. Are there any circumstances which help you to remember that it was the 26th day of February? A It was the night of the 26th at two o'clock. That would make it the 27th.
Q She was born at two o'clock after mid-night on the 26th? A Yes, sir. That would make it the 27th.
Q What day of the week was that? A The 26th was Saturday and the 27th was on Sunday if I remember it right. I am not positive it was that way.
Q What is the name of the father of that child? A C. A. Hancock.
Q Is he a citizen of any tribe in Indian Territory? A No, sir.
Q If that child has any right it comes through you? A Yes, sir.
Q Do you know whether your father was known by any other name? A No, sir.
Q Do you know whether your mother was known by any other name? A No, sir.
Q You don't know the Creek Indian Town you belong to? A No, sir.
Q You think you drew $21.00 at Muskogee, Indian Territory eight or nine years ago?
A Yes, sir, I think it was.
Q You don't know anything about the payments in the Creek Nation? A No, sir.
Q You say your post office is Checotah? A Yes, sir.
Q How long have you been in Indian Territory? A Never was out but once.
Q How long were you out of the Indian Territory? A Six months.
Q When was that? A That has ben two years ago.
Q Have you any brothers and sisters? A Margarette Wilson and J. E. Wilson.
Q Do you know a child of J. E. Wilson's? A Yes, sir.
Q What is the name of that child? A Earnest xxx[sic] Wilson.
Q Is it Earnest C. Wilson? A Yes, sir.
Q Where was this child born? A At Ireton.
Q What nation? A In the Chickasaw Nation.
Q You were enrolled as Hattie L. Wilson? A Yes, sir.
Q Is that your name? A Yes, sir.
Q Your name is then Hattie L. Hancock? A Yes, sir, since I married.
Q Why didn't you give it that way. You didn't sign your name Hattie L. Hancock, it is signed Hattie Hancock? No response
Q Did you make any record of this child's birth? A Yes, sir.
Q Where did you write it down? A In a little book but it is home.
Q What did you write that with? A A pencil.
Q That is the child which you have in your arms is it? A Yes, sir.

Applications for Enrollment of Creek Newborn
Act of 1905   Volume IX

Q What is its name? A Lizzie Hancock.
Q Have you referred to that record before coming up here to-day? A No, sir.
Q Did you look at it before you made the affidavit? A No, sir, I never.
Q Do you remember of going before a man named H. A. Stines and executing an affidavit? A Yes, sir.
Q How old was Lizzie then? A She was about a month old then, I believe.
Q The date of her birth was pretty fresh in your mind then? A Yes, sir.
Q Are you positive that the child was born in February and not in some other month? A Yes, sir.
Q Are you sure of that? A Yes, sir.

I, D. C. Skaggs, on oath state that the above and foregoing is a full and true transcript of my stenographic notes as taken in said cause on said date.

DC Skaggs

Subscribed and sworn to before me this 2 day of August 1905.

J McDermott
Notary Public.

BIRTH AFFIDAVIT.

DEPARTMENT OF THE INTERIOR.
COMMISSION TO THE FIVE CIVILIZED TRIBES.

IN RE APPLICATION FOR ENROLLMENT, as a citizen of the Creek Nation, of Lizzie Handcock[sic], born on the 27th day of February, 1905

Name of Father: C. A. Hancock   a citizen of the   U.S.   Nation.
Name of Mother: Hattie Hancock   a citizen of the   Creek   Nation.

Postoffice   Ireton I.T.

AFFIDAVIT OF MOTHER.

UNITED STATES OF AMERICA, Indian Territory, ⎫
  Southern   DISTRICT.   ⎬

I, Hattie Hancock, on oath state that I am 23 years of age and a citizen by blood, of the Creek Nation; that I am the lawful wife of C. A. Hancock, who is a citizen U.S., by Intermarried of the Creek Nation; that a Female child was born to

Applications for Enrollment of Creek Newborn
Act of 1905   Volume IX

me on   27th   day of February , 1905 , that said child has been named   Lizzie Hancock , and was living March 4, 1905.

            Hattie Hancock
Witnesses To Mark: nee Wilson
{

  Subscribed and sworn to before me this 4 day of April , 1905.

            A. J. Stein
            Notary Public.

AFFIDAVIT OF ATTENDING PHYSICIAN OR MID-WIFE.

UNITED STATES OF AMERICA, Indian Territory,
  Southern   DISTRICT.

  I, Mary E Handley , a Midwife , on oath state that I attended on Mrs. Hattie Hancock , wife of C. A. Hancock on the 27th day of   February , 1905 ; that there was born to her on said date a Female child; that said child was living March 4, 1905, and is said to have been named Lizzie Hancock

            Mary E Handley
Witnesses To Mark:
{

  Subscribed and sworn to before me this 4 day of April , 1905.

            A. J. Stein
            Notary Public.

DEPARTMENT OF THE INTERIOR

COMMISSIONER TO THE FIVE CIVILIZED TRIBES.

  In the matter of the enrollment of Lizzie Hancock as a citizen by blood of the Creek Nation.

AFFIDAVIT OF JAMES HENDERSON IN SUPPORT OF APPLICATION.

UNITED STATES OF AMERICA
INDIAN TERRITORY
SOUTHERN DISTRICT.

Applications for Enrollment of Creek Newborn
Act of 1905 Volume IX

I, James Henderson, state on oath that I am 45 years of age and live near Ireton, Ind. Ter, on the farm of John Ireton. I know Hattie Hancock and have known her for about a year. She was living in the home of John Ireton during this past spring and winter, and I was also employed on the same farm, living in the same house with Mrs. Hancock during the month of February, 1905. I was asked to go for a midwife for Mrs. Hancock on the night of February 26th, 1905, and I went to the home of Mrs. Handley, two miles distant, and she came to attend Mrs. Hancock, accompanied by her husband, Dave Handley. A child was born to Mrs. Hancock during the night and I saw the infant next day. The child was living on March 4, 1905, and is named Lizzie Hancock.

James Henderson

Subscribed and sworn to before me this 31St day of July 1905.

E Hamillon
Notary Public.
My commission expires Sept. 15, 1908

Affidavit of Nicholas M. Walthall.

INDIAN TERRITORY
SOUTHERN DISTRICT.

NICHOLAS M. WALTHALL, after being duly sworn, testifies as follows.

My name is Nicholas M. Walthall. My post office is Ireton, Ind. Ter. I am a Chickasaw Indian by blood and have taken lands in allotment. I live about two miles from the home of Mr. John Ireton, Indian Territory at whose house Mrs. Hattie Hancock has lived during this year. I am acquainted with Mrs. Hattie Hancock and have known here[sic] since some time in July, 1904.

I am a farmer and stock raiser. On the 1st day of March of this year I was looking for stray cattle and went to the home of John Ireton. They invited me to dinner and while there Mrs. Hattie Hancock showed me her new born child. She was still confined to bed.

I being a Chickasaw and knowing Mrs. Hancock to be a Creek, I asked her if the baby could get enrolled in the Creek Nation and take lands the same as our Chickasaw babies, and she replied that she did not know. This was March 1st, 1905.

Nick M. Walthall

Subscribed and sworn to before me this 27th day of July, 1905.

J. S. Gebsoy
Notary Public.

Applications for Enrollment of Creek Newborn
Act of 1905 Volume IX

COMMISSIONER TO THE FIVE CIVILIZED TRIBES
CREEK CITIZENSHIP DEPARTMENT

In re Enrollment of ( )
Mary Josephine Foster ( ) Affidavit as to birth
( )

Comes now A J Russell and shows that he is not of kin to the applicant for citizenship, Mary Josephine Foster; that he is not a party to the application nor nor[sic] interested in the result of said application.

Affiant shows that he knows that a female child was born to mrs.[sic] Mary E. Foster on or about the 19th day of September 1901 near Henryetta in the Creek Nation Indian Territory; that said child is named Mary Josephine Foster and is now alive and lives with her mother and father near Beggs in said nation and territory.

A J Russell

United States of America
 Western District
 Indian Territory

On this day personally appeared before me, a notary public in and for the Western District, Indian Territory A J Russell to me well known and having read the above and foregoing affidavit and having been duly sworn says that he has persoal[sic] knowledge of the facts therein stated and knows same to be true.

In testimony whereof witness my hand and seal of office at Muskogee Western District Indian Territory on this the 19th day of July A.D. 1905.

My Commission expires   Peter J. Zigler Jr.
 Jan -9-1908   Notary Public.

COMMISSIONER TO THE FIVE CIVILIZED TRIBES
CREEK CITIZENSHIP DEPARTMENT

In re Enrollment of ( )
Mary Josephine Foster ( ) Affidavit as to birth
( )

Applications for Enrollment of Creek Newborn
Act of 1905   Volume IX

Comes now   Mrs Maude Russell   and shows that he[sic] is not of kin to the applicant for citizenship, Mary Josephine Foster; that he[sic] is not a party to the application nor nor[sic] interested in the result of said application.

Affiant shows that he[sic] knows that a female child was born to mrs.[sic] Mary E. Foster on or about the 19th day of September 1901 near Henryetta in the Creek Nation Indian Territory; that said child is named Mary Josephine Foster and is now alive and lives with her mother and father near Beggs in said nation and territory.

Mrs. Maude Russell

United States of America
Western District
Indian Territory

On this day personally appeared before me, a notary public in and for the Western District, Indian Territory   Mrs Maude Russell   to me well known and having read the above and foregoing affidavit and having been duly sworn says that he[sic] has 233ersonal[sic] knowledge of the facts therein stated and knows same to be true.

In testimony whereof witness my hand and seal of office at   Muskogee Western District Indian Territory on this the   19th   day of   July   A.D. 1905.

My Commission expires   Peter J. Zigler Jr.
Jan -9-1908   Notary Public.

DEPARTMENT OF THE INTERIOR,
COMMISSION TO THE FIVE CIVILIZED TRIBES.

IN RE APPLICATION FOR ENROLLMENT, as a citizen of the Creek Nation, Mary Josephine Foster, born on the 19th day of September, 1901.

Name of father: George W. Foster, not a citizen of the Creek Nation.
Name of Mother: Mary E. Foster, a citizen of the Creek Nation.

Post Office Henryetta, Ind. Ter.

AFFIDAVIT OF MOTHER.

UNITED STATES OF AMERICA,   )
INDIAN TERRITORY,   ) ss.
WESTERN JUDICIAL DISTRICT.   )

Applications for Enrollment of Creek Newborn
Act of 1905 Volume IX

I, Mary E. Foster, states on oath that I am twenty-nine years of age and a citizen by blood of the Creek Nation; That I am the lawful wife of George W. Foster, who is not a citizen of the Creek Nation; that a female child was born to me on 19th day of September, 1901; that said child has been named Mary Josephine Foster, and is now living.

Mary E. Foster

Subscribed and sworn to before me this 4th, day of April, 1905.

Harry E Breese.
Notary Public.

My Commission expires July 7- 1907

AFFIDAVIT OF WILLIAM MOREY

UNITED STATES OF AMERICA)
INDIAN TERRITORY   ) ss.
WESTERN JUDICIAL DISTRICT)

I, William Morey, on oath state that I am the husband of Callie D. Morey now deceased, who attended on Mrs. Mary E. Foster, as mid-wife on the 19the[sic] day of September, 1901; that I was present and know that there was born to the said Mary E. Foster on said date a female child; that said Callie D. Morey died on the 11th day of February 1902; that said child is now living and said to have been named Mary Josephine Foster.

William Morey

Subscribed and sworn to before me this 4th day of April 1905.

Harry E. Breese
Notary Public.

My Commission expires July 7- 1907

EATON & HINNEN
Attorneys at Law   Henryetta, Indian Territory.

Applications for Enrollment of Creek Newborn
Act of 1905 Volume IX

NC-730

Muskogee, Indian Territory, August 15, 1905.

Daniel W. Polk,
Eufaula, Indian Territory.

Dear Sir:

In the matter of the application for the enrollment of your minor daughter, Ethel Polk, as a citizen by blood of the Creek Nation blood, it will be necessary for you to furnish this Office with the affidavit of Katie Polk, the mother of said child, relative to her birth. For that purpose, there is enclosed herewith blank for proof of birth, which has been filled out.

It will also be necessary for you to furnish this Office, in the matter of the enrollment of said child, the affidavits of two disinterested persons as to its birth. Said affidavits must set forth said child's name, the date of her birth, the names of her parents, and whether or not she was living on March 4, 1905.

Respectfully,

Acting Commissioner.

CTD-50
Env

BIRTH AFFIDAVIT.
DEPARTMENT OF THE INTERIOR.
COMMISSION TO THE FIVE CIVILIZED TRIBES.

IN RE APPLICATION FOR ENROLLMENT, as a citizen of the Creek Nation, of Ethel Polk, born on the 28 day of Feb., 1905

Name of Father: Daniel Polk   a citizen of the   Creek   Nation.
Ketchopatcky Town
Name of Mother: Katie Polk   a citizen of the   CreekNation.
Eufaula Canadian
                                        Postoffice   Eufaula, Ind Ter

235

Applications for Enrollment of Creek Newborn
Act of 1905   Volume IX

AFFIDAVIT OF MOTHER.

UNITED STATES OF AMERICA, Indian Territory, ⎱
Western   DISTRICT.   ⎰   Child is not present

I, Daniel Polk , on oath state that I am 32 years of age and a citizen by blood , of the Creek Nation; that I am the lawful ~~wife~~ husband of Katie Polk , who is a citizen, by blood of the Creek Nation; that a female child was born to ~~me~~ her on 28 day of February, 1905 , that said child has been named Ethel Polk , and was living March 4, 1905. That the mother is unable to appear personally to make application for the enrollment of the child on account of illness.

Daniel Polk

Witnesses To Mark:
{

Subscribed and sworn to before me this 5 day of April , 1905.

Drennan C Skaggs
Notary Public.

AFFIDAVIT OF ATTENDING PHYSICIAN OR MID-WIFE.

UNITED STATES OF AMERICA, Indian Territory, ⎱
Western   DISTRICT.   ⎰

I, Cinda Polk , a midwife , on oath state that I attended on Mrs. Katie Polk , wife of Daniel Polk on the 28 day of Feb. , 1905 ; that there was born to her on said date a female child; that said child was living March 4, 1905, and is said to have been named Ethel Polk   her
Cinda x Hope[sic]
Witnesses To Mark: mark
{ Alex Posey
{ DC Skaggs

Subscribed and sworn to before me 5 day of April, 1905.

Drennan C Skaggs
Notary Public.

Applications for Enrollment of Creek Newborn
Act of 1905 Volume IX

BIRTH AFFIDAVIT.
DEPARTMENT OF THE INTERIOR.
COMMISSION TO THE FIVE CIVILIZED TRIBES.

IN RE APPLICATION FOR ENROLLMENT, as a citizen of the Creek Nation, of Ethel Polk , born on the 28th day of February , 1905

Name of Father: Daniel W. Polk   a citizen of the   Creek   Nation.
Name of Mother: Katie Polk   a citizen of the   Creek   Nation.

Postoffice   Eufaula, I. T.

AFFIDAVIT OF MOTHER.

UNITED STATES OF AMERICA, Indian Territory,⎱
    Western   DISTRICT.   ⎰

I, Katie Polk , on oath state that I am 22 years of age and a citizen by blood , of the Creek Nation; that I am the lawful wife of Daniel W. Polk , who is a citizen, by blood of the Creek Nation; that a female child was born to me on 28th day of February , 1905 , that said child has been named Ethel Polk , and was living March 4, 1905.   her
                                                     Katie Polk x
Witnesses To Mark: mark
 ⎰ K.B. Turner
 ⎱ Jas. Sawyer

Subscribed and sworn to before me this 22th[sic] day of August , 1905.
Western
District   Geo M Porter
Indian Territory   Notary Public.

AFFIDAVIT OF ATTENDING PHYSICIAN OR MID-WIFE.

UNITED STATES OF AMERICA, Indian Territory,⎱
    Western   DISTRICT.   ⎰

I, Lucinda Polk , the mother as midwife , on oath state that I attended on Mrs. Katie Polk, wife of Daniel W Polk on the 28th day of February , 1905 ; that there was born to her on said date a female child; that said child was living March 4, 1905, and is said to have been named Ethel Polk   her
                                                     Lucinda Polk x
                                                          mark

Applications for Enrollment of Creek Newborn
Act of 1905 Volume IX

Witnesses To Mark:
{ K.B. Turner
{ Jas Sawyer

Subscribed and sworn to before me 22th[sic] day of August, 1905.

Western
District   Geo M Porter
Indian Territory   Notary Public.

NC-731

         Muskogee, Indian Territory, August 15, 1905.

George McGilbry,
  Checotah, Indian Territory.

Dear Sir:

  In the matter of the application for the enrollment of your minor son, George L. McGilbry, as a citizen by blood of the Creek Nation, it will be necessary for you to furnish this Office with either the original or a certified copy of the marriage license and certificate, showing marriage between you and Laura McGilbray[sic], the non-citizen mother of said child.

  It will also be advisable for you to furnish this Office with your affidavit as to the birth of said child, and a blank for that purpose, which has been filled out, is enclosed herewith.

         Respectfully,
                Acting Commissioner.
CTD-51
Env

MARRIAGE LICENSE.

United States of America
Indian Territory   SS.   No. 51
Western District

To any person authorized by law to solemnize marriage--Greeting

You are hereby commanded to solemnize the rite and publish the banns of matrimony between Mr. George McGilbray of Checotah in the Indian Territory, aged 27 years, and

Applications for Enrollment of Creek Newborn
Act of 1905 Volume IX

Mrs Laura Whaley of Checotah, in the Indian Territory, aged 26 years, according to law, and do you officially sign and return this license to the parties therein named.
Witness my hand and official seal at Muskogee Indian Territory this 21st day of A D July, 1902

R.P. Harrison
Clerk of the U.S. Court.

By A Z English deputy

CERTIFICATE OF MARRIAGE.

United States of America
   Indian Territory   ss
Western District

I, J.M. Amerson, a minister of the gospel, do hereby certify that on the 23 day of July AD 1902 did duly and according to law as commanded in the foregoing license solemnize the Rite and Publish the Banns of Matrimony between the parties therein named.
    WITNESS my hand this 24 day of July A D 1902
My credentials are recorded in the office of the Clerk of the United States Court in Indian Territory, Western District, Book A, page 52 or 54

J.M. Amerson
A Minister of the Gospel.

Note. This license and certificate of marriage must be returned to the office of the Clerk of the United States Court in the Western District Indian Territory, from when it was issued, within sixty days from the date thereof, or the party to whom the license was issued will be liable in the amount of one hundred dollars ($100.00)

CERTIFICATE OF RECORD.

United State of America
Indian Territory
Western District

    I, Robert P. Harrison, Clerk of the United States Court in the Western District, Indian Territory, do hereby certify that the instrument hereto attached was filed for record in my office the 14 day of Aug 1901 at --M and duly recorded in Book N marriage record page 160
Witness my hand and seal of said court at Muskogee in said Territory this 14 day of Aug. A D 1902

R.P. Harrison Clerk

By J.L. Peacock, Deputy

Applications for Enrollment of Creek Newborn
Act of 1905   Volume IX

Western Dist. Ind Ter
FILED
Aug 14 1902
R P Harrison
Clerk U.S. Courts

I, Anna Garrigues, hereby certify that the above is a true and correct copy of the original.

Anna Garrigues

Subscribed and sworn to before me this 18th day of July 1905

Edw C Griesel
Notary Public.

BIRTH AFFIDAVIT.
DEPARTMENT OF THE INTERIOR.
COMMISSION TO THE FIVE CIVILIZED TRIBES.

IN RE APPLICATION FOR ENROLLMENT, as a citizen of the Creek Nation, of George L. McGilbry, born on the 13th day of December, 1903

Name of Father: George McGilbry   a citizen of the   Creek   Nation.
Name of Mother: Laura McGilbry   a citizen of the United States Nation.

Postoffice   Checotah, I. T.

AFFIDAVIT OF MOTHER.

UNITED STATES OF AMERICA, Indian Territory,
Western   DISTRICT.

I, George McGilbry, on oath state that I am 30 years of age and a citizen by blood, of the Creek Nation; that I am the lawful ~~wife of~~ husband of Laura McGilbry, who is a citizen, ~~by~~ *(blank)* of the United States ~~Nation~~; that a male child was born to ~~me~~ us on 13th day of December, 1903, that said child has been named George L. McGilbry, and was living March 4, 1905.

George McGilbry

Witnesses To Mark:

Applications for Enrollment of Creek Newborn
Act of 1905 Volume IX

Subscribed and sworn to before me this 16$\underline{th}$ day of August, 1905.

J.B. Morrow
Notary Public.

BIRTH AFFIDAVIT.
DEPARTMENT OF THE INTERIOR.
COMMISSION TO THE FIVE CIVILIZED TRIBES.

IN RE APPLICATION FOR ENROLLMENT, as a citizen of the Creek Nation, of George L. McGilbry, born on the 13th day of December, 1903

Name of Father:	George McGilbry	a citizen of the Creek Nation.
Name of Mother:	Laura McGilbry	a citizen of the United States ~~Nation~~.

Postoffice   Checotah, Ind. Terr.

AFFIDAVIT OF MOTHER.

UNITED STATES OF AMERICA, Indian Territory,
Western   **DISTRICT.**

I, Laura McGilbry, on oath state that I am 29 years of age and a citizen xx xxxxxxxxxxxxxxxx, of the United States xxxx; that I am the lawful wife of George McGilbry, who is a citizen, by blood of the Creek Nation; that a male child was born to me on 13th day of December, 1903, that said child has been named George L. McGilbry, and was living March 4, 1905.   her

Witnesses To Mark: Laura x McGilbry
 { JB Morrow   mark
 { J B Lucas

Subscribed and sworn to before me this 6th day of April, 1905.

My commission expires   Charles Buford
July 3rd 1906.   Notary Public.

Applications for Enrollment of Creek Newborn
Act of 1905   Volume IX

AFFIDAVIT OF ATTENDING PHYSICIAN OR MID-WIFE.

UNITED STATES OF AMERICA, Indian Territory, }
Western   DISTRICT.

I, B. J. Vance, a physician and surgeon , a *(blank)* , on oath state that I attended on Mrs. Laura McGilbry , wife of George McGilbry on the 13th day of December , 1903 ; that there was born to her on said date a male child; that said child was living March 4, 1905, and is said to have been named George L McGilbry

                                                       B.J. Vance

Witnesses To Mark:
{

    Subscribed and sworn to before me this 6th day of April , 1905.

My commission expires   Charles Buford
July 3rd 1906.   Notary Public.

BIRTH AFFIDAVIT.
DEPARTMENT OF THE INTERIOR.
COMMISSION TO THE FIVE CIVILIZED TRIBES.

    IN RE APPLICATION FOR ENROLLMENT, as a citizen of the Creek Nation, of Lyeman Brightman , born on the 16 day of July , 1904

Name of Father: Earl Brightman   a citizen of the United States Nation.
Name of Mother: Fannie Brightman (nee Sanger)a citizen of the   Creek   Nation.
Coweta Town
                               Postoffice   Eufaula, Ind. Ter.

AFFIDAVIT OF MOTHER.

UNITED STATES OF AMERICA, Indian Territory, }
Western   DISTRICT. } Child is present

    I, Fannie Brightman (nee Sanger) , on oath state that I am 21 years of age and a citizen by blood , of the Creek Nation; that I am the lawful wife of Earl Brightman , who is a citizen, by *(blank)* of the United States ~~Nation~~; that a male child was born to me on 16 day of July , 1904 , that said child has been named Lyeman Brightman , and was living March 4, 1905.

Applications for Enrollment of Creek Newborn
Act of 1905   Volume IX

Fannie Brightman

Witnesses To Mark:
{

Subscribed and sworn to before me this 5 day of April , 1905.

Drennan C Skaggs
Notary Public.

BIRTH AFFIDAVIT.

Department of the Interior,
COMMISSION TO THE FIVE CIVILIZED TRIBES.

IN RE APPLICATION FOR ENROLLMENT, as a citizen of the Creek Nation, of Leyman B. Brightman , born on the 16th day of July , 1904

Name of Father: (blank)   a citizen of the non citizen Nation.
Name of Mother: Fanny Brightman   a citizen of the   Creek   Nation.
Formerly Fanny Sanger
                                Post-Office: Eufaula, Indian Territory

---

AFFIDAVIT OF MOTHER.

UNITED STATES OF AMERICA,
  INDIAN TERRITORY,   } SS
    Western   District.

I, Fanny Brightman , on oath state that I am *(blank)*   years of age and a citizen by Blood , of the Creek   Nation; that I am the lawful wife of Brightman , who is a citizen, by a non of the citizen Nation; that a male   child was born to me on   16th   day of   July , 1904 , that said child has been named   Leyman Brightman, and is now was living. That my former name prior to my marriage was Fanny Sanger.

(No signature given)

WITNESSES TO MARK:
{

Subscribed and sworn to before me this 3rd day of July, 1905.

(No signature given)
Notary Public.

243

Applications for Enrollment of Creek Newborn
Act of 1905 Volume IX

AFFIDAVIT OF ATTENDING PHYSICIAN OR MID-WIFE.

UNITED STATES OF AMERICA,
   INDIAN TERRITORY, } SS.
  Western   District.

    I, R. M. Counterman , a Physician , on oath state that I attended on Mrs. Fanny Brightman , wife of Brightman on the 16th day of July , 1904; that there was born to her on said date a male child; that said child is now living and is said to have been named Leyman Brightman

                                              R.M. Counterman, MD

WITNESSES TO MARK:
{

    Subscribed and sworn to before me this 3 *day of* April, *1905.*

                                          (Illegible) Haskell Jr.
My Commission Expires May 19" 1908.   Notary Public.

NC 733

                                  Muskogee, Indian Territory, August 15, 1905.

Lucy Fulsom,
    Care of Robert Fulsom,
        Sapulpa, Indian Territory.

Dear Madam:

    In the matter of the application for the enrollment of your minor son, Ladee Fulsom, born July 28, 1903, as a citizen by blood of the Creek Nation, it will be necessary for you to furnish this Office with the affidavits of two disinterested persons as to the birth of said child. These affidavits must set forth said child's name, the date of his birth, the names of his parents, and whether or not he was living on March 4, 1905.

    From the evidence on file, this Office is unable to identify you upon the final roll of citizens by blood of the Creek Nation. It is necessary that you be so identified before the rights of your minor child can be finally determined. You are therefore requested to immediately inform this Office the name under which you are finally enrolled, the names of your parents and other members of your family, the Creek Indian Town to which you belong, and if possible, your final roll number as the same appears upon your allotment certificates and deeds to land in the Creek Nation.

Applications for Enrollment of Creek Newborn
Act of 1905 Volume IX

Respectfully,
Acting Commissioner.

BIRTH AFFIDAVIT.
DEPARTMENT OF THE INTERIOR.
COMMISSION TO THE FIVE CIVILIZED TRIBES.

IN RE APPLICATION FOR ENROLLMENT, as a citizen of the CREEK Nation, of Ladee Fulsom, born on the 28" day of July, 1903

Name of Father:	Robert Fulsom	a citizen of the	Creek	Nation.
Name of Mother:	Lucy "	a citizen of the	"	Nation.

Postoffice   Sapulpa

(Child present)
AFFIDAVIT OF MOTHER.

UNITED STATES OF AMERICA, Indian Territory, }
WESTERN   DISTRICT.

I, Lucy Fulsom, on oath state that I am 30 years of age and a citizen by blood, of the Creek Nation; that I am the lawful wife of Robert Fulsom, who is a citizen, by blood of the Creek Nation; that a male child was born to me on 28" day of July, 1903, that said child has been named Ladee Fulsom, and is now living.
There was no midwife present

Witnesses To Mark:
{ J H Bense
{ EC Griesel

her
Lucy x Fulsom
mark

Subscribed and sworn to before me   11" day of April, 1905.

Edw C Griesel
Notary Public.

Affidavid[sic]

Where as Cassey Tiger and Lewis Cumsey First being duly sworn testified as follows Deposes and says that they are personaly[sic] acquainted with Lucy Fulsom and her Husband Robert Fulsom and that they are well acquainted with there[sic] child Ladee Fulsom and that they are well known to the fact that the said Child was Borned[sic] to the said parents on the 28th day of July 1903 and that it was living on the 4th day of March

Applications for Enrollment of Creek Newborn
Act of 1905 Volume IX

1905 and that it is living att[sic] the present time And that Lucy Fulsom was on the Roll as Lucy or Conthlany Brown

Subscribed and Sworn to this 17th day August 1905

Cassey Tiger

My Commision[sic] Expires June 3rd, 1909   Lewis Cumsey

E. L. Drake
Notray[sic] Public

Lucy Fulsom formerly Conthlany Brown
her father's name is Behen = Juda Behen
mother's name - member of Euchee Town
Roll Number, 2869. Deed for Conthlany Brown (#Lucy Fulsom) allottment[sic] was delivered to her on Nov. 30th. 1904. Commission No. 26433. File No. 13412.

BIRTH AFFIDAVIT.
DEPARTMENT OF THE INTERIOR
COMMISSION TO THE FIVE CIVILIZED TRIBES.

In Re Application for Enrollment, as a citizen of the Creek Nation, of Ladee Fulsom , born on the 28th day of July , 1903

Name of Father: Robert Fulsom   a citizen of the   Creek   Nation.
Name of Mother: Lucy Fulsom   a citizen of the   Creek   Nation.

Postoffice   Sapulpa Ind. Ter.

Affidavit of Mother

UNITED STATES OF AMERICA, INDIAN TERRITORY,⎱
Western   DISTRICT. ⎰

I, Lucy Fulsom , on oath state that I am 30 years of age and a citizen by Indian Blood , of the Creek Nation; that I am the lawful wife of Robert Fulsom , who is a citizen, by Blood of the Creek Nation; that a Boy child was born to me on 28th day of July , 1903 , that said child has been named Ladee Fulsom , and was living March 4, 1905.

Lucy Fulsom

Applications for Enrollment of Creek Newborn
Act of 1905 Volume IX

WITNESSES TO MARK:
{ EL Drake
{ Arther[sic] Fox

Subscribed and sworn to before me this 17th day of August, 1905.

E L Drake
Notary Public.

Affidavit of Attending Physician or Mid-Wife

UNITED STATES OF AMERICA, INDIAN TERRITORY,}
Western DISTRICT.}

I, Cassey Tiger , a Midwife , on oath state that I attended on Mrs. Lucy Fulsom , wife of Robert Fulsom on the 28 day of July , 1903 ; that there was born to her on said date a Boy child; that said child was living March 4, 1905, and is said to have been named Ladee Fulsom

Cassey Tiger

WITNESSES TO MARK:
{ EL Drake
{ Arther[sic] Fox

Subscribed and sworn to before me this 17th day of August, 1905.

My Commission Expires
June 3rd 1909

E L Drake
Notary Public.

DEPARTMENT OF THE INTERIOR,
COMMISSION TO THE FIVE CIVILIZED TRIBES.
Eufaula, I. T., April 7, 1905.

In the matter of the application for the enrollment of Ella Manahwe as a citizen by blood of the Creek Nation.

CINDA MANAHWE, being duly sworn, testified as follows:

BY COMMISSION:
Q What is your name? A Cinda Manahwe.
Q How old are you? A Thirty-seven.
Q What is your post office address? A Burney.

247

Applications for Enrollment of Creek Newborn
Act of 1905 Volume IX

Q Are you a citizen of the Creek Nation? A Yes, sir.
Q To what town do you belong? A Tulwathlocco.
Q Do you make application for the enrollment of your minor child, Ella Manahwe, as a citizen by blood of the Creek Nation? A Yes, sir.
Q Who is the father of the child? A John Manahwe.
Q Is he a citizen of the Creek Nation? A Yes, sir.
Q To what town does he belong? A Hickory Ground.
Q Is he your lawful husband? A Yes, sir, he was my lawful husband at the time the child was born but we have since separated and he has married again.
Q When was Ella born? A the 1st of November.
Q What year? A I do not know.
Q How old is she? A Passed four.
Q Was the child four years old the first of last November? A Yes, sir.
Q She will be five years old next November will she? A Yes, sir.
Q Why is it that you have not heretofore made application for the enrollment of this child? A Because I was advised that a child born at the time my child was born was not entitled to enrollment.
Q Who gave you such advise[sic]? A I was advised by the authorities at Muskogee. I do not know whether the advise[sic] was from the Indian Agent or the Dawes Commission.
Q Do you know whether or not the Town Officers of your town made application for the enrollment of Ella? A Sam Haines appeared before the Commission at Muskogee, Indian Territory at my request, and made application but he informed me that the child could not be enrolled.
Q When did he make the application? A I think he made the application sometime in September, last year, and informed me that the child could not be enrolled, during the Creek Council at Okmulgee last October.
Q Did you ever execute an affidavit about Ella? A No, sir.
Q Have you the letter to which you referred? A I do not know whether I have or not. Perhaps it has been lost or destroyed by this time.
Q When did you receive that letter? A In October last year
Q Did any one attend on you at the birth of the child? A No one attended on me as mid-wife or physician, but two women were present that are now dead.
Q Would any one in your neighborhood know when the child was born? A No, sir, we have no immediate neighbors where I live.

I, D. C. Skaggs, on oath state that the above and foregoing is a full and true transcript of my stenographic notes as taken in said cause on said date.

DC Skaggs

Subscribed and sworn to before me this 22 day of July, 1905.

J McDermott
Notary Public.

Applications for Enrollment of Creek Newborn
Act of 1905 Volume IX

NC-734

DEPARTMENT OF THE INTERIOR,
COMMISSIONER TO THE FIVE CIVILIZED TRIBES.

Muskogee, Indian Territory, December 15, 1905.

In the matter of the application for the enrollment of Ella Monahwee[sic] as a citizen by blood of the Creek Nation.

John Monahwee, being duly sworn, testified as follows:

EXAMINATION BY THE COMMISSION:
Q What is your name? A John Monahwee.
Q How old are you? A 33, going on 34.
Q What is the name of your father? John David Monahwee.
Q What is the name of your mother? A Milley.
Q What Creek Indian Town do you belong to? A Hickory Ground. My mother is.[sic]

The witness is identified as John Monahwee, on Creek Indian card, Field No. 2208, opposite Roll No. 6746.

Q What is your postoffice? A Okmulgee.
Q Did you have a child named Ella Monahwee? A Yes sir.
Q What is the name of her mother? A Cinda.
Q She was your wife? A She was not my wife by law, just taking up together.
Q Do you remember the name of her mother--Cinda's? A Susan.
Q Her father's name? A March Thompson.

Cynda Monahwee is enrolled opposite No. 6737.

Q After you first took up with her, how long did you live with her before you separated? A Six years.
Q What year did you separate from her? A In 1903.
Q What month? A In January.
Q How old was Ella when you separated? A I forgot about a little over a year old.
Q When was Ella Monahwee born? A On November 1, 1901.
Q If that is true, and you separated from your wife in January, 1901, and the child was a little over a year old, it could not have been born, as you state in an affidavit here, in November, 1901, because from November, 1901 to January, 1902, is only about two months. Are you certain what year Ella was born in? A Yes, I am certain, but then since I left--I don't know what year it was I left.
Q That's how you made a mistake. It must have been 1903.

Applications for Enrollment of Creek Newborn
Act of 1905   Volume IX

Q Cynda Monahwee has made affidavit stating that the child was born November 1, 1900; isn't that correct? A No, it wasn't correct. It was 1901, November 1.
Q How old would it be if it was living now? It is now living? A No sir.
Q How old would it be? A Little over three years old.
Q You surely must be mistaken, because if it would be only three years old, it would have been born in 1902. A Little over four years old, I mean, 1905 now--- four years old.
Q Ella is now living, is she? A No sir.
Q When did she die? A Died last August, about the 15th.
Q The 15th of last August? A Yes sir.
Q 1905? A 1905.

The witness is again advised, as he was by letter on a former occasion, that this Office requires the affidavits of two disinterested witnesses relative to the birth of said child, in lieu of the affidavit of the midwife.

Q There was no midwife present? A No, sir, there was no midwife, just myself, two little girls. Lizzie was one of the people. She is dead.
Q Witness was advised in said letter to bring in witnesses to this Office to be examined under oath. A Yes, I got the letter, but then I don't know what one; we were with the girl; I couldn't find her and then--
Q You are enrolled here as Monahwee; is that the correct name? A Yes, that is the correct name.
Q Who had this child--taking care of it at the time it was dead, you or the woman? A I did.

INDIAN TERRITORY, Western District.

I, J. Y. Miller, a stenographer to the Commission to the Five Civilized Tribes, do hereby certify that the above and foregoing is a true and complete translation of my notes as same appear in my stenographic report of this case.

JY Miller

Sworn to and subscribed before me
this the 20th day of December,
1905.

J McDermott
Notary Public.

Applications for Enrollment of Creek Newborn
Act of 1905 Volume IX

N.C. 734.

DEPARTMENT OF THE INTERIOR,
COMMISSIONER TO THE FIVE CIVILIZED TRIBES.
Muskogee, I.T., January 5, 1906.

In the matter of the application for the enrollment of Ella Monahwee as a citizen by blood of the Creek Nation.

JOHN MONAHWEE, being duly sworn, testified as follows:

Through Alex Posey Official Interpreter:

BY THE COMMISSIONER:
Q What is your name? A John Manahwee[sic].
Q You have heretofore testified in this case, have you not? A Yes, sir.
Q In what year was your child, Ella, born? A I think she was born in the early part of November, 1901.
Q How many years ago was she born? A I have not counted the years, and can't tell you.
Q Were you living with the mother of the child at the time it was born? A Yes, sir.
Q How long after the birth of the child before you separated from her? A I think it was something like a year.

JOHN SMITH, being duly sworn, testified as follows:

Through Alex Posey Official Interpreter:

BY THE COMMISSIONER:
Q What is your name? A John Smith.
Q How old are you? A I do not know, but I think I am about thirty.
Q What is your post office address? A Senora.
Q Are you a citizen of the Creek Nation? A Yes, sir.
Q Do you know John Monahwee and his wife Cinda? A Yes, sir.
Q Did you know a child of theirs named Ella Monahwee? A Yes, sir.
Q Is she living? A No, sir, the child is now dead.
Q How old was she when she died? A She was about five years old, I think, when she died.
Q When did she die? A August 14, 1905.
Q When was Ella born? A She was born on the first or second day of November, 1901.
Q Well, that would have made her only four years old then, instead of five? A I think she was near about 5 years old. I don't know whether she was five years old or not but she was something like five years old.
Q From November, 1901, to August, 1905, the dates of the birth and death of this child, as you give them, is less than four years? A I am certain of the dates of the child's birth and death. I have told you the truth about the date of the child's birth.

Applications for Enrollment of Creek Newborn
Act of 1905   Volume IX

Q How do you fix the dates of the birth and death? A I simply know when she was born, the names of her parents and whether or not she was living on March 4, 1905 because I was living, breathing and seeing at that time.
Q The mother of the child made out an affidavit, and also gave testimony, to the effect that the child was born in November, 1900? A I am simply telling you what I know, I don't care what she states. She told you what she knew and I am telling you what I know.
Q Do you remember when the first Creek treaty was ratified? A yes, sir. I remember, but I don't know the date on which the treaty was ratified. I know the child died after that treaty was ratified.
Q Do you know whether or not the child was born in the same year the treaty was ratified? A I don't know whether it was in the same year or not, but I know the child was born after the treaty was ratified.
Q Are you any relation to this child? A No, sir.
Q Are you interested in this case in any way? A I have no interest in the case.

---oooOOOooo---

I, D. C. Skaggs, on oath state that the above and foregoing is a full and true transcript of my stenographic notes as taken in said cause on said date.

DC Skaggs

Subscribed and sworn to before me this 6 day of Jan , 1906.

J McDermott
Notary Public.

N.C. 734.   F.H.W.
DEPARTMENT OF THE INTERIOR,
COMMISSIONER TO THE FIVE CIVILIZED TRIBES.

In the matter of the application for the enrollment of Ella Monahwee, deceased, as a citizen by blood of the Creek Nation.

DECISION.

The record in this case shows that on April 7, 1905, application was made, in affidavit form, for the enrollment of Ella Monahwee, deceased, as a citizen by blood of the Creek Nation, under the provisions of the Act of Congress approved March 3, 1905 (33 Stats., 1048). Supplemental affidavits as to the birth and death of said applicant; one executed on April 13, 1905, another December 15, 1905, and a third January 5, 1906, are attached to and made part of the record herein. Further proceedings were had April 7, and December 15, 1905 and January 5, 1906.

The evidence shows that the said Ella Monahwee, deceased, was the child of John Monahwee and Cynda Monahwee, whose names appear upon a schedule of citizens by

Applications for Enrollment of Creek Newborn
Act of 1905 Volume IX

blood of the Creek Nation approved by the Secretary of the Interior March 28, 1902, opposite Nos. 6736 and 6737 respectively.

The testimony is conflicting as to the date of birth of the said Ella Monahwee but a preponderance of the evidence established said date as November 1, 1901.

The evidence further shows that said child died on August 15, 1905.

The Act of Congress approved March 3, 1905 (33 Stat. L., 1048), provided in part as follows:

"That the Commission to the Five Civilized Tribes is authorized for sixty days after the date of the approval of this Act to receive and consider applications for enrollment of children born subsequent to May twenty five, nineteen hundred and one, and prior to March fourth, nineteen hundred and five, and living on said latter date, to citizens of the Creek tribe of Indians whose enrollment has been approved by the Secretary of the Interior prior to the approval of this act; and to enroll and make allotments to such children."

It is therefore, ordered and adjudged that the said Ella Monahwee, deceased, is entitled to be enrolled as a citizen by blood of the Creek Nation, in accordance with the provisions of law above quoted, and the application for her enrollment as such is accordingly granted.

Tams Bixby Commissioner.
Muskogee, Indian Territory.
JAN 3 1907

BIRTH AFFIDAVIT.
DEPARTMENT OF THE INTERIOR.
COMMISSION TO THE FIVE CIVILIZED TRIBES.

IN RE APPLICATION FOR ENROLLMENT, as a citizen of the Creek Nation, of Ella Manahwe, born on the 1 day of November, 1900

Name of Father: John Manahwe   a citizen of the   Creek   Nation.
Hickory Ground Town
Name of Mother: Cinda Manahwe   a citizen of the   Creek   Nation.
Tulwathlocco Town

                Postoffice   Burney, Ind. Terr

Applications for Enrollment of Creek Newborn
Act of 1905   Volume IX

AFFIDAVIT OF MOTHER.

UNITED STATES OF AMERICA, Indian Territory,
Western   DISTRICT.

I, Cinda Manahwe , on oath state that I am 37 years of age and a citizen by blood , of the Creek Nation; that I am the lawful wife of John Manahwe , who is a citizen, by blood of the Creek Nation; that a female child was born to me on 1 day of November , 1900 , that said child has been named Ella Manahwe , and was living March 4, 1905. that no one attended physician or midwife at the birth of the child.

                                              her
                                   Cinda x Manahwe
Witnesses To Mark: mark
{ DC Skaggs
{ *(Name Illegible)*

Subscribed and sworn to before me this 7 day of April , 1905.

                                 Drennan C Skaggs
                                 Notary Public.

                See Duplicate for Aff of Mother -
BIRTH AFFIDAVIT.   Parents have parted
                DEPARTMENT OF THE INTERIOR.
COMMISSION TO THE FIVE CIVILIZED TRIBES.

IN RE APPLICATION FOR ENROLLMENT, as a citizen of the Creek Nation, of Ella Monahwee , born on the 1 day of November , 1901

Name of Father: John Monahwee   a citizen of the   Creek   Nation.
(Hickory Ground)
Name of Mother: Cinda   "   (Thompson) a citizen of the   Creek   Nation.
(Tulwathlocco)
                              Postoffice   Okmulgee

AFFIDAVIT OF ~~MOTHER~~.
                                Father
UNITED STATES OF AMERICA, Indian Territory,
Western   DISTRICT.

I, John Monahwee , on oath state that I am 32 years of age and a citizen by blood, of the Creek Nation; that I am the lawful ~~wife~~ Husband of Cinda Monahwee , who is a citizen, by blood of the Creek Nation; that a female child was born to me on 1 day of Nov , 1901 , that said child has been named Ella Monahwee , and is now living.

Applications for Enrollment of Creek Newborn
Act of 1905 Volume IX

John Monahwee

Witnesses To Mark:

Subscribed and sworn to before me this 13 day of April, 1905.

        (Seal)   Edw C Griesel
                                      Notary Public.

Western District
Indian Territory   SS
   I   I am
We, the undersigned, on oath state that we are personally acquainted with Cinda Monahwee wife of John Monahwee ; and that on or about the 1 day of Nov , 19 01 , a female child was born to them and has been named Ella Monahwee ; and that said child was living March 4, 1905.
   I   I
   We further state that we have no interest in the above case.

                                          John Smith

Witness to mark:

Subscribed and sworn to before
me this 5 day of Jan 19 06
                                          Alex Posey
                                          Notary Public

Form 80   TESTIMONY.

Be it remembered, That on this .... day of ...., 190
at ...., within the .... District of the
Indian Territory, personally appeared before me ...., a
Commissioner for the United States Court in said Territory, within and for said District thereof, ...
...., I. T.; my age is .... years. ....
....

                                     Okmulgee IT Apr 10 1905

H G Hains   Chief Creek Enrollment Division
  Muskogee   Com. to Five Civilized Tribes

Applications for Enrollment of Creek Newborn
Act of 1905 Volume IX

Dear Sir:

John Manahwee, of Hickory Ground Town, desires to know if his daughter Ella Manahwee has been enrolled by the Commission. The mother of the child is Cindy Manahwee, of Tulwa Thlocco Town. She executed an affidavit at Eufaula that the child was born Nov. 1, 1900. The father claims that he made application for the child sometime ago. It occurs to us that the application *(illegible)* made an enrollment case but → do not now remember what disposition was made of it.

Very respectfully,
Alex Posey

DEPARTMENT OF THE INTERIOR.
COMMISSION TO THE FIVE CIVILIZED TRIBES.

In the matter of the death of Ella Monahwee a citizen of the Creek Nation, who formerly resided at or near Okmulgee , Ind. Ter., and died on the 15" day of August , 1905

AFFIDAVIT OF RELATIVE.

UNITED STATES OF AMERICA, Indian Territory,
Western DISTRICT.

I, John Monahwee , on oath state that I am 33 years of age and a citizen by blood , of the Creek Nation; that my postoffice address is Okmulgee , Ind. Ter.; that I am father of Ella Monahwee who was a citizen, by blood , of the Creek Nation and that said Ella Monahwee died on the 15" day of August , 1905.

John Monahwee

Witnesses To Mark:

Subscribed and sworn to before me this 15" day of December, 1905.

Henry G Hains
Notary Public.

Applications for Enrollment of Creek Newborn
Act of 1905   Volume IX

NC-734

Muskogee, Indian Territory, August 16, 1905.

John Monahwee,
Okmulgee, Indian Territory.

Dear Sir:

In the matter of the application for the enrollment of your minor daughter, Ella Monahwee, as a citizen by blood of the Creek Nation, you are advised that before the rights of said child as a citizen can be finally determined, it will be necessary for you, and two disinterested witnesses who have knowledge of the date of the birth of said child, to appear before the Commissioner to the Five Civilized Tribes, at his office in Muskogee, Indian Territory, for the purpose of being examined under oath. Such appearances should be made as soon as possible.

Respectfully,

Acting Commissioner.

NC-734

Muskogee, Indian Territory, October 18, 1905.

John Monahwee,
Okmulgee, Indian Territory.

Dear Sir:

In the matter of the application for the enrollment of your minor daughter, Ella Monahwee, as a citizen by blood of the Creek Nation, you are again advised that, before the rights of said child as a citizen can be finally determined, it will be necessary for you and two disinterested witnesses who have knowledge of the date of the birth of said child, to appear before the Commissioner to the Five Civilized Tribes, at his office in Muskogee, Indian Territory, for the purpose of being examined under oath.

Such appearances should be made as soon as possible.

Respectfully,

Commissioner.

Applications for Enrollment of Creek Newborn
Act of 1905   Volume IX

NF-552

Muskogee, Indian Territory, September 15, 1905.

Millie C. Davis,
    Care of Redmond C. Davis,
        Newby, Indian Territory.

Dear Madam:

    In the matter of the application for the enrollment of your minor child, Mack Davis, as a Creek Freedman, you are advised that this Office is unable to identify you on its rolls of Creek Freedman.

    You are requested to write this Office, at an early date, giving your maiden name, the names of your parents, the Creek Indian Town to which you belong, and, if possible, your name and roll number as same appear on your deeds to land in the Creek Nation.

                        Respectfully,
                                  Acting Commissioner.

(The letter below typed as given)

                                      Newby Ind Ter Sept 19 1905

Wm O. Beall,
    Muskogee, I.T.

Sir:

    Receipt is hereby acknowledged of yours of a recent date through which you request of me to write at that place at an early date giving my maden name & parents the Creek Indian town to which I belong I will say in reply to the same that my parents name is Barnetts my fathers[sic] name is Anston Barnett My mother name is Lizzie Barnett both are dead I and my mother belong to the Alabama town I myself are not a freedman my husbands[sic] is Redmond C Davis he belongs to the canady town he is a colored freedman

    I doant know name my mother filed under as my father died first and my mother marid to a man by the name of Hartridge her name may be Lizie Hartridge So if you knwwd any more please let me or us know as I havent got my deed it is at Bristow and I dont[sic] remember the Nos

    Hoping this will give satisfactory
                              I remain as ever
                            Millie C. Davis by
                              R.D.Davis

Applications for Enrollment of Creek Newborn
Act of 1905   Volume IX

BIRTH AFFIDAVIT.

DEPARTMENT OF THE INTERIOR,
COMMISSION TO THE FIVE CIVILIZED TRIBES.

In Re- Application for Enrollment, as a citizen of the Creek Nation, of   Mack Davis , born on the 3 day of Feby , 1904

Name of Father: Redmond C Davis   a citizen of the Creek   Nation.
Name of Mother: Millie C Davis   a citizen of the Creek   Nation.

Post-office   Newby Ind. Tery.

AFFIDAVIT OF MOTHER.

UNITED STATES OF AMERICA,
INDIAN TERRITORY,
Western   District.

I, Millie C Davis , on oath state that I am 32 years of age and a citizen by birth , of the Creek Nation; that I am the lawful wife of Redmond C. Davis , who is a citizen, by birth of the Creek Nation; that a male child was born to me on 3 day of Feby , 1904 , that said child has been named Mack Davis , and is now living.

Millie C Davis

Witnesses To Mark:

W F Malley

Subscribed and sworn to before me this 4 day of April, 1905.

E.W. Sims
Notary Public.

AFFIDAVIT OF ATTENDING PHYSICIAN OR MID-WIFE.

UNITED STATES OF AMERICA,
INDIAN TERRITORY,
Western   District.

I, Adline Barnett , a Midwife , on oath state that I attended on Mrs. Millie C Davis , wife of Edmond C Davis on the 3 day of Feby , 1904; that there was born to her on said date a male child; that said child is now living and is said to have been named Mack Davis

Adline Barnett

Applications for Enrollment of Creek Newborn
Act of 1905 Volume IX

Witnesses To Mark:

{ W F Malley

Subscribed and sworn to before me this 4 day of April, 1905.

E.W. Sims
Notary Public.

NC-737.

Muskogee, Indian Territory, October 18, 1905.

Louvina Wiley,
    c/o Monroe Wiley,
        Texanna, Indian Territory.

Dear Madam:

    In the matter of the application for the enrollment of your minor daughter Bertha Wiley as a citizen by blood of the Creek Nation this office is unable to identify you upon the final roll of citizens by blood of said nation. It is necessary that you be so identified before the rights of said child can be finally determined.

    You are requested to inform this office of the name under which you are finally enrolled, the names of your parents and other members of your family, the Creek Indian town to which you belong and if possible your roll number as the same appears upon your allotment certificate and deeds.

                        Respectfully,
                                    Commissioner.

NC 737.

Muskogee, Indian Territory, January 13, 1907.

Louvina Wiley (or Watts),
    Texanna, Indian Territory.

Dear Madam:

    You have been repeatedly advised in the matter of the application for the enrollment of your minor child, Bertha Wiley as a citizen by blood of the Creek Nation, that this office cannot identify you upon the final rolls of citizens by blood of said Nation, and you are requested to inform this office within ten days of the name under which you

Applications for Enrollment of Creek Newborn
Act of 1905 Volume IX

are finally enrolled as a citizen of the Creek Nation, the names of your parents and of other members of your family, and if possible, your roll number as same appears upon your allotment certificates or deeds to land in the Creek Nation.

Respectfully,
Commissioner.

NC 737.

Muskogee, Indian Territory, January 13, 1907.

Amanda Wiley,
Texanna, Indian Territory.

Dear Madam:

You are requested to inform this office of the name under which Louvina Wiley, wife of Monroe Wiley, is enrolled as a citizen of the Creek Nation, the names of her parents, and other members of her family, the Creek Indian town to which she belongs and if possible, the roll numbers as same appear on her allotment certificates or deeds to land in the Creek Nation, if she is in fact enrolled as a citizen of said Nation.

Respectfully,
Commissioner.

REFER IN REPLY TO THE FOLLOWING:
Cherokee
N B 2027

DEPARTMENT OF THE INTERIOR,
COMMISSIONER TO THE FIVE CIVILIZED TRIBES.

(N.C. 737)

Muskogee, Indian Territory, January 26, 1907.

Chief Clerk,
Creek Enrollment Division.

Dear Sir:

In compliance with your verbal request you are advised that the name of Bertha Wiley, born September 28, 1903, daughter of Monroe Wiley, a non-citizen of the Cherokee Nation, and Louvenia Wiley, whose name appears upon an approved roll of citizens by blood of the Cherokee Nation opposite, No. 16923, appears upon an approved roll of citizens of the Cherokee Nation enrolled under the Act of April 26, 1905, opposite No. 2560.

Respectfully,
Tams Bixby   Commissioner.

GHL

Applications for Enrollment of Creek Newborn
Act of 1905   Volume IX

(COPY)
Texanna, Ind. Ter.
Dec. 21, 1907.

Commissioner to the Five Civilized Tribes,

Your communication of the 14th received. In reply will say that in regard to the application for the enrollment of my child Bertha Wiley Which application I made about two years ago - - Was never approved of. I supposed the matter was decided That she could of be enrolled in the Creek Nation - - I am enrolled in the Cherokee Nation. My father Thomas Watts, is a Cherokee. My mother Mary Watts, is a Creek Indian. I am the wife of Monroe Wiley, deceased, a citizen of the United States.

Respectfully,
Louvena Wiley.

BIRTH AFFIDAVIT.
DEPARTMENT OF THE INTERIOR.
COMMISSION TO THE FIVE CIVILIZED TRIBES.

IN RE APPLICATION FOR ENROLLMENT, as a citizen of the Creek Nation, of Bertha Wiley, born on the 28 day of September, 1903

Name of Father: Monroe Wiley   a citizen of the United States Nation.
Name of Mother: Louvina Wiley (nee Watts)   a citizen of the   Creek   Nation.
Coweta Town
                         Postoffice   Texanna, Ind. Ter.

AFFIDAVIT OF MOTHER.

UNITED STATES OF AMERICA, Indian Territory,
      Western   DISTRICT.   Child is present

I, Louvina Wiley , on oath state that I am 36 years of age and a citizen by blood , of the Creek Nation; that I am the lawful wife of Monroe Wiley , who is a citizen, by *(blank)* of the United States Nation; that a female child was born to me on 28 day of September , 1903 , that said child has been named Bertha Wiley , and was living March 4, 1905.

Louvena Wiley

Witnesses To Mark:

Applications for Enrollment of Creek Newborn
Act of 1905 Volume IX

Subscribed and sworn to before me this 4 day of April, 1905.

Drennan C Skaggs
Notary Public.

AFFIDAVIT OF ATTENDING PHYSICIAN OR MID-WIFE.

UNITED STATES OF AMERICA, Indian Territory,
Western   DISTRICT.

I, Amanda Wiley, a midwife, on oath state that I attended on Mrs. Louvina Wiley, wife of Monroe Wiley on the 28 day of September, 1903; that there was born to her on said date a female child; that said child was living March 4, 1905, and is said to have been named Bertha Wiley

her
Amanda x Wiley
mark

Witnesses To Mark:
- Alex Posey
- DC Skaggs

Subscribed and sworn to before me 4 day of April, 1905.

Drennan C Skaggs
Notary Public.

DEPARTMENT OF THE INTERIOR,
COMMISSION TO THE FIVE CIVILIZED TRIBES.
Eufaula, I.T. April 3, 1905.

In the matter of the application for the enrollment of Jessie Eulalie Wadsworth, as a citizen by blood of the Creek Nation.

P.J. WADSWORTH, being duly sworn, testified as follows:

BY COMMISSION:
Q What is your name? A P.J. Wadsworth.
Q How old are you? A 35.
Q What is your post office address? A Cathay.
Q Are you a citizen of the Creek Nation? A No, sir, I am a Seminole.
Q Do you make application for the enrollment of your minor child, Jessie Eulalie Wadsworth, as a citizen of the Creek Nation? A Yes, sir.
Q What is the name of the mother of that child? A Mattie Wadsworth

Applications for Enrollment of Creek Newborn
Act of 1905 Volume IX

Q Is she living? A She is dead.
Q Was she your lawful wife? A Yes sir.
Q Was she a citizen of the Creek Nation? A Yes sir.
Q To what town did she belong? A Hitchite.
Q If it should be found that your child Jessie Eulalie Wadsworth is entitled to enrollment in either the Creek or Seminole Nation, in which Nation do you elect to have her enrolled? A In the Creek Nation.

   I, D. C. Skaggs, on oath, state that the above and foregoing is a full and true transcript of my stenographic notes as taken in said cause on said date.

DC Skaggs

Subscribed and sworn to before me this 20th day of July, 1905.

J McDermott
Notary Public.

BIRTH AFFIDAVIT.

Department of the Interior,
COMMISSION TO THE FIVE CIVILIZED TRIBES.

   IN RE APPLICATION FOR ENROLLMENT, as a citizen of the Creek Nation, of Jessie Eulalie Wadsworth , born on the 23 day of February , 1902

Name of Father:	P.J. Wadsworth	a citizen of the Seminole	Nation.
Name of Mother:	Mattie Wadsworth	a citizen of the Creek	Nation.
Hitchitee Town			
	Post-Office:	Cathay, Ind. Terr.	

Father
AFFIDAVIT OF <s>MOTHER</s>.
Child present

UNITED STATES OF AMERICA,
 INDIAN TERRITORY,
 Western District.

   I, P.J. Wadsworth , on oath state that I am 35 years of age and a citizen by blood , of the Seminole Nation; that I <s>am</s> was the the lawful <s>wife</s> husband of Mattie Wadsworth , who is a citizen, by blood of the Creek Nation; that a female child was born to me on 23 day of February , 1902, that said child has been named Jessie Eulalie Wadsworth , and <s>is now</s> was living. on March 4, 1905.
That the mother, Mattie Wadsworth, is dead.

P.J. Wadsworth

Applications for Enrollment of Creek Newborn
Act of 1905   Volume IX

WITNESSES TO MARK:
{

Subscribed and sworn to before me this 3 day of April, 1905.

Drennan C Skaggs
Notary Public.

AFFIDAVIT OF ATTENDING PHYSICIAN OR MID-WIFE.

UNITED STATES OF AMERICA,
INDIAN TERRITORY,
Western   District.

I, Josephine Berryhill , a mid-wife , on oath state that I attended on Mrs. Mattie Wadsworth, wife of P.J. Wadsworth on the 23 day of February , 1902; that there was born to her on said date a   female   child; that said child is now was living on March 4, 1905 and is said to have been named Jessie Eulalie Wadsworth That the mother, Mattie Wadsworth, is dead.

Josephine Berryhill

WITNESSES TO MARK:
{

Subscribed and sworn to before me this 3 day of April, 1905.

Drennan C Skaggs
Notary Public.

NC. 738.

Muskogee, Indian Territory, July 15, 1905.

Chief Clerk,
    Seminole Enrollment Division,
        Muskogee, Indian Territory.

Dear Sir:

April 7, 1905, application was made to the Commission to the Five Civilized Tribes for the enrollment of Eulalie Wadsworth, born February 23, 1902, as a citizen by blood of the Creek Nation. It is stated in said application that the father of said child is P. J. Wadsworth, a citizen of the Seminole Nation, and that the mother is Mattie Wadsworth, a citizen of the Creek Nation.

Applications for Enrollment of Creek Newborn
Act of 1905   Volume IX

You are requested to inform the Creek Enrollment Division as to whether application has been made for the enrollment of said Eulalie Wadsworth, as a citizen of the Seminole Nation, and if so, what disposition has been made of the same.

Respectfully,
Commissioner.

W.F.
DEPARTMENT OF THE INTERIOR.
COMMISSION TO THE FIVE CIVILIZED TRIBES.

Muskogee, Indian Territory, July 19, 1905.

Chief Clerk,
      Creek Enrollment Division.

Dear Sir:

Receipt is acknowledged of your letter of July 15, 1905 (NC-738) stating that application was made to the Commission to the Five Civilized Tribes for the enrollment of Eulalie Wadsworth, born February 23, 1902, child of P. J. Wadsworth, a citizen of the Seminole Nation, and Mattie Wadsworth, a citizen of the Creek Nation, as a citizen by blood of the Creek Nation and requesting to be informed as to whether application was made for the enrollment of said child as a citizen of the Seminole Nation.

In reply to your letter you are advised that it does not appear from an examination of the records of this office that any application was ever made for the enrollment of said Eulalie Wadsworth as a citizen of the Seminole Nation.

Respectfully,
            Tams Bixby   Commissioner.

NC 738

Muskogee, Indian Territory, November 13, 1906

Chief Clerk,
      Seminole Enrollment Division,
            General Office.

Dear Sir:

You are hereby advised that the name of Jessie Eulalie Wadsworth, born February 23, 1902 to P. J. Wadsworth an alleged citizen of the Seminole Nation and Mattie Wadsworth a citizen by blood of the Creek Nation, is contained in schedule of

Applications for Enrollment of Creek Newborn
Act of 1905   Volume IX

minor citizens by blood of the Creek Nation, approved by the Secretary of the Interior, September 27, 1905 opposite Roll number 680.

Respectfully,

Commissioner.

NC-739

Muskogee, Indian Territory, August 16, 1905.

Willie Brink, (or Ka-ko-con-ney)
    Kellyville, Indian Territory.

Dear Sir:

    In the matter of the application for the enrollment of your minor daughter Lizzie Brink, as a citizen by blood of the Creek Nation, it will be necessary for you to furnish this Office with the affidavits of two disinterested persons as to the birth of said child. Said affidavits must set forth said child's name, the date of her birth, the names of her parents, and whether or not she was living on March 4, 1905. Said affidavits must also set for the source of the knowledge of the affiants.

Respectfully,

Acting Commissioner.

N C 739

COPY
Sapulpa, I. T. Sept. 9, 1905.

The Commissioner to the Five Civilized Tribes,
    Muskogee, I. T.

Dear Sir:-

    Referring to your favor of the 7th instant you suggest that the mother of Lizzie Brink write that office relative to the correct spelling of her name, I have to say, at the request of the mother, that the correct spelling of her name is Lusanna Brink, and that her name was formerly Lusanna Daniel. She does not speak English, an she has asked me through her husband, who speaks a little English to write for her.

    She has her allotment deeds, and her name is given in them as Lusanna Daniel.

Yours very truly,
(Signed). E. B. Hughes.

Applications for Enrollment of Creek Newborn
Act of 1905 Volume IX

BIRTH AFFIDAVIT.

DEPARTMENT OF THE INTERIOR.
COMMISSION TO THE FIVE CIVILIZED TRIBES.

IN RE APPLICATION FOR ENROLLMENT, as a citizen of the Creek Nation, of Lizzie Brink, born on the 1st day of March, 1905

Name of Father: Willie Brink (Ka-ko-con-ney) a citizen of the Creek Nation. Euchee
Name of Mother: Lusanna Brink   a citizen of the Creek Nation. Euchee   formerly Daniel
Postoffice   Kellyville I.T.

AFFIDAVIT OF MOTHER.

UNITED STATES OF AMERICA, Indian Territory,
Western   DISTRICT.

I, Lusanna Brink, formerly Daniel, on oath state that I am 36 years of age and a citizen by blood, of the Creek Nation; that I am the lawful wife of Willie Brink, Ka-ko-con-ney, who is a citizen, by blood of the Creek Nation; that a female child was born to me on 1st day of March, 1905, that said child has been named Lizzie Brink, and was living March 4, 1905.

                                her
                        Lusanna x Brink
Witnesses To Mark: mark
 { David Shelby
 { Jesse McDermott

Subscribed and sworn to before me this 24 day of April, 1905.

(Seal)   Edw C Griesel
                            Notary Public.

AFFIDAVIT OF ATTENDING PHYSICIAN OR MID-WIFE.

UNITED STATES OF AMERICA, Indian Territory,
Western   DISTRICT.

I, Willie Brink (Ka-ko-con-ney), a -----, on oath state that I attended on Mrs. Lusanna Brink formerly Daniel my, wife of ----- on the 1st day of March, 1905; that there was born to her on said date a *(blank)* child; that said child was living March 4, 1905, and is said to have been named Lizzie Brink

Applications for Enrollment of Creek Newborn
Act of 1905   Volume IX

Witnesses To Mark:
{ David Shelby
{ Jesse McDermott

         his
     Willie x Brink
     mark (Ka-ko-con-ney)

Subscribed and sworn to before me this 24 day of April, 1905.

(Seal)   Edw C Griesel
                 Notary Public.

United States of America,)
Indian Territory   ) ss.
Western District   )

  I, Willie Littlehead, being first duly sworn, on oath state, that I am 32 years of age, that I am a citizen of the Creek Nation, that I was present at the home of William Brink near Kelleyville[sic], I. T., on the first day of March, 1905, when a female child was born to Lusanna Brink, wife of the said William Brink, that said child was named Lizzie Brink, that said child was living on March 4, 1905; that I am not in any way interested in the enrollment of the said child as a citizen of the Creek Nation. That said child is now living, and I have this day seen said child.

                   Willie Littlehead

Subscribed and sworn to before me this 25th day of March, 1905.

                  EB Hughes
                  Notary Public.
My commission expires May 18, 1909

United States of America,)
Indian Territory   ) ss.
Western District   )

  I, Dixon Brown, being first duly sworn, on oath state, that I am 48 years of age, that I am a citizen by blood of the Creek Nation, that I was present at the home of William Brink near Kelleyville[sic], I. T., on March first, 1905, when a female child was born to Lusanna D. Brink, the wife of said William Brink; that said child was named Lizzie Brink; and that said child was living on the 4th day of March, 1905; that I am not in any way interested in the enrollment of said child as a citizen of the Creek Nation.

Witness to mark:-   his
EB Hughes   Dixon x Brown
Willie Littlehead   mark

Applications for Enrollment of Creek Newborn
Act of 1905 Volume IX

Subscribed and sworn to before me this 25th day of August, 1905.

                        EB Hughes
My commission expires May 18, 1909   Notary Public.

United States of America,)
Indian Territory   ) ss.
Western District   )

     I, Willie Littlehead, being first duly sworn state on oath that I understand and speak both the Euchee and English languages; that fully and correctly interpreter and explained the above and foregoing affidavit to Dixon Brown, who subscribed the same, and that said Dixon Brown stated to me that he understood the same, and that the statements therein contained are true.

                                    Willie Littlehead

Subscribed and sworn to before me this 25th day of August, 1905.

                        EB Hughes
My commission expires May 18, 1909   Notary Public.

BIRTH AFFIDAVIT.
DEPARTMENT OF THE INTERIOR.
COMMISSION TO THE FIVE CIVILIZED TRIBES.

     IN RE APPLICATION FOR ENROLLMENT, as a citizen of the Creek Nation, of Lizzie Brink, born on the first day of March, 1905

Name of Father:	William Brink	a citizen of the	Creek	Nation.
Name of Mother:	Lusanna D. Brink	a citizen of the	Creek	Nation.

                        Postoffice   Kelleyville[sic], I. T.

                        AFFIDAVIT OF MOTHER.

UNITED STATES OF AMERICA, Indian Territory,
Western District   DISTRICT.

     I, Lusanna D. Brink, on oath state that I am 36 years of age and a citizen by blood, of the Creek Nation; that I am the lawful wife of William Brink, who is a citizen, by blood of the Creek Nation; that a female child was born to me on first day of March, 1905, that said child has been named Lizzie Brink, and was living

Applications for Enrollment of Creek Newborn
Act of 1905 Volume IX

March 4, 1905, and that there was no mid-wife or attending physician present at the birth of said child.

Witnesses To Mark:
{ Willie Littlehead
{ EB Hughes

her
Lusanna D x Brink
mark

Subscribed and sworn to before me this 25th day of August, 1905.

My commission expires May 18, 1909

EB Hughes
Notary Public.

AFFIDAVIT OF ATTENDING PHYSICIAN OR MID-WIFE.

United States of America,)
Indian Territory) ss.
Western District)

I, Willie Littlehead, being first duly sworn state on oath that I understand and speak both the Euchee and English languages; that fully and correctly interpreter and explained the above and foregoing affidavit to Lusanna D. Brink, who subscribes the same, and that said Lusanna D. Brink stated to me that she understood the same, and that the statements therein contained are true.

Willie Littlehead

Subscribed and sworn to before me this 25th day of August, 1905.

My commission expires May 18, 1909

EB Hughes
Notary Public.

BIRTH AFFIDAVIT.

DEPARTMENT OF THE INTERIOR.
COMMISSION TO THE FIVE CIVILIZED TRIBES.

IN RE APPLICATION FOR ENROLLMENT, as a citizen of the Creek (Euchee) Nation, of Lizzie Brink , born on the First day of March , 1905

Name of Father: William Brink   a citizen of the   Creek   Nation.
Name of Mother: Susannah Brink, nee Daniel   a citizen of the   Creek   Nation.

Postoffice   Kellyville, Ind. Terr.

Applications for Enrollment of Creek Newborn
Act of 1905 Volume IX

AFFIDAVIT OF MOTHER.

UNITED STATES OF AMERICA, Indian Territory, ⎱
  Western District   DISTRICT. ⎰

I, Susanna D. Brink , on oath state that I am 35 years of age and a citizen by blood , of the Creek Nation; that I am the lawful wife of   William Brink , who is a citizen, by blood of the Creek Nation; that a female child was born to me on First day of March, A.D. 1905 , that said child has been named Lizzie Brink , and was living March 4, 1905.

                                                  her
                          Susanna Brink x
Witnesses To Mark: mark
⎰ Laslie Cloud
⎱ Lee Foster

Subscribed and sworn to before me this 7th day of April, 1905.

                        T. W. Flynn
                        Notary Public.

                  Father
AFFIDAVIT OF ~~ATTENDING PHYSICIAN OR MID-WIFE~~.

UNITED STATES OF AMERICA, Indian Territory, ⎱
  Western   DISTRICT. ⎰

I, William Brink , a *(blank)*   , on oath state that I attended on Mrs. Susanna Brink , wife of William Brink on the First day of March , 1905 ; that there was born to her on said date a female child; that said child was living March 4, 1905, and is said to have been named Lizzie Brink

                                                his
                        William Brink x
Witnesses To Mark: mark
⎰ Laslie Cloud
⎱ Lee Foster

Subscribed and sworn to before me this 7th day of April, 1905.

                        T. W. Flynn
                        Notary Public.

Applications for Enrollment of Creek Newborn
Act of 1905   Volume IX

NC-740

Muskogee, Indian Territory, August 16, 1905.

Kogee Leverett,
Lenna, Indian Territory.

Dear Madam:

In the matter of the application for the enrollment of your minor daughter, Bessie Leverett, as a citizen by blood of the Creek Nation, it will be necessary for you to furnish this Office with the proper proof of birth of said child, and a blank for that purpose, which has been filled out, is enclosed herewith. In having same executed, be careful to see that the notary public before whom the affidavits are sworn to, attaches his name and seal to each affidavit. Care should also be exercised on the part of those signing the affidavits that their names appear in the body of the affidavits the same as in the signatures. In case any signature is by mark, the same must be attested by two witnesses.

Respectfully,

Acting Commissioner.

CTD-52
Env

BIRTH AFFIDAVIT.

DEPARTMENT OF THE INTERIOR.
COMMISSION TO THE FIVE CIVILIZED TRIBES.

IN RE APPLICATION FOR ENROLLMENT, as a citizen of the Creek Nation, of Bessie Levitt , born on the 18 day of September , 1902

Name of Father: Walter Levitt   a citizen of the United States Nation.
Name of Mother: Cogee Levitt   a citizen of the   Creek   Nation.
Coweta Town
                         Postoffice   Lenna, Ind. Terr.

AFFIDAVIT OF ATTENDING PHYSICIAN OR MID-WIFE.

UNITED STATES OF AMERICA, Indian Territory,
    Western   DISTRICT.

I, Mary McCombs , a Mid-wife , on oath state that I attended on Mrs. Cogee Levitt , wife of Walter Levitt on the 18 day of September , 1902 ; that there was born to her on said date a female child; that said child was living March 4, 1905, and is said

Applications for Enrollment of Creek Newborn
Act of 1905 Volume IX

to have been named Bessie Levitt. That the mother Cogee Levitt, is sick and unable to leave her bed. And that the father, Walter Levitt, is dead.

Mary McCombs

Witnesses To Mark:
{

Subscribed and sworn to before me 4 day of April, 1905.

Drennan C Skaggs
Notary Public.

BIRTH AFFIDAVIT.

DEPARTMENT OF THE INTERIOR.
COMMISSION TO THE FIVE CIVILIZED TRIBES.

IN RE APPLICATION FOR ENROLLMENT, as a citizen of the Creek Nation, of Bessie Leverett, born on the 18th day of September, 1902

Name of Father: Walter Leverett a citizen of the United States ~~Nation~~.
Name of Mother: Kogee Leverett (2655) a citizen of the Creek Nation.

Postoffice   Lenna, I.T.

AFFIDAVIT OF MOTHER.

UNITED STATES OF AMERICA, Indian Territory,}
Western   DISTRICT.

I, Kogee Leverett, on oath state that I am 30 years of age and a citizen by blood, of the Creek Nation; that I ~~am~~ was the lawful wife of Walter Leverett, deceased, who ~~is~~ was a citizen, ~~by~~ *(blank)* of the United States ~~Nation~~; that a female child was born to me on 18th day of September, 1902, that said child has been named Bessie Leverett, and was living March 4, 1905.

My Commission Expires July 20, 1907   Kogee Leverett

Witnesses To Mark:
{ Louisa Morrison

Subscribed and sworn to before me this 23rd day of August, 1905.

Henry L. McDaniel
Notary Public.

Applications for Enrollment of Creek Newborn
Act of 1905   Volume IX

AFFIDAVIT OF ATTENDING PHYSICIAN OR MID-WIFE.

UNITED STATES OF AMERICA, Indian Territory,
Western   DISTRICT.

I, Mary McCombs, a mid-wife , on oath state that I attended on Mrs. Kogee Leverett , wife of Walter Leverett on the 18th day of September , 1902 ; that there was born to her on said date a female child; that said child was living March 4, 1905, and is said to have been named Bessie Leverett

My Commission Expires July 20, 1907   Mary McCombs

Witnesses To Mark:
Louisa Morrison

Subscribed and sworn to before me this 23rd day of August , 1905.

Henry L. McDaniel
Notary Public.

Muskogee, Indian Territory, July 1, 1905.

Joe Reynolds,
Price, Indian Territory.

Dear Sir:

The Commission is in receipt of your letter of June 19, 1905, relative to the application for the enrollment of your minor child, Earnest Reynolds, as a citizen of the Creek Nation. You ask when you can file for said child.

In reply you are advised that there is on file with the Commission an affidavit relative to the enrollment of said Earnest Reynolds, and that he has been listed for enrollment as a citizen of the Creek Nation.

You are further advised that at the present time no reservation of land can be made for new-born children.

Respectfully,
Commissioner.

Applications for Enrollment of Creek Newborn
Act of 1905 Volume IX

(The above letter is given again, but dated July 5, 1905.)

NC-741

Muskogee, Indian Territory, August 16, 1905.

Delphie Reynolds,
    Care of Joseph A. Reynolds,
        Bearden, Indian Territory.

Dear Madam:

    There is on file with the records of this Office an application for the enrollment of your minor son, Earnest Reynolds, as a citizen by blood of the Creek Nation. In your affidavit as to the birth of said child your name appears as Delphie McCoy, and you state that you are the lawful wife of Joseph Reynolds. If you are the lawful wife of Joseph Reynolds, it must necessarily follow that your name is Delphie Reynolds, and not Delphie McCoy.

    It is, therefore, necessary for you to furnish this Office with your affidavit as to the birth of said child, which will correct the discrepancy appearing in your affidavit which is now on file, and a blank for proof of birth, which has been filled out, is enclosed. You are requested to appear before a notary public, and if the affidavit as filled out correctly states the facts in regard to the birth of said child, swear to same, and when sworn to, return it to this Office in the enclosed envelope.

                Respectfully,

                                   Acting Commissioner.

CTD-53
Env

BIRTH AFFIDAVIT.

DEPARTMENT OF THE INTERIOR.
COMMISSION TO THE FIVE CIVILIZED TRIBES.

    IN RE APPLICATION FOR ENROLLMENT, as a citizen of the Creek Nation, of Ernest Reynolds, born on the 12th day of July, 1903

Name of Father: Joseph Reynolds   <u>not</u> a citizen of the   Creek   Nation.
Name of Mother: Delphie McCoy   a citizen of the   Creek   Nation.
(Euchee Town)

                      Postoffice   Bearden, Indian Territory

Applications for Enrollment of Creek Newborn
Act of 1905 Volume IX

AFFIDAVIT OF MOTHER.

UNITED STATES OF AMERICA, Indian Territory,
Western   DISTRICT.

I, Delphie McCoy , on oath state that I am 25 years of age and a citizen by blood , of the Creek Nation; that I am the lawful wife of Joseph Reynolds , who is not a citizen, by blood or otherwise of the Creek Nation; that a male child was born to me on 12th day of July , 1903 , that said child has been named Ernest Reynolds , and was living March 4, 1905.

Delphie McCoy her + mark

Witnesses To Mark:
- Bernard B. Mooney
- Harold E Boudinot

Subscribed and sworn to before me this 7th day of April , 1905.

(Name Illegible)
Notary Public.

AFFIDAVIT OF ATTENDING PHYSICIAN OR MID-WIFE.

UNITED STATES OF AMERICA, Indian Territory,
Western   DISTRICT.

I, Elizabeth Barnett , a mid-wife , on oath state that I attended on Mrs. Joseph Reynolds , wife of Joseph Reynolds on the 12th day of July , 1903 ; that there was born to her on said date a male child; that said child was living March 4, 1905, and is said to have been named Ernest Reynolds

Elizabeth Barnett, her + mark

Witnesses To Mark:
- Bernard B. Mooney
- Harold E Boudinot

Subscribed and sworn to before me this 7th day of April , 1905.

(Name Illegible)
Notary Public.

Applications for Enrollment of Creek Newborn
Act of 1905   Volume IX

BIRTH AFFIDAVIT.

DEPARTMENT OF THE INTERIOR.
COMMISSION TO THE FIVE CIVILIZED TRIBES.

IN RE APPLICATION FOR ENROLLMENT, as a citizen of the Creek Nation, of Ernest Reynolds, born on the 12th day of July, 1903

Name of Father: Joseph Reynolds a citizen of the United States Nation.
Name of Mother: Delphie Reynolds a citizen of the   Creek   Nation.

Postoffice   Bearden, I. T.

AFFIDAVIT OF MOTHER.

UNITED STATES OF AMERICA, Indian Territory,
    Western   **DISTRICT.**

I, Delphie Reynolds, on oath state that I am 25 years of age and a citizen by blood, of the Creek Nation; that I am the lawful wife of Joseph Reynolds, who is a citizen, ~~by~~ *(blank)* of the United States Nation; that a male child was born to me on 12th day of July, 1903, that said child has been named Ernest Reynolds, and was living March 4, 1905.

                    Delphie + Reynolds

Witnesses To Mark:
  { G.H. Van Dyke
  { CW Holmes

Subscribed and sworn to before me this 21st day of August, 1905.

                    (No name given)
                        Notary Public.

My Commission Expires Dec. 10, 1906.

Applications for Enrollment of Creek Newborn
Act of 1905 Volume IX

BIRTH AFFIDAVIT.
DEPARTMENT OF THE INTERIOR.
COMMISSION TO THE FIVE CIVILIZED TRIBES.

IN RE APPLICATION FOR ENROLLMENT, as a citizen of the (Muskogee) Creek Nation, of Ind Ter , born on the 15 day of July, 1902

Name of Father: Willie Tiger a citizen of the Creek Nation.
Name of Mother: Hannah Tiger a citizen of the Creek Nation.

Postoffice Wetumka Ind. Ter.

AFFIDAVIT OF MOTHER.

UNITED STATES OF AMERICA, Indian Territory,
Western Judicial DISTRICT.

I, Hannah Tiger , on oath state that I am 25 years of age and a citizen by Birth , of the Creek Nation; that I am the lawful wife of Willie Tiger , who is a citizen, by Birth of the Creek Nation; that a Female child was born to me on 15 day of July , 1902 , that said child has been named Lillie Tiger , and ~~was living March 4, 1905~~.
16 Oct 1903

Hannah Tiger

Witnesses To Mark:
{ William Buck
{ Nat Williams

Subscribed and sworn to before me this 18 day of Aug , 1905.

My Commission Expires Aug 15 1906   B.H. Mills
Notary Public.

AFFIDAVIT OF ATTENDING PHYSICIAN OR MID-WIFE.

UNITED STATES OF AMERICA, Indian Territory,
Western Judicial DISTRICT.

I, Willie Tiger , a Creek Indian , on oath state that I attended on Mrs. Hannah Tiger , wife of Willie Tiger on the 15 day of July , 1902 ; that there was born to her on said date a Female child; that said child was living ~~March 4, 1905~~, and is said to have been named Lillie Tiger   Oct 16 1903

Willie Tiger

Applications for Enrollment of Creek Newborn
Act of 1905 Volume IX

Witnesses To Mark:
{ Chas Coachman
{ B H Mills

Subscribed and sworn to before me 14 day of April, 1905.

B.H. Mills
Notary Public.

N.C. 742. F.H.W.
DEPARTMENT OF THE INTERIOR, A.G.
COMMISSIONER TO THE FIVE CIVILIZED TRIBES.

In the matter of the application for the enrollment of Lillie Tiger, deceased, as a citizen by blood of the Creek Nation.

STATEMENT AND ORDER.

The record in this case shows that on August 19, 1905, an application was filed, in affidavit form, for the enrollment of Lillie Tiger, deceased, as a citizen by blood of the Creek Nation.
The evidence shows that said Lillie Tiger was born July 15, 1902.
The evidence further shows that on the birth affidavit the clause "was living March 4, 1905" has been cancelled and October 16, 1903, substituted therefor. It is therefore clear that the said Lillie Tiger died about the 16 or 17 of October, 1903, and was not living March 4, 1905. Several unsuccessful efforts have been made by this office to secure further evidence as to the death of the said applicant.
It is, therefore, adjudged that there is no authority of law for the enrollment of the said Lillie Tiger, deceased, as a citizen by blood of the Creek Nation, and that the application for her enrollment as such is hereby ordered dismissed.

Tams Bixby Commissioner.
Muskogee, Indian Territory.
JAN 26 1907

Applications for Enrollment of Creek Newborn
Act of 1905 Volume IX

N.C. 742   I.D.
DEPARTMENT OF THE INTERIOR,
COMMISSIONER TO THE FIVE CIVILIZED TRIBES.

In the matter of the application for the enrollment of Lillie Tiger as a citizen by blood of the Creek Nation.

ORDER

The record in this case shows that on August 19, 1905, there was filed with the Commissioner to the Five Civilized Tribes, at Muskogee, Indian Territory, the application of Hannah Tiger for the enrollment of her minor child, Lillie Tiger, as a citizen by blood of the Creek Nation.

The evidence shows that said Lillie Tiger was born July 15, 1902, and an examination or the records of this Office shows that no application, other than the one filed August 19, 1905, has been made for her enrollment as a citizen by blood of the Creek Nation.

The act of Congress approved March 3, 1905, (Public No. 212), provides:

"That the Commission to the Five Civilized Tribes is authorized for sixty days after the date of the approval of this act to receive and consider applications for enrollment, of children, born subsequent to May twenty-fifth, nineteen hundred and one, and prior to March fourth, nineteen hundred and five, and living on said latter date, to citizens of the Creek tribe of Indians whose enrollment has been approved by the Secretary of the Interior prior to the approval of this act; and to enroll and make allotments to such children."

It is, therefore, ordered that there is no authority of law for the enrollment of the said Lillie Tiger as a citizen by blood of the Creek Nation, and that the application for her enrollment as such should be and the same is hereby dismissed.

                                                                    Commissioner.
Muskogee, Indian Territory.

Applications for Enrollment of Creek Newborn
Act of 1905 Volume IX

NC 742.

Muskogee, Indian Territory, January 29, 1907.

Hannah Tiger,
   c/o Willie Tiger,
      Wetumka, Indian Territory.

Dear Madam:

    There is herewith enclosed one copy of the statement and order of the Commissioner to the Five Civilized Tribes, dated January 26, 1907, dismissing the application made by you for the enrollment of your minor child, Lillie Tiger, deceased, as a citizen of the Creek Nation.

                                   Respectfully,

                                                 Commissioner.

Register.
LM-23.

NC-744

Muskogee, Indian Territory, August 16, 1905.

Lillie Robertson,
   Care of I. W. Robertson,
      Dustin, Indian Territory.

Dear Madam:

    In the matter of the application for the enrollment of your minor son, Andrew Jackson Robertson, as a citizen by blood of the Creek Nation, it appears from yourmaffidavit[sic] and the affidavit of Hattie Brownlee, midwife, that said child was born August 22, 1905, which is apparently an error.

    In order that this error may be corrected, there is herewith enclosed blank for proof of birth, which has been filled out with the exception of the date of the birth of said child. You are requested to fill in the date of the birth of the child in the affidavits, appear before a notary public with Hattie Brownlee, the midwife who attended you at the birth of said child, swear to same, and when sworn to, return same to this Office in the enclosed envelope.

    You are requested to inform this Office as to the name under which you are finally enrolled, the names of your parents and other members of your family, and, if possible, your final roll number as the same appears upon your allotment certificates and

Applications for Enrollment of Creek Newborn
Act of 1905 Volume IX

deeds to land in the Creek Nation. Please also state the Creek Indian Town to which you belong.

                        Respectfully,

                                        Acting Commissioner.

CTD-54
Env

N C 744   COPY

                         Dustin, I. T., 8/17 1905

Commissioner to the Five Civilized Tribes

In reply to yours Aug. 16th my maiden name was Benson. My father's name was Dave Benson, and my mother was not enrolled She died 1895. One bro. Willie Benson two sisters Lena Benson Johnson Tiger's wife Hattie Benson, B. B. Brownlee wife Roll No. on Deed 66.

The Creek Indian Town to which I belong is Cheya ha.

                        Respt.

                        (Signed) Lillie Robertson.

BIRTH AFFIDAVIT.
DEPARTMENT OF THE INTERIOR.
COMMISSION TO THE FIVE CIVILIZED TRIBES.

    IN RE APPLICATION FOR ENROLLMENT, as a citizen of the Creek Nation, of Andrew Jackson Robertson, born on the 22 day of August, 1904

Name of Father: I. W. Robertson   a citizen of the United States Nation.
Name of Mother: Lilly Robertson   a citizen of the   Creek   Nation.

                    Postoffice   Dustin, I. T.

AFFIDAVIT OF MOTHER.

UNITED STATES OF AMERICA, Indian Territory, ⎱
    Western   DISTRICT.   ⎰

    I, Lilly Robertson, on oath state that I am 26 years of age and a citizen by blood, of the Creek Nation; that I am the lawful wife of I. W. Robertson, who is a

Applications for Enrollment of Creek Newborn
Act of 1905 Volume IX

citizen, ~~by~~ *(blank)* of the United States Nation; that a male child was born to me on 22 day of August, 1904 , that said child has been named Andrew Jackson Robertson , and was living March 4, 1905.

             Lilly Robertson

Witnesses To Mark:
{

  Subscribed and sworn to before me this 17th day of August, 1905.

My Com Expires May 20 1907   *(Name Illegible)*
                 Notary Public.

AFFIDAVIT OF ATTENDING PHYSICIAN OR MID-WIFE.

UNITED STATES OF AMERICA, Indian Territory, }
  Western   DISTRICT.

  I, Hattie Brownlee , a mid-wife , on oath state that I attended on Mrs. Lilly Robertson , wife of I. W. Robertson on the 22 day of August , 1904 ; that there was born to her on said date a male child; that said child was living March 4, 1905, and is said to have been named Andrew Jackson Robertson

             Hattie Brownlee

Witnesses To Mark:
{

  Subscribed and sworn to before me this 17th day of August, 1905.

My Com Expires May 20th 1907   *(Name Illegible)*
                 Notary Public.

BIRTH AFFIDAVIT.
DEPARTMENT OF THE INTERIOR.
COMMISSION TO THE FIVE CIVILIZED TRIBES.

  IN RE APPLICATION FOR ENROLLMENT, as a citizen of the Creek Nation, of Andrew Jackson Robertson , born on the 22nd day of August , 1904

Name of Father:	I. W. Robertson	a citizen of the	US	Nation.
Name of Mother:	Lilly Robertson	a citizen of the	Creek	Nation.

          Postoffice Dustin, I.T.

Applications for Enrollment of Creek Newborn
Act of 1905 Volume IX

AFFIDAVIT OF MOTHER.

UNITED STATES OF AMERICA, Indian Territory, }
Western DISTRICT.

I, Lilly Robertson , on oath state that I am 26 years of age and a citizen by blood , of the Creek Nation; that I am the lawful wife of I. W. Robertson , who is a citizen, by *(blank)* of the *(blank)* Nation; that a male child was born to me on 22 day of August, 1904 , that said child has been named Andrew Jackson Robertson , and was living March 4, 1905.

Lilly Robertson

Witnesses To Mark:

{

Subscribed and sworn to before me this 3rd day of Apr , 1905.

My Com Exp Mch 5th 1907   Horace Wilson
                                    Notary Public.

AFFIDAVIT OF ATTENDING PHYSICIAN OR MID-WIFE.

UNITED STATES OF AMERICA, Indian Territory, }
Western DISTRICT.

I, Hattie Brownlee , a female , on oath state that I attended on Mrs. Lilly Robertson , wife of I. W. Robertson on the 22 day of Aug , 1904 ; that there was born to her on said date a Male child; that said child was living March 4, 1905, and is said to have been named Andrew Jackson Robertson

~~Mrs B B B~~
Hattie Brownlee

Witnesses To Mark:

{

Subscribed and sworn to before me this 3rd day of Apr , 1905.

My Com Exp Mch 5th 1907   Horace Wilson
                                    Notary Public.

Applications for Enrollment of Creek Newborn
Act of 1905 Volume IX

N.C. 745.
DEPARTMENT OF THE INTERIOR,
COMMISSIONER TO THE FIVE CIVILIZED TRIBES.
Muskogee, Indian Territory, October 3, 1906.

In the matter of the application for the enrollment of Annie Matoy as a citizen by blood of the Creek Nation.

CHARLES MATOY, being duly sworn by Henry G. Hains, a Notary Public, testifies as follows:

BY THE COMMISSIONER:

Q What is your name? A Charles Matoy.
Q How old are you? A 31.
Q What is your postoffice address? A Eufaula.
Q To what Creek Indian town do you belong? A Tookabathche[sic].
Q What is the name of your father? A John Matoy.
Q What is the name of your mother? A Martha Walker, now Martha Matoy.

The witness is identified as Charles Matoy opposite Creek Indian roll No. 5889.

Q What is the name of this little girl here? A Annie.
Q Annie Matoy? A Yes sir.
Q This your child is it? A Yes sir.
Q When was it born? A Born 16th of July, 1901.
Q What is the name of her mother? A Maud Matoy.
Q Is Maud Matoy a citizen of any of the five tribes? A No sir.
Q White woman? A Yes sir.
Q Is Maud living? A Yes sir.
Q Is this the lady here? A Yes sir.
Q You remember going before Mr. Posey down there at Eufaula in the field? A Yes sir.
Q About April 6, 1905? A April sometime?
Q Who were[sic] with you at that time to make affidavit? A Charley Gibson was with me, and then I went over to his place and got his wife to go over and sign--
Q Modenia? A Yes sir.
Q Were those affidavits made out in a hurry? A No sir, dont[sic] think they were.
Q How do you explain that the affidavit intended for Charley Matoy is signed by Modenia Gibson, and the affidavit written out for Modenia Gibson is signed by Charley Matoy; how did that mistake happen? A I signed where he showed me.
Q Who showed you, Charley Gibson? A No sir, Mr. Posey.
Q Mr. Posey is a notary, was it he? A Mr. Skaggs was there.

Applications for Enrollment of Creek Newborn
Act of 1905   Volume IX

[sic] How do you account for the fact that in the body of the affidavit it states Maud Matoy, your wife, is dead? A That must have been a mistake of Posey's, because I never told him she was dead.
Q Did Charley Gibson do any talking at that time? A No sir, dont[sic] remember.
Q He was there with you? A Yes sir, he was there with me.
Q Dont[sic] you know a man isnt[sic] going to presume a certain person is dead; dont[sic] you know how that happened? A No sir, do not.
Q Then afterwards on February 21, 1906, there was an affidavit executed by Maud Matoy; is that your wife? A Yes sir.
Q And instead of Modenia Gibson, whom you intended to have for one of the affiants the first time, you then has the affidavit of R. M. Donaldson, physician? A Yes sir.
Q Was he the doctor that was present at the time the child was born? A Yes sir.
Q In his affidavit the name of the child is given as Anna, and in the affidavit of the mother as Annie Matoy? A Yes sir.
Q The affidavit of the mother-- this child's name was Annie and was born on the date given? A Yes sir.

WITNESS EXCUSED.

MAUD MATOY, being duly sworn by Henry G. Hains, a Notary Public, testifies as follows:

BY THE COMMISSIONER:

Q What is your name? A Maud Matoy.
Q What was your name before it was Matoy? A Brashears.
Q How old are you? A I am 25.
Q What is your postoffice address? A Eufaula.

The witness is identified as Maud Matoy from marriage license on file, in which it is stated that Mr. Charles Matoy was married to Miss Maud Brashears.

Q Did you sign this affidavit, Mrs. Matoy? A Yes sir.
Q M-a-u-d- Matoy? A Yes sir.
Q This is a true and correct affidavit? A Yes sir.
Q In the doctor's affidavit the name is written Anna; that isnt[sic] right, is it Annie? A Yes sir.

WITNESS EXCUSED.

Cora Moore, being duly sworn, states that as stenographer to the Commissioner to the Five Civilized Tribes she reported the proceedings had in the above entitled cause on October 3, 1906, and that the above and foregoing is a true and correct transcript of her stenographic notes taken in said cause on said date.

Cora Moore

Applications for Enrollment of Creek Newborn
Act of 1905 Volume IX

Subscribed and sworn to before me this October 4, 1906.

Walter W. Chappell
Notary Public.

MARRIAGE LICENSE.

, , ,

UNITED STATES OF AMERICA,)
INDIAN TERRITORY,) ss No. 1 1461.
Northern District.)

To Any Person Authorized by Law to Solemnize Marriage---Greeting:

YOU ARE HEREBY COMMANDED to solemnize the Rite and publish the Banns of Matrimony between Mr. Chas Matoy of Eufaula, in the Indian Territory, aged 24 years, and Miss Maude Brashar, of Eufaula, in the Indian Territory, aged 20 years, according to law, and do you officially sign and return this License to the parties therein named.
WITNESS my hand and official seal at Muscogee[sic], Indian Territory, this 28" day of December, A. D. 1900.

(Signed)   Chas A Davidson
Clerk of the U.S. Court.
(SEAL)
By P. M. Ford Deputy.

CERTIFICATE OF MARRIAGE.

, , ,

UNITED STATES OF AMERICA,)
INDIAN TERRITORY,) ss
Northern District.)

I, Fletcher E. Shanks, a Minister of the Gospel, DO HEREBY CERTIFY, that on the Eighth day of Jan A. D. 1901, I did duly and according to law as commanded in the foregoing License, solemnize the Rite and publish the Banns of Matrimony between the parties therein named.
WITNESS my hand this Eighth day of Jan , A. D. 1901.
My credentials are recorded in the office of the Clerk of the United States Court, Indian Territory, Soth[sic] District, Third Division, Book A, Page 58.

(Signed)   F. E. Shanks.
A Minister of the Gospel.

Applications for Enrollment of Creek Newborn
Act of 1905   Volume IX

In the M. E. Church South.

I, Harriett E. Arbuckle, state on oath that the above and foregoing is a true and exact copy of the original.

Harriett E Arbuckle

Subscribed and sworn to before me this February 27, 1905.

Drennan C Skaggs
Notary Public.

BIRTH AFFIDAVIT.

DEPARTMENT OF THE INTERIOR.
COMMISSION TO THE FIVE CIVILIZED TRIBES.

IN RE APPLICATION FOR ENROLLMENT, as a citizen of the Creek Nation, of Annie Matoy, born on the 16 day of July, 1901

Name of Father: Charley Matoy   a citizen of the   Creek   Nation.
Tuckabatche Town
Name of Mother: Maud Matoy   a citizen of the United States Nation.

Postoffice   Eufaula, Ind. Ter.

AFFIDAVIT OF MOTHER.

UNITED STATES OF AMERICA, Indian Territory,
   Western   DISTRICT.   Child is not present

I, Charley Matoy, on oath state that I am 29 years of age and a citizen by blood, of the Creek Nation; that I am the lawful ~~wife~~ husband of Maud Matoy, deceased, who is a citizen, ~~by~~ (blank) of the United States ~~Nation~~; that a female child was born to me on 16 day of July, 1901, that said child has been named Annie Matoy, and was living March 4, 1905.

Modenia Gibson

Witnesses To Mark:

Subscribed and sworn to before me this 6 day of April, 1905.

Drennan C Skaggs
Notary Public.

Applications for Enrollment of Creek Newborn
Act of 1905   Volume IX

AFFIDAVIT OF ATTENDING PHYSICIAN OR MID-WIFE.

UNITED STATES OF AMERICA, Indian Territory, ⎫
   Western   DISTRICT.   ⎬
                                      ⎭

    I, Modenia Gibson , a——, on oath state that I attended on Mrs. Maud Matoy deceased , wife of Charley Matoy on the 16 day of July , 1901 ; that there was born to her on said date a female child; that said child was living March 4, 1905, and is said to have been named Annie Matoy

                                                                Charley Matoy

Witnesses To Mark:
{

    Subscribed and sworn to before me 6 day of April, 1905.

                                        Drennan C Skaggs
                                              Notary Public.

BIRTH AFFIDAVIT.
DEPARTMENT OF THE INTERIOR.
COMMISSION TO THE FIVE CIVILIZED TRIBES.

    IN RE APPLICATION FOR ENROLLMENT, as a citizen of the Creek Nation, of Annie Matoy, born on the 16th. day of July, 1901

Name of Father: Charley Matoy   a citizen of the   Creek   Nation.
Name of Mother: Maud Matoy   a citizen of the United States Nation.

                             Postoffice   Eufaula Indian Territory.

AFFIDAVIT OF MOTHER.

UNITED STATES OF AMERICA, Indian Territory, ⎫
   Western   DISTRICT.   ⎬
                                      ⎭

    I, Maud Matoy , on oath state that I am 25 years of age and a citizen by of the U. S. , of the *(blank)* Nation; that I am the lawful wife of Charley Matoy , who is a citizen, by Blood of the Creek Nation; that a female child was born to me on the 16th. day of July , 1901 , that said child has been named Annie Matoy , and is now living.

                                               Maud Matoy

Witnesses To Mark:
{

Applications for Enrollment of Creek Newborn
Act of 1905   Volume IX

Subscribed and sworn to before me this 21st day of February, 1906.

My Commission Expires Jan. 30, 1909.

Frank W. Rushing
Notary Public.

AFFIDAVIT OF ATTENDING PHYSICIAN OR MID-WIFE.

UNITED STATES OF AMERICA, Indian Territory,
Western   DISTRICT.

I, R. M. Counterman, a Physician, on oath state that I attended on Mrs. Maude Matoy, wife of Charles Matoy on the 16 day of July, 1901 ; that there was born to her on said date a female child; that said child is now living and is said to have been named Anna Matoy

R.M. Counterman, M.D.

Witnesses To Mark:

Subscribed and sworn to before me this 19 day of February, 1906.

My Commission Expires Jan. 30, 1909.

Frank W. Rushing
Notary Public.

NC-745.

Muskogee, Indian Territory, October 18, 1905.

Charley Matoy,
 Eufaula, Indian Territory.

Dear Sir:

In the matter of the application for the enrollment of your minor daughter Annie Matoy, as a citizen by blood of the Creek Nation blood, you are again advised that it will be necessary for you to furnish this office with the proper proof of birth of said child and a blank for that purpose, properly filled out, is herewith inclosed. You should be careful to sign the affidavit as your name appears in the body thereof.

The affidavits now on file as to the birth of said child are defective, inasmuch as the midwife, Modenia Gibson, signed the affidavit which was filled out for you, and you signed the affidavit which was meant for her signature.

It will also be necessary for you to furnish this office, in the matter of the enrollment of said child, the affidavits of two disinterested persons who are acquainted with the circumstances attending the birth of said child. Said affidavits of the

Applications for Enrollment of Creek Newborn
Act of 1905   Volume IX

disinterested parties must set forth said child's birth, her name, the names of her parents and whether or not she was living on March 4, 1905.

You are also requested to furnish this office with evidence of your marriage to Maud Matoy, the noncitizen mother of said child. The evidence of marriage may consist of either the original or a certified copy of your marriage license and certificate.

Respectfully,
Commissioner.

CTD-5.
Env.

NC-745

Muskogee, Indian Territory, December 14, 1905.

Charley Matoy,
    Eufaula, Indian Territory.

Dear Sir:

In the matter of the application for the enrollment of your minor child, Annie Matoy, born July 16, 1901, as a citizen by blood of the Creek Nation, you are again advised that it will be necessary for you to furnish this Office with proper proof of the birth of said child, and a blank for that purpose is herewith enclosed.

The affidavits now on file as to the birth of said child are defective, inasmuch as the midwife, Modenia Gibson, signed the affidavit which was filled out for you, and you signed the affidavit which was meant for her signature.

It will also be necessary for you to furnish this Office, in the matter of the enrollment of said child, the affidavits of two disinterested persons who are acquainted with the circumstances attending the birth of said child. A blank for that purpose is herewith enclosed.

You are further requested to furnish this Office with evidence of the marriage between you and Maud Matoy, the noncitizen mother of said child. Such evidence of marriage may consist of either the original or a certified copy of your marriage license and certificate. In the event that you are not married to said Maud Matoy, or that you were married to her with a license, it will be necessary for you to execute an affidavit to the effect that you are the father of said child.

This matter should receive your immediate attention.

Respectfully,
Commissioner.

1 B A
Dis

Applications for Enrollment of Creek Newborn
Act of 1905   Volume IX

FRANK W. RUSHING
LAWYER
Eufaula, Ind. Ter.

Office over
Eufaula National Bank.

February 21, 1906.

TDanna[sic] H. Kelsey,
   United States Indian Agent,
      Muskogee, I. T.
Dear Sir:-

     Enclosed please find Certificate of Charley Matoy, Duly certified to by his wife and the attending physician, who attended the wife of the said Charley Matoy, when the child was born. Also find a marriage certificate which you will please return to me when the same is duly inspected.

Hoping the evidence herein sufficient, I, am,

                Yours truly,
                (Signed)   Charley Matoy.

                                      JWH

N C 745
                Muskogee, Indian Territory, March 1, 1907.

Charles Matoy,
   Eufaula, Indian Territory.

Dear Sir :--

     You are hereby advised that on February 15, 1906, the Secretary of the Interior approved the enrollment of your minor child, Annie Matoy, as a citizen by blood of the Creek Nation, and that the name of said child appears upon the roll of New Born citizens by blood of the Creek Nation, enrolled under the Act of Congress approved March 3, 1905, as number 1167.

     This child is now entitled to allotment and application therefor should be made without delay at the Creek Land Office, Muskogee, Indian Territory.

                Respectfully,
                            Commissioner.

Applications for Enrollment of Creek Newborn
Act of 1905   Volume IX

NC 749.

Muskogee, Indian Territory, January 29, 1907.

Blanche Williams Payton,
   c/o L.C. Payton,
      Holdenville, Indian Territory.

Dear Madam:

    There is herewith enclosed one copy of the statement and order of the Commissioner to the Five Civilized Tribes, dated January 26, 1907, dismissing the application made by you for the enrollment of your minor child, Clara Payton, as a citizen by blood of the Creek Nation.

                Respectfully,

                        Commissioner.

Register.
LM-25.

BIRTH AFFIDAVIT.

DEPARTMENT OF THE INTERIOR.
COMMISSION TO THE FIVE CIVILIZED TRIBES.

    IN RE APPLICATION FOR ENROLLMENT, as a citizen of the Creek Nation, of Clara Payton, born on the 28 day of January, 1902

Name of Father: L. C. Payton   a citizen of the United States Nation.
Name of Mother: Blanche Williams Payton   a citizen of the   Creek   Nation.
Hickory Ground Town
                    Postoffice   Holdenville, Ind. Ter.

AFFIDAVIT OF MOTHER.

UNITED STATES OF AMERICA, Indian Territory, }
    Western   DISTRICT.   Child is present

    I, Blanche Williams Payton , on oath state that I am   31   years of age and a citizen by blood , of the Creek   Nation; that I am the lawful wife of L. C. Payton , who is a citizen, ~~by~~ *(blank)* of the United States   Nation; that a female child was born to me on 28 day of January , 1902 , that said child has been named Clara Payton , and was living March 4, 1905.

                          Blanche Williams Payton

Witnesses To Mark:

Applications for Enrollment of Creek Newborn
Act of 1905 Volume IX

Subscribed and sworn to before me this 31 day of March, 1905.

Drennan C Skaggs
Notary Public.

AFFIDAVIT OF ATTENDING PHYSICIAN OR MID-WIFE.

UNITED STATES OF AMERICA, Indian Territory,
Western DISTRICT.

I, F. E. Waterfield, a physician, on oath state that I attended on Mrs. Blanche Williams Payton, wife of L. C. Payton on the 28 day of January, 1902; that there was born to her on said date a female child; that said child was living March 4, 1905, and is said to have been named Clara Payton

F. E. Waterfield

Witnesses To Mark:

Subscribed and sworn to before me 31 day of March, 1905.

Drennan C Skaggs
Notary Public.

N.C. 749.

F.H.W.
AG

DEPARTMENT OF THE INTERIOR, COMMISSIONER TO THE FIVE CIVILIZED TRIBES.

In the matter of the application for the enrollment of Clara Payton as a citizen by blood of the Creek Nation.

STATEMENT AND ORDER.

The record in this case shows that an application was made, in affidavit form, April 4, 1905, for the enrollment of Clara Payton as a citizen by blood of the Creek Nation.

It appears from the evidence that the said Clara Payton is the child of L. C. Payton, a citizen of the United States, and Blanche Williams Payton.

It further appears from the records of this office that on March 15, 1905, a decision was rendered by the Commission to the Five Civilized Tribes denying the right to enrollment of Blanche Williams Payton, the mother of the applicant.

It further appears that on December 8, 1905, the Department of the Interior affirmed said decision.

Applications for Enrollment of Creek Newborn
Act of 1905 Volume IX

Inasmuch as the records of this office fail to show that either the father or the mother of the said applicant is a duly enrolled citizen of the Creek Nation, or has an application for enrollment pending at the present time, there is no authority of law for the enrollment of said Clara Payton.

It is therefore, ordered that the said application for the enrollment of Clara Payton as a citizen by blood of the Creek Nation, be, and the same is hereby dismissed.

Muskogee, Indian Territory,   Tams Bixby   Commissioner.
JAN 26 1907

BIRTH AFFIDAVIT.

DEPARTMENT OF THE INTERIOR.
COMMISSION TO THE FIVE CIVILIZED TRIBES.

IN RE APPLICATION FOR ENROLLMENT, as a citizen of the CREEK Nation, of Ethel May Churchill, born on the 14th day of September, 1904

Name of Father: Avery Churchill   a citizen of the United States Nation.
Name of Mother: Maude M. Churchill   a citizen of the   Creek   Nation.

                      Postoffice   Checotah Ind. Ter.

AFFIDAVIT OF MOTHER.

UNITED STATES OF AMERICA, Indian Territory,
    WESTERN   DISTRICT.

I, Maude M. Churchill (nee McNulty), on oath state that I am 18 years of age and a citizen by Blood, of the Creek Nation; that I am the lawful wife of Avery Churchill, who is a citizen, by *(blank)* of the United States Nation; that a Female child was born to me on 14th day of September, 1904, that said child has been named Ethel May Churchill, and is now living.   (nee McNulty)
                          Maude M Churchill
Witnesses To Mark:

Subscribed and sworn to before me this 6$^{\underline{th}}$ day of April, 1905.

My Commission Expires July 1, 1905.   J.B. Morrow
                                  Notary Public.

Applications for Enrollment of Creek Newborn
Act of 1905 Volume IX

AFFIDAVIT OF ATTENDING PHYSICIAN OR MID-WIFE.

UNITED STATES OF AMERICA, Indian Territory,
WESTERN DISTRICT.

I, A. B. Montgomery, a Physician, on oath state that I attended on Mrs. Maude M. Churchill, wife of Avery Churchill on the 14th day of September, 1904; that there was born to her on said date a Female child; that said child is now living and is said to have been named Ethel May Churchill

A. B. Montgomery

Witnesses To Mark:

{

Subscribed and sworn to before me this 6th day of April, 1905.

My Commission Expires July 1, 1905.   J.B. Morrow
                                            Notary Public.

NC-752.

Muskogee, Indian Territory, October 18, 1905.

Daniel Lewis,
    Eufaula, Indian Territory.

Dear Sir:

In the matter of the application for the enrollment of your minor child, Mattie Lewis, born July 20, 1902, as a citizen by blood of the Creek Nation it is necessary for you to file with this office the affidavit of the midwife or physician in attendance at the birth of said child and a blank for that purpose is inclosed herewith.

In the event that no midwife or physician was present at the birth of said child or that for any reason you are unable to obtain the affidavit of said midwife or physician it will be necessary for you to file with this office the affidavits of two disinterested witnesses relative to the birth of said child. Said affidavits to set forth said child's name, the date of her birth, the names of her parents and whether or not she was living on March 4, 1905.

Applications for Enrollment of Creek Newborn
Act of 1905 Volume IX

Respectfully,
Commissioner.
B C
Env.

Witnesses

AFFIDAVIT OF ~~ATTENDING PHYSICIAN OR MID-WIFE~~.

UNITED STATES OF AMERICA, Indian Territory,
Western   DISTRICT.

                                  we are acquainted with
I, Mr Tobe Belcher & Wm Francis , a   (blank) , on oath state that ~~I attended on~~
Mrs. Pollie Lewis , wife of Daniel Lewis on the 20$^{\underline{th}}$ day of July , 1902 ; that there was born to her on said date a female child; that said child is now living and is said to have been named Mattie Lewis   his
                                  Tobe Belcher   x
                                        mark
Witnesses To Mark: William Francis
{ Winnie Turner
  J. Montgomery

    Subscribed and sworn to before me this 28th day of Oct, 1905.

                                      Thos. F. *(Illegible)*
                                            Notary Public.

BIRTH AFFIDAVIT.
DEPARTMENT OF THE INTERIOR.
COMMISSION TO THE FIVE CIVILIZED TRIBES.

    IN RE APPLICATION FOR ENROLLMENT, as a citizen of the Creek Nation, of Mattie Lewis , born on the 20 day of July , 1902

Name of Father: Daniel Lewis   a citizen of the   Creek   Nation.
Eufaula Canadian Town
Name of Mother: Pollie Lewis   a citizen of the   Creek   Nation.
Eufaula Canadian Town
                               Postoffice   Eufaula, I. T.

Applications for Enrollment of Creek Newborn
Act of 1905 Volume IX

Child present.
AFFIDAVIT OF MOTHER.

UNITED STATES OF AMERICA, Indian Territory, ⎫
Western   DISTRICT.   ⎬
                                      ⎭

I, Pollie Lewis , on oath state that I am about 27 years of age and a citizen by blood , of the Creek Nation; that I am the lawful wife of Daniel Lewis , who is a citizen, by blood of the Creek Nation; that a female child was born to me on 20 day of July , 1902 , that said child has been named Mattie Lewis , and was living March 4, 1905.

Polly Lewis

Witnesses To Mark:

Subscribed and sworn to before me this 6 day of April , 1905.

Drennan C Skaggs
Notary Public.

AFFIDAVIT OF ATTENDING PHYSICIAN OR MID-WIFE.

UNITED STATES OF AMERICA, Indian Territory, ⎫
Western   DISTRICT.   ⎬
                                      ⎭

my wife
I, Daniel Lewis , a (blank) , on oath state that I attended on ^ Mrs. Pollie Lewis , wife of (blank) on the 20 day of July , 1902 ; that there was born to her on said date a female child; that said child was living March 4, 1905, and is said to have been named Mattie Lewis

Daniel Lewis

Witnesses To Mark:

Subscribed and sworn to before me this 6 day of April, 1905.

Drennan C Skaggs
Notary Public.

**Applications for Enrollment of Creek Newborn
Act of 1905 Volume IX**

NC 753.

Muskogee, Indian Territory, January 17, 1907.

Bettie McGirt,
    Barnard, Indian Territory.

Dear Madam:

    There is herewith enclosed one copy of the Statement and Order of the Commissioner to the Five Civilized Tribes, dated January 15, 1907, dismissing the application made by you for the enrollment of your minor child, Minnie McGirt, deceased, as a citizen by blood of the Creek Nation.

                     Respectfully,

                                 Commissioner.

LM-70.

**DEPARTMENT OF THE INTERIOR.
COMMISSION TO THE FIVE CIVILIZED TRIBES.**

    In the matter of the death of   Minnie McGirt   a citizen of the Creek Nation, who formerly resided at or near   Barnard   , Ind. Ter., and died on the 9th day of December   , 1904   <u>Born</u> Dec 6th 1904

AFFIDAVIT OF RELATIVE.

UNITED STATES OF AMERICA, Indian Territory, ⎱
    (blank)   DISTRICT. ⎰

    I, Bettie McGirt , on oath state that I am 23 years of age and a citizen by blood , of the Creek Nation; that my postoffice address is   Barnard   , Ind. Ter.; that I am the Mother   of Minnie McGirt   who was a citizen, by blood   , of the Creek   Nation and that said   Minnie McGirt   died on the   9th day of December   , 1904   her

                                   Bettie x McGirt
Witnesses To Mark: mark
⎰ Goliah Jones
⎱ Timmie Stidham

    Subscribed and sworn to before me this 27 day of March, 1905.

                                  J. R. Dunzy
                                      Notary Public.

Applications for Enrollment of Creek Newborn
Act of 1905   Volume IX

AFFIDAVIT OF ACQUAINTANCE.

UNITED STATES OF AMERICA, Indian Territory, }
(blank)   DISTRICT.

I, Nancy Leader, on oath state that I am 27 years of age, and a citizen by blood of the Creek Nation; that my postoffice address is Barnard, Ind. Ter.; that I was personally acquainted with Minnie McGirt who was a citizen, by blood, of the Creek Nation; and that said Minnie McGirt died on the 9th day of December, 1904

her
Nancy x Leader
mark

Witnesses To Mark:
{ Goliah Jones
{ Timmie Stidham

Subscribed and sworn to before me this 27 day of March, 1905.

J. R. Dunzy
Notary Public.

NC 753   DEPARTMENT OF THE INTERIOR,   JLD
COMMISSIONER TO THE FIVE CIVILIZED TRIBES.

In the matter of the application for the enrollment of Minnie McGirt, deceased, as a citizen by blood of the Creek Nation.

. . . .

STATEMENT AND ORDER.

The record in this case shows that on April 1, 1905, application was made, in affidavit form, for the enrollment of Minnie McGirt, deceased, as a citizen by blood of the Creek Nation, under the provisions of the Act of Congress approved March 3, 1905.

It appears from the evidence filed in this matter that said Minnie McGirt, deceased, was born December 6, 1904, and died December 9, 1904.

The Act of Congress approved March 3, 1905, (33 Stats., 1048), provides:
"That the Commission to the Five Civilized Tribes is authorized for sixty days after the date of the approval of this act to receive and consider applications for enrollment, of children, born subsequent to May twenty-fifth, nineteen hundred and one, and prior to March fourth, nineteen hundred and five, and living on said latter date, to citizens of the Creek tribe of Indians whose enrollment has been approved by the Secretary of the Interior prior to the approval of this act; and to enroll and make allotments to such children."

Applications for Enrollment of Creek Newborn
Act of 1905   Volume IX

It is, therefore, ordered that the application for the enrollment of said Minnie McGirt, deceased, as a citizen by blood of the Creek Nation, be, and the same is hereby dismissed.

Muskogee, Indian Territory.
JAN 15 1907

Tams Bixby Commissioner.

BIRTH AFFIDAVIT.
DEPARTMENT OF THE INTERIOR.
COMMISSION TO THE FIVE CIVILIZED TRIBES.

IN RE APPLICATION FOR ENROLLMENT, as a citizen of the Creek Nation, of Samuel Webster Howell, born on the 16 day of June, 1903

Name of Father: Tollie H. Howell   a citizen of the United States ~~Nation~~.
Name of Mother: Lizzie Howell (nee Hawkins) a citizen of the   Creek   Nation. Ketchopatcky Town
             Postoffice   Brush Hill, Ind. Ter.

AFFIDAVIT OF MOTHER.

UNITED STATES OF AMERICA, Indian Territory, }
  Western   DISTRICT.   }   Child is present

I, Lizzie Howell , on oath state that I am 24 years of age and a citizen by blood, of the Creek Nation; that I am the lawful wife of Tollie H. Howell , who is a citizen, ~~by~~ *(blank)* of the United States Nation; that a male child was born to me on 16 day of June , 1903 , that said child has been named Samuel Webster Howell , and was living March 4, 1905.

Lizzie Howell

Witnesses To Mark:
{

Subscribed and sworn to before me this 4 day of April , 1905.

Drennan C Skaggs
Notary Public.

302

Applications for Enrollment of Creek Newborn
Act of 1905 Volume IX

AFFIDAVIT OF ATTENDING PHYSICIAN OR MID-WIFE.

UNITED STATES OF AMERICA, Indian Territory, ⎱
    Western   DISTRICT.   ⎰

I, Lucinda Hawkins , a midwife , on oath state that I attended on Mrs. Lizzie Howell , wife of Tollie H. Howell on the 16 day of June , 1903 ; that there was born to her on said date a male child; that said child was living March 4, 1905, and is said to have been named Samuel Webster Howell

                                                                her
Witnesses To Mark: Lucinda x Hawkins
⎰ Samuel C. *(Illegible)*   mark
⎱ Lewis Pittman

Subscribed and sworn to before me 5 day of April, 1905.

                                         Preston Janway
                                         Notary Public.

BIRTH AFFIDAVIT.
DEPARTMENT OF THE INTERIOR.
COMMISSION TO THE FIVE CIVILIZED TRIBES.

IN RE APPLICATION FOR ENROLLMENT, as a citizen of the Creek Nation, of Emma Lewis, born on the 7th day of Sept, 1904

Name of Father: Harley Lewis	a citizen of the	Creek	Nation.
Name of Mother: Effie Lewis	a citizen of the	Creek	Nation.

                          Postoffice   Oktaba[sic], Indian Territory

Applications for Enrollment of Creek Newborn
Act of 1905   Volume IX

AFFIDAVIT OF MOTHER.

UNITED STATES OF AMERICA, Indian Territory, ⎱
    Western   DISTRICT.   ⎰

I, Effie Lewis , on oath state that I am 22 years of age and a citizen by blood , of the Creek Nation; that I am the lawful wife of Harley Lewis , who is a citizen, by blood of the Creek Nation; that a female child was born to me on 7th day of September , 1904 , that said child has been named Emma Lewis , and was living March 4, 1905.

                                                her
Witnesses To Mark: Effie x Lewis
                                           mark
⎰ Clarina Chapman
⎱ Annie Carter

Subscribed and sworn to before me this 15th day of April , 1905.

                                        A.M. Darling
                                                Notary Public.

AFFIDAVIT OF ATTENDING PHYSICIAN OR MID-WIFE.

UNITED STATES OF AMERICA, Indian Territory, ⎱
    Western   DISTRICT.   ⎰

I, A.J. Snelson , a physician , on oath state that I attended on Mrs. Effie Lewis , wife of Harley Lewis on the 7th day of September , 1904 ; that there was born to her on said date a female child; that said child was living March 4, 1905, and is said to have been named Emma Lewis

                                          A.J. Snelson
Witnesses To Mark:

⎰
⎱ Subscribed and sworn to before me this 15th day of April , 1905.

                                        A.M. Darling
                                                Notary Public.

Applications for Enrollment of Creek Newborn
Act of 1905 Volume IX

2101 B
DEPARTMENT OF THE INTERIOR,
COMMISSION TO THE FIVE CIVILIZED TRIBES.
April 19, 1905, Bristow, I.T.

In the matter of the application for the enrollment of Mahala Hamilton, as a citizen by blood of the Creek Nation.

Clarence Douglass, being duly sworn, by E.C. Griesel, a Notary Public, testified as follows:

By Commission:
Q What is your name? A Clarence Douglass.
Q How old are you? A About 40.
Q What is your post office? A Bristow.
Q Are you a citizen of any Nation in the Indian Territory? A No sir.
Q You are a State man? A Yes sir.
Q Do you know a child named Mahala Hamilton? A Yes sir.
Q Do you know when that child was born? A I do.
Q When was that child born? A March 4, 1905.
Q Would that be on the night of Saturday? A (No answer).
Q How do you know that this child was born on the 4th? A Because I saw it on the 5th.
Q How do you know that this child was not born a week before you saw it? A Because I saw the mother on the 4th and she didn't have the child then. I saw her in the evening, for she was standing on her feet.
Q Had Peter Hamilton gone for the midwife when you saw the mother standing there on the 4th? A Yes, sir he had returned with her, for she was there at the same time.
Q How did you know that this was the 4th day of March, 1905? A I made a contract on the 4th of March with J.W. Williams to farm on shares; the man living on Peter's place, is the reason I am so positive.
Q Did you report the birth of this child on the day following, that is, on the 5th to anyone? A I told J.W. Williams and Mrs. B.B. Williams, whose post office is Bristow.

E.C. Griesel, being duly sworn, on his oath states that the above and foregoing is a true and correct transcript of his stenographic notes as taken in said cause on said date.

Edw C Griesel

Subscribed and sworn to before me this 5 day of May, 1905.

Zera E. Parrish
Notary Public.

Applications for Enrollment of Creek Newborn
Act of 1905   Volume IX

N.C. 757
DEPARTMENT OF THE INTERIOR,
COMMISSIONER TO THE FIVE CIVILIZED TRIBES.
Muskogee, Indian Territory, November 8, 1905.

In the matter of the application for the enrollment of Mary and Mahala Hamilton as citizens by blood of the Creek Nation.

Mrs. S.V. Williams being duly sworn testified as follows:

Q What is your name? A Mrs. S.V. Williams
Q What is your age? A 39 next June
Q What is your post office address? [sic] Bristow.
Q Are you a citizen of any nation in Indian Territory? A No, sir I am a white woman.
Q Do you know a child named Mahala Hamilton? A Yes, sir.
Q What is the name of her father? A Peter Hamilton
Q Is he living? A Yes, sir
Q Is she a citizen of the Creek Nation? A No, sir
Q Were you present when that child was born? A No, sir
Q How long after its birth before you saw it? A About a week.
Q When was it born? A In the first part of March on Saturday night.
Q Are you sure it was Saturday night? A I couldn't swear whether it was born in the fore or after part of the night. Peter Hamilton's brother-in-law had some hogs that had been getting in our fields and my husband and I came from town and he was away from home, we stopped to notify him about the hogs, and we went on down and Peter Hamilton was in town to get a woman to take care of this child's birth.
Q Do you remember what time you started on that trip? A In the afternoon on the way home we meant to go back to tell this Mr. Mann and we went on home and my husband told the hired man to go down by Peter Hamilton's and this midwife was there and his wife was sick in bed and Sunday morning the hired man, Clarence Douglass said he would go down and ask Peter Hamilton if the child was there and when Peter saw him he hollered and told him they had a new cook, meaning Mahala, and that was Sunday morning.
Q You are sure that was in March? A I know it was in March, along the first part of the month
Q Are you sure it was a Saturday in March that you made that trip? A Yes, sir, I named the child but I didn't see it for a week
Q And you are sure it was on Saturday that you went on the trip when you saw them looking for the midwife? A Yes, sir
Q And you are sure it was a Saturday in March that your hired man went down and was told they had a new cook? A Yes, sir
Q Do you know anything about their other child Mary? A I think it was born on the 20th of February, it was two last February I believe.
Q Are you sure it was not a Saturday or Sunday in February that this other child was born? A I am sure it was in March

Applications for Enrollment of Creek Newborn
Act of 1905   Volume IX

Nancy Murray being duly sworn testified as follows:

Q What is your name? A Nancy Murray.
Q You testified before in this case? A Yes, sir
Q Were you the midwife when this child was born? A Yes,[sic]
Q You testified before that it was the first part of March, that you didn't know the date. A Yes, sir
Q And you testified that it was either Sunday or Monday? A Yes, sir
Q Is that the best you know now? A Yes, sir
Q Are you sure it was a Sunday or Monday in March? A Yes, I think it was, it was born in the night, it must have been the last part of Saturday night or Sunday morning, I think it was born about two o'clock Saturday night, but the day of the month I don't know.
Q You made out an affidavit before our notary public at the same time Ellen Hamilton did and you stated in it, "about the first of March" you didn't know the date that was the reason you said about. You didn't know the exact date? A No, sir, I wouldn't swear the date because I didn't know. I knew it was born the first part of March.

Peter Hamilton being duly sworn testified as follows:

Q What is your name? A Peter Hamilton
Q What was the name of your father? A Alec Hamilton
Q What was the name of your mother? A Sallie Knoll
Q Has she a child named Dora Knoll? A Yes, sir

Witness is identified as Peter Hamilton on Creek Indian card, field No. 850 opposite roll No. 2748

Q Your wife testified before about your children, Mahala and Mary? A Yes, sir
Q She was asked this question on what day of the week was this child Mahala born and she said on Saturday, do you know what month it was? A I think it was on the 4th of March
Q Your wife made out an affidavit in which she said it was born the first part of March, she didn't mean the first day of March? A No, sir
Q You think now it was the 4th of March, about the 4th of March? A Yes, sir
Q You are sure it was the first part of March on a Saturday night? A Yes, sir
Q We will look in the calendar and tell you the first Saturday in March was March 4th, you think that is when it was born do you[sic] A Yes, sir
Q Was it born in the night time? A Yes, sir
Q Who was the midwife? A Nancy Murray
Q Do you know Mrs. Williams? A Yes, she lives on our place about five years
Q She says it was born Saturday night too in the first part of March; she says Sunday morning her hired man went down to your place and you told him you had a new cook in your family, meaning Mahala, that's right she did that? A Yes, sir

Applications for Enrollment of Creek Newborn
Act of 1905 Volume IX

Ellan[sic] Hamilton being duly sworn testified as follows:

Q What is your name? A Ellan Hamilton
Q You are not a citizen of any nation in Indian Territory? [sic] No, sir
Q You testified in this case before? A Yes, sir
Q When was your child Mahala born? A The first part of March
Q Do you know what day of the week? A No, sir I dont[sic], but as soon as I counted it up it was on the 4th of March
Q You made an affidavit and stated the child was born on the first day of March is that correct? A No, sir I didn't mean on the first day, I meant in the first part and since I figured it up, it was the 4th of March.
Q Can you read and write? [sic] A little
Q You signed your name to the affidavit, looks like Ellan is that right? A Yes, sir
Q Is your child Mary Hamilton living? A Yes, sir
Q You are sure now that Mahala was born on the 4th of March? A Yes, sir

I will have you make out a new affidavit and give the correct date.

I, Anna Garrigues, state on oath that the above and foregoing is a true and correct transcript of my stenographic notes as taken in said case on said date.

Anna Garrigues

Subscribed and sworn to before me
this 10th day of November, 1905.

J McDermott
Notary Public.

BIRTH AFFIDAVIT.

DEPARTMENT OF THE INTERIOR.
COMMISSION TO THE FIVE CIVILIZED TRIBES.

IN RE APPLICATION FOR ENROLLMENT, as a citizen of the Creek Nation, of Mary Hamilton, born on the 20 day of Feb, 1903

Name of Father:	Peter Hamilton	a citizen of the	Creek	Nation.
(Tuskegee)				
Name of Mother:	Ellen " (nee White)	a citizen of the	U.S.	Nation.

Postoffice Bristow

Applications for Enrollment of Creek Newborn
Act of 1905   Volume IX

AFFIDAVIT OF MOTHER.

UNITED STATES OF AMERICA, Indian Territory, }   Child Present
Western   DISTRICT.

I, Ellen Hamilton , on oath state that I am 32 years of age and a citizen by -----, of the U. S. Nation; that I am the lawful wife of Peter Hamilton , who is a citizen, by blood of the Creek Nation; that a female child was born to me on 20 day of Feb , 1903 , that said child has been named Mary Hamilton , and is now living.

Ellen Hamilton

Witnesses To Mark:
{

Subscribed and sworn to before me this 18 day of April , 1905.

Edw C Griesel
Notary Public.

AFFIDAVIT OF ATTENDING PHYSICIAN OR MID-WIFE.

UNITED STATES OF AMERICA, Indian Territory, }
Western   DISTRICT.

I, Nancy Murray , a Midwife , on oath state that I attended on Mrs. Ellen Hamilton , wife of Peter Hamilton on the 20 day of Feb , 1903 ; that there was born to her on said date a female child; that said child is now living and is said to have been named Mary Hamilton

Nancy Murray

Witnesses To Mark:
{ Subscribed and sworn to before me this 18 day of April , 1905.

Edw C Griesel
Notary Public.

BIRTH AFFIDAVIT.

DEPARTMENT OF THE INTERIOR.
COMMISSION TO THE FIVE CIVILIZED TRIBES.

IN RE APPLICATION FOR ENROLLMENT, as a citizen of the Creek Nation, of Mahala Hamilton , born on the 4" day of March , 1905

Applications for Enrollment of Creek Newborn
Act of 1905 Volume IX

Name of Father: Peter Hamilton   a citizen of the   Creek   Nation.
Name of Mother: Ellan Hamilton   a citizen of the   U.S.   Nation.

                        Postoffice   Bristow

AFFIDAVIT OF MOTHER.

UNITED STATES OF AMERICA, Indian Territory, ⎫
Western   DISTRICT.   ⎭

    I, Ellan Hamilton , on oath state that I am 32 years of age and a citizen by -----, of the U. S. Nation; that I am the lawful wife of Peter Hamilton , who is a citizen, by blood of the Creek Nation; that a female child was born to me on 4" day of March, 1905 , that said child has been named Mahala Hamilton , and was living March 4, 1905.

                                   Ellen Hamilton

Witnesses To Mark:
{

    Subscribed and sworn to before me this 8 day of November , 1905.

                                   Henry G Hains
                                       Notary Public.

BIRTH AFFIDAVIT.
                    DEPARTMENT OF THE INTERIOR.
          COMMISSION TO THE FIVE CIVILIZED TRIBES.

    IN RE APPLICATION FOR ENROLLMENT, as a citizen of the Creek Nation, of Mahala Hamilton , born on the 1 day of March, 1905

Name of Father: Peter Hamilton   a citizen of the   Creek   Nation.
          (Tuskegee)
Name of Mother: Ellen Hamilton   a citizen of the   U.S.   Nation.

                        Postoffice   Bristow

Applications for Enrollment of Creek Newborn
Act of 1905   Volume IX

AFFIDAVIT OF MOTHER.

UNITED STATES OF AMERICA, Indian Territory, } Child Present
Western   DISTRICT.

I, Ellen Hamilton , on oath state that I am 32 years of age and a citizen by -----, of the U. S. Nation; that I am the lawful wife of Peter Hamilton , who is a citizen, by blood of the Creek Nation; that a female child was born to me on 1 day of March , 1905 , that said child has been named Mahala Hamilton , and is now living.

Ellen Hamilton

Witnesses To Mark:
{

Subscribed and sworn to before me this 18 day of April , 1905.

Edw C Griesel
Notary Public.

AFFIDAVIT OF ATTENDING PHYSICIAN OR MID-WIFE.

UNITED STATES OF AMERICA, Indian Territory, }
Western   DISTRICT.

I, Nancy Murray , a Midwife , on oath state that I attended on Mrs. Ellen Hamilton , wife of Peter Hamilton on or about the 1 day of March , 1905 ; that there was born to her on said date a female child; that said child is now living and is said to have been named Mahala Hamilton

Nancy Murray

Witnesses To Mark:
{
Subscribed and sworn to before me this 18 day of April , 1905.

Edw C Griesel
Notary Public.

Muskogee, Indian Territory, June 22, 1906.

Ellen Hamilton,
  Bristow, Indian Territory.

Dear Madam:

In the matter of the application for the enrollment of your minor child, Mahala Hamilton, as a citizen of the Creek Nation, you are advised that it is required that you

Applications for Enrollment of Creek Newborn
Act of 1905   Volume IX

furnish this office with the affidavits of yourself and the midwife in attendance at its birth. For this purpose there is inclosed blank form of birth affidavit. Said affidavit should show the name of the child, the names of its parents, the date of its birth and whether or not it was living on March 4, 1906.

This matter should receive your prompt attention.

Respectfully,
BA
Commissioner.

N.C. 557[sic]

Muskogee, Indian Territory, October 18, 1905.

Peter Hamilton,
Bristow, Indian Territory.

Dear Sir:

In the matter of the application for the enrollment of Mary and Mahala Hamilton as citizens by blood of the Creek Nation, this office desires evidence of your marriage to Ellen Hamilton, the said mother of said children. Such evidence may consist of either the original or a certified copy of the marriage license and certificate.

It appears from the testimony now on file with this office that you[sic] said child, Mahala Hamilton, was born in the first part of March 1905.

You are requested to appear before this office with the mother of said Mahala Hamilton, the midwife in attendance at her birth and at least one other witness who knows the exact date and the exact time of the day or night in which said child was born.

You will be allowed twenty days from date within which to appear.

Respectfully,
Commissioner.

NC. 758.

Muskogee, Indian Territory, July 15, 1905.

Chief Clerk,
Cherokee Enrollment Division,
Muskogee, Indian Territory.

Applications for Enrollment of Creek Newborn
Act of 1905 Volume IX

Dear Sir:

April 11, 1905, application was made to the Commission to the Five Civilized Tribes for the enrollment of Cecil Raymond Carr born November 16, 1904, as a citizen by blood of the Creek Nation. It is stated in said application that the father of said child is William M. Carr, a citizen of the Creek Nation, and that the mother is Vida Carr, a citizen of the Cherokee Nation.

You are requested to inform the Creek Enrollment Division as to whether application has been made for the enrollment of said Cecil Raymond Carr as a citizen of the Cherokee Nation, and if so, what disposition has been made of the same.

Respectfully,

Commissioner.

REFER IN REPLY TO THE FOLLOWING:

DEPARTMENT OF THE INTERIOR,
COMMISSIONER TO THE FIVE CIVILIZED TRIBES.

Muskogee, Indian Territory, July 18, 1905.

Chief Clerk,
    Creek Enrollment Division,
        Muskogee, Indian Territory.

Dear Sir:

Replying to your letter of July 1, 1905, (NC. 758) asking to be advised whether or not any application has ever been made for the enrollment, as a citizen of the Cherokee Nation, of Cecil Raymond Carr, a child of William M. Carr, a citizen of the Creek Nation, and Vida Carr, a citizen of the Cherokee Nation, you are advised that from an examination of the records of the Cherokee Enrollment Division it does not appear that any application has ever been made for the enrollment of said child as a citizen of that nation.

Respectfully,

Tams Bixby Commissioner.

Applications for Enrollment of Creek Newborn
Act of 1905 Volume IX

CERTIFICATE OF RECORD.

United States of America
Indian Territory
Northern District   SS

I, Charles A. Davidson, Clerk of the United States Court in the Northern District, Indian Territory, do hereby certify that the instrument hereto attached was filed for record in my office the 6 day of December 1900 at --M and duly recorded in Book J. Marriage record, Page 410

         Witness my hand and seal of said Court at Muscogee[sic],
         in said Territory
                This 18 day of Mch A.D. 1901

                     Chas A Davidson Clerk

                     By   Deputy

I, Anna Garrigues, state on oath that the above and foregoing is a true and correct copy of the original.

                     Anna Garrigues

Subscribed and sworn to before me this 25 day of October 1905.

                     J. McDermott
                     Notary Public.

MARRIAGE LICENSE

United States of America,
    Indian Territory,   SS.   No. 1391
    Northern District.

To Any Person Authorized by Law to Solemnize Marriage-Greeting:
      You are hereby commanded to Solemnize the Rite and publish the Banns of Matrimony between Mr. William M. Carr of Checotah in the Indian Territory, aged 27 years, and Miss Vida Mulkey of Checotah in the Indian Territory, aged 19 years, according to law and do you officially sign and return this License to the parties therein named.
      Witness my hand and official seal at Muscogee[sic], Indian Territory, this 4" day of December, A. D. 1900

               (SEAL)   Chas A Davidson
                                         Clerk of the U.S. Court.
By P.M. Ford Deputy.

Applications for Enrollment of Creek Newborn
Act of 1905   Volume IX

CERTIFICATE OF MARRIAGE.

United States of America
Indian Territory   SS.
Northern District

I, Youngs Coleman, a Minister of the Gospel, Do Hereby Certify, that on the Fifth day of December A.D. 1900 I did duly and according to law as commanded in the foregoing License, solemnize the Rite and publish the Banns of Matrimony between the parties therein named.
Witness my hand this Fifth day of December A. D. 1900
My credentials are recorded in the office of the Clerk of the United States Court, Indian Territory, Central District Book A page 31

                              Youngs Coleman
                              A Minister of the Gospel

NC-758.

                        Muskogee, Indian Territory, October 18, 1905.

Vida Carr,
      c/o William Carr,
            Checotah, Indian Territory.

Dear Madam:

      In the matter of the application for the enrollment of your minor child, Cecil Raymond Carr, born November 16, 1904, as a citizen by blood of the Creek Nation, it will be necessary for you to furnish this office with evidence of your marriage to William Carr, the father of said child.

      Such evidence may consist of either the original or a certified copy of your marriage license.
                          Respectfully,
                                      Commissioner.

N.C. 758

                        Muskogee, Indian Territory, October 26, 1905.

William M. Carr,
      Checotah, Indian Territory.

Dear Sir:

Applications for Enrollment of Creek Newborn
Act of 1905   Volume IX

There is herewith returned to you, your marriage license and certificate, a copy of which has been made for the files of this office.

Respectfully,

Commissioner.

M-2

NC 758

Muskogee, Indian Territory, November 13, 1906

Chief Clerk,
    Cherokee Enrollment Division,
        General Office,

Dear Sir:

You are hereby advised that the name of Cecil Raymond Carr, born November 16, 1904 to William M. Carr, a citizen by blood of the Creek Nation and Vida Carr, an alleged citizen of the Cherokee Nation, is contained in schedule of minor citizens by blood of the Creek Nation, approved by the Secretary of the Interior, November 27, 1905, opposite Roll number 755.

Respectfully,

Commissioner.

BIRTH AFFIDAVIT.
DEPARTMENT OF THE INTERIOR.
COMMISSION TO THE FIVE CIVILIZED TRIBES.

IN RE APPLICATION FOR ENROLLMENT, as a citizen of the Creek Nation, of Cecil Raymond Carr, born on the 16 day of November, 1904

Name of Father: William M. Carr   a citizen of the   Creek   Nation.
Cussehta Town
Name of Mother: Vida Carr   a citizen of the   Cherokee   Nation.

                Postoffice   Checotah I.T.

Applications for Enrollment of Creek Newborn
Act of 1905 Volume IX

AFFIDAVIT OF MOTHER.

UNITED STATES OF AMERICA, Indian Territory, }
Western   DISTRICT.

I, Vida Carr, on oath state that I am 23 years of age and a citizen by Blood, of the Cherokee Nation; that I am the lawful wife of William M. Carr, who is a citizen, by blood of the Creek Nation; that a male child was born to me on 16th day of November, 1904, that said child has been named Cecil Raymond Carr, and was living March 4, 1905.

Vida Carr

Witnesses To Mark:
{

Subscribed and sworn to before me this 5th day of April, 1905.

J.B. Morrow
Notary Public.

My Commission Expires July 1, 1906.

AFFIDAVIT OF ATTENDING PHYSICIAN OR MID-WIFE.

UNITED STATES OF AMERICA, Indian Territory, }
Western   DISTRICT.

I, J. M. *(Illegible)*, a Physician, on oath state that I attended on Mrs. Vida Carr, wife of William M. Carr on the 16th day of November, 1904; that there was born to her on said date a male child; that said child was living March 4, 1905, and is said to have been named Cecil Raymond Carr

J. M. *(Illegible)* M.D.

Witnesses To Mark:
{

Subscribed and sworn to before me this 5th day of April, 1905.

J.B. Morrow
Notary Public.

My Commission Expires July 1, 1906.

Applications for Enrollment of Creek Newborn
Act of 1905   Volume IX

DEPARTMENT OF THE INTERIOR,
COMMISSION TO THE FIVE CIVILIZED TRIBES.
Muskogee, Ind. Ter., September 19, 1902.

SUPPLEMENTARY TESTIMONY In the matter of the application of Nar-wal-le-pe-se for the enrollment of herself, her three minor children, Mary, Walter and Willie Washington, and her three minor grandchildren, Harry, Sam and Annie Dougherty, as citizens, by blood. of the Creek Nation.

John B. Hosey, being first duly sworn, testified as follows:

Examination by the Commission:

Q What is your full name? A John B. Hosey.
Q What is your age? A Thirty-one years.
Q What is your post office address? A Stroud, Oklahoma.
Q Are you a citizen of the Creek Nation? A Yes, sir.
Q Have you been enrolled by this Commission as a citizen of the Creek Nation?
A Yes, sir

The records of the commission examined and it appears therefore that John B. Hosey is listed for enrollment, as a citizen of the Creek Nation, on Creek Indian Card, Field No. 778.

Q Are you acquainted with Thomas Washington? A Yes, sir.
Q Where does he reside? A He lives in the Creek Nation, within about a couple of miles of the old Hosey post office, which has been discontinues.
Q Is Thomas Washington a citizen of the Creek Nation? A No, sir; I couldn't say for sure, but they claim not.
Q Is he a Shawnee Indian? A Yes, sir; that is my understanding.
Q Do you know his wife? A Yes, sir; I know her when I see her.
Q What is her name? A Well, sir; I couldn't tell you. She can't speak a word of English--good enough to talk to me, anyway.
Q Do you know what she is called? A Solo, the Shawnee Indians call her--that is what her son told me, about a month ago.
Q Have you heard her called by any other name? A No, sir.
Q Did you ever hear her called Nar-wal-le-pe-se? A No, sir; never heard any one call her that.
Q How long has Solo been living with Thomas Washington? A I couldn't tell you.
Q How long has Thomas Washington and his wife lived near you? A Why, I moved near them; they were there when I went there about eight years ago.
Q You reside near the old Hosey post office? A Yes, sir; I live right there in the house.
Q Thomas Washington and his wife are near neighbors, then? A Yes, sir.
Q They have resided near you continuously ever since you have been living at Hosey?
A Yes, sir; they have been living there ever since I got acquainted with them.

Applications for Enrollment of Creek Newborn
Act of 1905 Volume IX

Q Did you ever hear of Thomas Washington having any other wife besides Solo? A I never heard any one speak of it--Well, I suppose so by the oldest children are married around are not his wife's that he is living with now; I suppose if he hadn't had another woman, he wouldn't have two sets of children.
Q Has his present wife, Solo, any children? A Yes, sir; it is my understanding. I have seen her carrying children around with her. It is my understanding.
Q How many children has Thomas Washington by Solo? A I couldn't say.

2 Supplemental Testimony In Re application for enrollment of Nar-wal-le-pe-se et al., as citizens by blood of the Creek Nation.

John B. Hosey, witness.

Examination by the Commission.

Q Do you know the name of any of the children? A No, sir; they are all small, it is my understanding.
Q Did you ever hear of Thomas Washington having any children by the name of Mary, Willie and Walter Washington? A Not only what I heard here. I have seen them carrying them around, that is all I know. I never did ask what their names are.
Q Well, has this woman Solo ever received an allotment in the Shawnee Country?
A That is my understanding; yes, sir.
Q How do you know that she has received a Shawnee allotment? A Just what the Indians told me, and the agent.
Q Do you know whether any of Thomas Washington's youngest children have received Shawnee allotments? A No, sir; I couldn't say. I never made no inquiry about it.
Q Can you positively identify this woman Sola, you speak of, as the same person who makes application for the enrollment of herself, and her three minor children, and her three minor grandchildren, under the name of Nar-wal-le-pe-se, as citizens of the Creek Nation? A I couldn't say--I never seen them come down here, but I know the woman who lives there, and stays there, is the one that takes allotment; of course, I wasn't here when they come down, and I couldn't say whether it is the same woman or not.
Q Did you say that the United States Indian Agent of the Sac and Fox agency, who was agent at the time allotments were made to Thomas Washington and Solo in the Shawnee country, informed you that Solo had received an allotment in that country? A Why, I don't remember who it was that was agent at that time, it has been several years ago and, of course, I wasn't living out in there at that time and I never made an inquiry.
Q Who told you that Solo had receive d an allotment? A Lee Patrick, was the agent's name; he---I believe, last winter, he resigned, I think.
Q Where does Lee Patrick live now? A He lives at Chandler, I think.
Q Well, who is the present agent of the Sac and Fox Agency? A I couldn't tell you. He told me, but I never put the name down, and I have forgotten it.
Q Would a letter reach him addressed to the United States Indian Agency, Sac and Fox Agency, Oklahoma Territory? A Yes, sir; he would get it that way.
Q Do you know who the United States Indian Agent is at Shawnee? A I have his name at home, but I never brought it with me, and I can't think of that.

Applications for Enrollment of Creek Newborn
Act of 1905 Volume IX

Q Can you secure a certificate from the United States Indian Agent, showing that Solo is the wife of Thomas Washington? A I suppose so, yes, sir; they are living together, and they don't claim anything else. That is what it says on the rolls, I know.

Q Are you quite positive that Solo, and Nar-wal-le-pe-se who has made application to the Commission for the enrollment of herslef[sic] and three minor children and three minor grandchildren, are one and the same person? A I couldn't say, but I am satisfied that is my understanding--well, I couldn't say that m understanding is this is his wife--Solo is Thomas Washington's wife; and it was my understanding it was Thomas Washington's wife came down were and applied for enrollment; I suppose it is the same one.

Q Do you know about how old Solo is? A It is hard telling about these Indians. Some look young and they claim to be old. I suppose somewhere along hear about forty or fifty--somewhere along there. Thomas Washington is grayheaded. He is a good bit older. I don't think she is turning gray yet.

3 Supplemental Testimony In Re application for the enrollment of Nar-wal-le-pe-se et al. as citizens by blood of the Creek Nation.

John B. Hosey, witness.

Examination by the Commission.

Q Are there any other women living with Thomas Washington? A His daughter, Martin Dougherty's wife, a son-in-law, and Willie Mark, living with one of Thomas Washington's girls--they are all living there together, son-in-laws and grown children.
Q Will you endeavor to secure the certificates from the United States Indian Agent, herein referred to, and forward the same to the Commission here? A Yes, sir.
Q You stated that Thomas Washington had two sets of children? A That is my understanding. The oldest ones were married. I don't think that is his wife's children who is living with him now. It is my understanding that he has two sets of children. I suppose she died before that had taken allotments over there, because Solo[sic], because Solo taken allotment with him over there, because I examined the rolls--the agent and me--to look after that thing.
Q Is this Solo the mother of Thomas Washington's youngest children? A I think so, but I couldn't say about that, but these oldest ones, it is my understanding, they told me they were Thomas Washington's grown children, but when I went over there, I think the agent told me they were on the rolls there as his children.

The undersigned, being first duly sworn, upon his oath states, that, as stenographer for the Commission to the Five Civilized Tribes, he reported all the proceedings had in the above entitled cause, on the 19th day of September, 1902, and that the above and foregoing is a full, true and correct transcript of his stenographic notes of said proceedings had on said date.

                                  Oliver C. Hinkle

Applications for Enrollment of Creek Newborn
Act of 1905   Volume IX

Subscribed and sworn to before me this 30 day of September, 1902, at Muskogee, Indian Territory.

                                W.S. Boren
                                Notary Public.

BIRTH AFFIDAVIT.

See En 2112 for grandmother

DEPARTMENT OF THE INTERIOR.
COMMISSION TO THE FIVE CIVILIZED TRIBES.

IN RE APPLICATION FOR ENROLLMENT, as a citizen of the Creek Nation, of Arthur Rollette, born on the 21 day of May, 1904

Name of Father: Wm Rollette   a citizen of the   Shawnee   Nation.

Name of Mother: Hattie " (nee Washington) a citizen of the ~~Creek~~ Shawnee Nation.
Fok paf key
                       Postoffice   Sac & Fox Agency, O.T.

                    AFFIDAVIT OF MOTHER.   (Child Present)

UNITED STATES OF AMERICA, Indian Territory, ⎫
    Western   DISTRICT.   ⎭

    I, Hattie Rollette (Washington), on oath state that I am 27 years of age and a citizen by blood, of the Shawnee Nation; that I am the lawful wife of William Rollette, who is a citizen, by blood of the Shawnee Nation; that a male child was born to me on 21 day of May, 1904, that said child has been named Arthur Rollette, and is now living.
                                        her
                              Hattie x Rollette
Witnesses To Mark: mark
  ⎰ EC Griesel
  ⎱ Jesse McDermott

    Subscribed and sworn to before me this 17" day of April, 1905.

       (Seal)   J McDermott
                                   Notary Public.

Applications for Enrollment of Creek Newborn
Act of 1905   Volume IX

AFFIDAVIT OF ATTENDING PHYSICIAN OR MID-WIFE.

UNITED STATES OF AMERICA, Indian Territory, }
Western DISTRICT.

I, Nar-wal-la-pe-se , a midwife , on oath state that I attended on Mrs. Hattie Rollette (nee Washington), wife of Wm Rollette on the 21 day of May , 1904 ; that there was born to her on said date a male child; that said child is now living and is said to have been named Arthur Rollette

                          her
                          x Nar-wal-la-pe-se

Witnesses To Mark: mark
{ EC Griesel
{ Jesse McDermott

Subscribed and sworn to before me this 17" day of April, 1905.

                          J. McDermott
                          Notary Public.

N.C. 759.   EK.
DEPARTMENT OF THE INTERIOR,
COMMISSIONER TO THE FIVE CIVILIZED TRIBES.

In the matter of the application for the enrollment of Arthur Rollette, as a citizen by blood of the Creek Nation.

STATEMENT AND ORDER.

The record in this case shows that on April 20, 1905, application was filed, in affidavit form, for the enrollment of Arthur Rollette as a citizen by blood of the Creek Nation.

It appears from the evidence that Arthur Rollette is the child of William and Hattie Rollette, citizens by blood of the Shawnee Nation.

Inasmuch as, the records of this office fail to show that either of the parents of the said Arthur Rollette are duly enrolled citizens of the Creek Nation, and there is no application pending for their enrollment as such, there is no authority of law for the enrollment of said applicant as a citizen of the Creek Nation.

It is, therefore, ordered that the said application for the enrollment of Arthur Rollette, as a citizen by blood of the Creek Nation, be, and the same is hereby dismissed.

                        Tams Bixby COMMISSIONER.
Muskogee, Indian Territory.
JAN 26 1907

Applications for Enrollment of Creek Newborn
Act of 1905   Volume IX

HGH

REFER IN REPLY TO THE FOLLOWING:

NC 759.

DEPARTMENT OF THE INTERIOR,
COMMISSIONER TO THE FIVE CIVILIZED TRIBES.

Muskogee, Indian Territory, January 29, 1907.

Hattie Rollette,
   c/o William Rollette,
      Sac and Fox Agency,
         Oklahoma Territory.

Dear Madam:

    There is herewith enclosed one copy of the statement and order of the Commissioner to the Five Civilized Tribes, dated January 26, 1907, dismissing the application made by you for the enrollment of your minor child, Arthur Rollette, as a citizen of the Creek Nation.

                              Respectfully,
                                Tams Bixby   Commissioner.

Register.
LM-759.

NC-760.

Muskogee, Indian Territory, October 18, 1905.

Sally Tahlosa (or Tarloshaw),
   Eufaula, Indian Territory.

Dear Madam:

    In the matter of the application for the enrollment of your minor child, Louisa Tahlosa this office is unable to identify you upon the final roll of citizens by blood of the Creek Nation. It is necessary that you be so identified before the rights of Louisa Tahlosa can be finally determined.

    You are, therefore, requested to advise this office as to your maiden name, the names of your parents, the Creek Indian Town to which you belong and your roll number as the same appears on your allotment certificate and deeds.

    Tahlosa, whom you state is the father of said Louisa Tahlosa, has been identified upon the final roll of citizens by blood of the Creek Nation as Tarloshaw. If

Applications for Enrollment of Creek Newborn
Act of 1905 Volume IX

you lawfully married to Tarloshaw your surname and the surname of your child Louisa must necessarily be Tarloshaw.

For the purpose of correcting the above discrepancy there is inclosed herewith an affidavit which has been properly filled out. You are requested to have the same executed and when executed to return it to this office in the inclosed envelope.

       Respectfully,

CTD-6.   Commissioner.
Env.

N C 760   JWH

      Muskogee, Indian Territory, March 1, 1907.

Sally Tar-lo-shaw,
 % Tar-lo-shaw,
   Raiford, Indian Territory.

Dear Madam :--

  You are hereby advised that on February 15, 1907, the Secretary of the Interior approved the enrollment of your minor child, Louisa Tar-lo-shaw, as a citizen by blood of the Creek Nation, and that the name of said child appears upon the roll of New Born citizens by blood of the Creek Nation, enrolled under the Act of Congress approved March 3, 1905; as number 1168.

  This child is now entitled to allotment and application therefor should be made without delay at the Creek Land Office, Muskogee, Indian Territory.

       Respectfully,

            Commissioner.

N.C. 446.

    DEPARTMENT OF THE INTERIOR,
  COMMISSIONER TO THE FIVE CIVILIZED TRIBES,
     RAIFORD, I. T., August 27, 1906.

  In the matter of the application for the enrollment of an unnamed child of Tarlossa or Spana Harjo, and Sallie Harjo, as a citizen by blood of the Creek Nation.

Applications for Enrollment of Creek Newborn
Act of 1905 Volume IX

SALLIE HARJO being duly sworn testified as follows:

Through Alex Posey Official Interpreter.

BY THE COMMISSIONER:

Q What is your name? A Sallie ~~Harjo~~. Tarlossa
Q How old are you? A I do not know my age. (Witness appears to be about 22 years old).
Q What is your postoffice address? A Raiford.
Q Are you a citizen of the Creek Nation? A Yes sir.
Q To what Creek town do you belong? A Okfuske Canadian.
Q We have information that you have a minor child for which you have not made application. Have you such child? A Yes sir.
Q What is the child's name? A Mista.
Q Is the child a boy or girl? A A boy.
Q When was the child born? A I do not know but I have a record showing the date of its birth.

The witness presents a piece of paper on which appears the following record written in Creek.
"The child was born December 12, 1905".

Q Who made this record? A My husband.
Q When did he make the record? A At the time the child was born.
Q Who is your husband? A Tarlossa.
Q Is he sometimes known as Spana Harjo? A Yes sir, but his real name is Tarlossa.
Q To what Creek town does he belong? A Tallahassoche.
Q Is he your lawful husband? A Yes sir, we procured a license and was married by Luke McIntosh. We turned the license over to Luke McIntosh and I do not know whatever became of it.
Q What was hour[sic] name before you were married to Tarlossa? A Sallie Fixico.
Q Who were your parents? A Nocus Fixico was my father, I do not know my mother. She died while I was a baby.
Q Under what name are you enrolled? A I am enrolled as Sallie Fixico.
Q Have you any other children by Tarlossa? A I have one other child, Louisa.
Q Is Louisa enrolled? A Yes sir.

Witness is advised that this office requires either the original or certified copy of her marriage license.

James B. Myers, being first duly sworn, states, that as stenographer to the Commissioner to the Five Civilized Tribes, he recorded the testimony in the foregoing proceedings, and that the above is a true, and coreect[sic] transcript of his stenographic notes thereof.

Applications for Enrollment of Creek Newborn
Act of 1905 Volume IX

James B. Myers

Subscribed and sworn to before me this 30 day of August, 1906.

Alex Posey
Notary Public.

JBM

N.C. 760.

F.H.W.

DEPARTMENT OF THE INTERIOR,
COMMISSIONER TO THE FIVE CIVILIZED TRIBES.

In the matter of the application for the enrollment of Louisa Tarloshaw as a citizen by blood of the Creek Nation.

DECISION.

The record in this case shows that on April 6, 1905, application was made, in affidavit form, for the enrollment of Louisa Tarloshaw, under the provisions of the act of Congress approved March 3, 1905 (33 Stats., 1048). A copy of testimony taken August 27, 1906, in the matter of the application for the enrollment of an unnamed child of Tarloshaw, or Spana Harjo, and Sallie Harjo as a citizen by blood of the Creek Nation, is made a part of the record herein.

The evidence shows that Louisa Tarloshaw is the child of Tarloshaw and Sallie Tarloshaw, nee Fixico, whose names appear on a schedule of citizens by blood of the Creek Nation approved by the Secretary of the Interior March 28, 1902, opposite Nos. 7952 and 8741 respectively.

It is in evidence that the surname of said child is variously spelled, to-wit: Tahlosa, Tarlosa etc. but inasmuch as the name of the father of the applicant appears on the approved roll as Tarloshaw, the said child Louisa will hereafter in the consideration of this case be known as Louisa Tarloshaw.

The evidence further shows that she was born March 23, 1903, and was living on April 6, 1905.

The Act of Congress approved March 3, 1905, (33 State., 1048), provides in part as follows:

"That the Commission to the Five Civilized Tribes is authorized for sixty days after the date of the approval of this act to receive and consider applications for enrollment, of children, born subsequent to May twenty-fifth, nineteen hundred and one, and prior to March fourth, nineteen hundred and five, and living on said latter date, to citizens of the Creek tribe of Indians whose enrollment has been approved by the Secretary of the Interior prior to the approval of this act; and to enroll and make allotments to such children."

Applications for Enrollment of Creek Newborn
Act of 1905   Volume IX

It is, therefore, ordered and adjudged that said Louisa Tarloshaw is entitled to be enrolled as a citizen by blood of the Creek Nation, in accordance with the provisions of law above quoted, and the application for her enrollment as such is accordingly granted.

Muskogee, Indian Territory,
JAN 7 1907

Tams Bixby   COMMISSIONER.

BIRTH AFFIDAVIT.

DEPARTMENT OF THE INTERIOR.
COMMISSION TO THE FIVE CIVILIZED TRIBES.

IN RE APPLICATION FOR ENROLLMENT, as a citizen of the Creek Nation, of Louisa Tahlosa, born on the 23 day of March, 1903

Name of Father: Tahlosa (Tarlosa)   a citizen of the   Creek   Nation.
Tallahassoche Town
Name of Mother: Sally Tahlosa   a citizen of the   Creek   Nation.
Okfusky[sic] Canadian Town

Postoffice   Eufaula, Ind. Ter.

AFFIDAVIT OF MOTHER.

UNITED STATES OF AMERICA, Indian Territory, }   Child is present
   Western   DISTRICT.

I, Sally Tahlosa, on oath state that I am 25 years of age and a citizen by blood, of the Creek Nation; that I am the lawful wife of Tahlosa, who is a citizen, by blood of the Creek Nation; that a female child was born to me on 23 day of March, 1903, that said child has been named Louisa Tahlosa, and was living March 4, 1905.

            her
         Sally x Tahlosa
Witnesses To Mark: mark
{ Alex Posey
  DC Skaggs

Subscribed and sworn to before me this 6 day of April, 1905.

        Drennan C Skaggs
        Notary Public.

Applications for Enrollment of Creek Newborn
Act of 1905 Volume IX

AFFIDAVIT OF ATTENDING PHYSICIAN OR MID-WIFE.

UNITED STATES OF AMERICA, Indian Territory,
Western DISTRICT.

I, Nachunka Chisholm , a midwife , on oath state that I attended on Mrs. Sally Tahlosa , wife of Tahlosa on the 23 day of March , 1903 ; that there was born to her on said date a female child; that said child was living March 4, 1905, and is said to have been named Louisa Tahlosa

Witnesses To Mark:
    Alex Posey
    DC Skaggs

                    her
         Nachunka x Chisholm
                   mark

Subscribed and sworn to before me 6 day of April, 1905.

                    Drennan C Skaggs
                    Notary Public.

Index

ADAMS
  Anna 169,187
  Annie 171,177,179,188,189
  G Washington 24
  George W 23
  Lewis 167,168,172,177,178,179,
  180,181,187,188,189
  Sarah 23
  Sarrah 24
  Theodore 23,24
AMERSON
  J M 239
ANSELL
  Roxie 50
  Samuel E 50
ANSIEL
  Arnecie 196
  Henry F 51,52
  John 56
  John G 55,57,58
  Lula 55,57,58
  Necie 192
  Roxie 51,52
  Sam 51,52
  Samuel E O 55,57,58
ANSILL
  Henry F 50,51
  Roxie 50
  Samuel E 50,51
ARBUCKLE
  Harriett E 107,289
ARNETT
  Mrs Albert W 146
ATKINSON
  America 53,54

BACKBUN
  Arnecie 191,192,193,196
  Cal 189,190,194,195,196
  Calvin 191,192,193
  Ella May 195
  Etta May 189,190,191,192,193,196
  Lecie 196
  Necie 192,195
  Neecie 189,190
BACKMAN 196
  Cal 192

  Etta May 192
  Necie 192
BAILEY
  E G 215
BALLARD
  Perry A 220,222
BARNES
  Nora 201
BARNETT
  Adline 259
  Anston 258
  Billy 119
  Elizabeth 277
  Harley 167
  Harlie 174,184
  Lizzie 258
BARR
  D M 222
BAYNE
  R A 95,201
BEALL
  Wm O 34,48,152,258
BEAR
  Annie 209,210,211,212
  Lewis 208,209,210,211,212
  Turner 208,209,210,211,212
BEDFORD
  Edwin G 97
BEHEN
  Juda 246
BELCHER
  Tobe 298
BENSE
  J H 245
BENSON
  Dave 283
  Hattie 283
  Lena 283
  Willie 283
BENTLEY
  W S 222
BERRYHILL
  Josephine 4,265
BEWLEY
  Elizabeth 29
BIG MOSKETER 19
BIG MOSQUITO 17,18,20

Index

Jennie 17,18,20
Jensey 17,18,20
BIXBY
  Tams 2,26,28,33,49,61,76,83,101,
  115,140,145,149,164,165,174,176,194,
  253,261,266,280,296,302,313,322,
  323,327
BLACKBUN
  Cal 194
  Etta May 194
  Necie 194
BLAKEMAN
  J L 122
BOONE
  Josie 214
BOREN
  W S 321
BOUDINOT
  Harold E 277
BOYD
  A Lee 96
BRASHAR
  Maude 288
BRASHEARS
  Maud 287
BREESE
  Harry E 234
BREMER
  J M 63
BRIGHTMAN 243,244
  Earl 242
  Fannie 242,243
  Fanny 243,244
  Leyman 243,244
  Leyman B 243
  Lyeman 242
BRINK
  Lizzie 267,268,269,270,271,272
  Lusanna 267,268,269
  Lusanna D 270
  Susanna 272
  Susanna D 272
  Susannah 271
  William 269,270,272
  Willie 267,268,269
BROWN
  Alex 197

Conthlany 246
Dave 197
Dixon 269,270
Earl 24
Lucy 246
Maria 197
Mariah 197
BROWNLEE
  B B 283
  Hattie 282,284,285
BUCK
  William 279
BUFORD
  Charles 144,146,147,241,242
  Chas 146
BULLETT
  Bailey 61,62,63,64,65
  Millie 62,63,64,65
  Solomon 61,62,63,64,65
BURGESS
  Nora 13,14,15
BURNETT
  E H 220,221,222
  Joseph L 220,221,222
  Vinita 220,221,222
CAIN
  W A 36,37,38,39
CAMPBELL
  J B 158
CANARD
  Roman 227
  Washington 227,228
CARLOS
  C C Dan 18
CARR
  Cecil Raymond 313,315,316
  Cecil Raymond Carr 317
  Vida 313,315,316,317
  William 315
  William M 313,314,315,316,317
CARTER
  Annie 304
CASEY
  Alvro Edgar 38,39
  Eli 36
  John 36,37,38,39

330

Index

Savanah 36,37,38,39
Savannah 36
Vera Irene 37,38
CHAMBLEN
   Sarah 168,169,170,177,179,180,
   182,183,184,186
CHANDLER
   T A 224
CHAPMAN
   Clarina 304
CHAPPELL
   Walter W 288
CHARLESEY 137,138,139,140,141
   Ellen 136,137,138,139,140
   Flora 136,137,139,140,141
   Martha 136,137,138,139,141
CHISHOLM
   Nachunka 328
CHISSOE
   Lena 205,206,207
   Lena E 204
   Pleas 202
   Please E 205
   Please S 204
   Sam 202,203,205,206,207
   Sam, Jr 203,206,207
   Samuel W 204
CHURCHILL
   Avery 296,297
   Ethel May 296,297
   Maude M 296,297
CINDA 249
CLARK
   Alex 39,40,41,43,44
   George 39,40,41,43,44
   Louisa 39,40,41,43,44
CLARKE
   Alex 42
   George 42
   Louisa 42
CLAWSON
   (Illegible) D 132
CLOUD
   Laslie 272
COACHMAN
   Chas 280
COLBERT

Ella 107,109,110
Ellen 106,107,108,110,111
Kizzie 106,107,108,109,110,111
Thompson 107,108,109,110,111
COLEMAN
   Youngs 315
COLLINS
   Lewis 90
   Lou 227
COMSTOCK 169
   Fred 168,170,184,186,187
   George 168
COODEY
   Levena 102,104,105,106
   Luvena 101
   W M S 105
   W S 103
   Walter Lee 101,102,104,105,106
   William S 102,104,106
   Wm S 101
COODY
   Levena 104
COREY
   Cordelia 212,215,216
   Drank 213
   Frank 212,213,214,215,216,217
   Josie 213,214,215,216,217
   Jossie 215
   Tom 212,213,214,215,217
COUNTERMAN
   Dr R M 22
   R M 97,244,291
   R M, MD 22,244,291
CRITES
   Allye 95
CROW
   George 25,27
   Melissa 27,28
   Tommie 25
   Tommy 27,28
CULLER
   Tom 130,131
CULLY
   Bessie 138,140,141
CUMSEY
   Lewis 245,246

Index

DANIEL
  Lusanna 267,268
  Susannah................................... 271
DARLING
  A M 304
DAVIDSON
  Charles A 55,314
  Chas A 56,102,103,224,288,314
DAVIS
  Bettie 79
  J W 13,14
  Mack.................................... 258,259
  Millie C 258,259
  Nancy 11
  Nancy W 13,14,16
  Nora...................................... 13,14
  R D 258
  Redmond C...................... 258,259
  Sam'l C 98
  Saml C 99
DEER
  Lewis 208
  Sarfarcher 45
DEERE
  Lawyer..................................... 125
DERISAW
  Maggie.................................... 171
DONALDSON
  R M.. 287
DOUGHERTY
  Annie 318
  Harry....................................... 318
  Martin 320
  Sam 318
DOUGLASS
  Clarence........................... 305,306
DRAKE
  E L 246,247
DREW
  Clifton C 20,21
  Emma 20,21
  Moses Warrener..................... 20
  Moses Warrner 21
DUCKWORTH
  Robert D 99,100
  Ruth E.................................. 99,100
  Vera Oma 99,100

DUNN
  Tupper 46
DUNZY
  J R 300,301
EATON & HINNEN 234
ELDER
  Robert... 7
ENGLISH
  A Z 239
ESKRIDGE
  C C 63,64
EVANS
  Lettie 36,37,38
  Lillie 39
FACTOR
  Fanny...................................... 153
  Joe 153
  Youthlechee........................... 153
FANNING
  Bob........................... 12,13,15,16,17
  Nancy 11,16
  Nancy W.................... 12,13,15,16,17
  Nora................. 11,12,13,14,15,16,17
FAUBION
  Cecil 222
FISH
  Nicey 32,33
FIXICO 45,49
  Bassta 49
  Basta.................................. 44,45
  Bastie............................. 45,47,48
  Fannie.................................... 150
  Fanny........ 151,152,153,154,155,156
  Jeffy........... 150,151,152,153,154,155
  Jemima 45,47,48,49
  Jemmima 47
  Nocus 325
  Rhoda 133,134,135
  Roley 44,45,47,48,49
  Tarlossa................................. 325
  Watty 150,151,152,154,155,156
  Winey 150,151,152,153,155,156
FLYNN
  T W 19,20,272
FORD

Index

? M 56
P M 288,314
FOSTER
  Betsey 81
  George W 233,234
  Lee 272
  Mary E 232,233,234
  Mary Josephine.............. 232,233,234
  Sukey 81
FOX
  Arther 247
FRANCIS
  William 298
  Wm 298
FULSOM
  Ladee 244,245,246,247
  Lucy 244,245,246,247
  Robert 244,245,247

GARRIGUES
  Anna 201,240,308,314
GAYLOR
  Lavina 103
GEBSOY
  J S 231
GIBSON
  Charley 286,287
  Modenia..... 286,287,289,290,291,292
GILLIS
  Elizabeth 221
GILLISS
  Elizabeth 222
GIVENS
  Annie 78,79
  Harper 78,79
  Kizzie 27,28,31
  William 78,79
GOAT
  Alfred 116,117,118
  Alice Sukey 116
  Angeline 117,118
  Eddielinie 83,84
  A G 160,161,162
  John K 160,161,162
  Minnie 83,84,116,118
  Racheal 116,117,118
  Wadley 83,84

GORDEN
  Vinita 220
GORDON
  G R 143
  George R 143
  Vinita 221
GOVEY
  Mrs R M 7
  R M 7
GRACE
  R C 103
GRAYSON
  Alice ... 144,145,146,147,148,149,150
  Allice 146
  Clearance 149
  Joe 146
  Joseph 144,147
  Judy 197
  Louisa 111,113
  Mamie 144,145,147,148,149,150
  Mr and Mrs 146
  Vinnie Ree 149
  Winey 112,113,114,115
GREEN
  Leah 218,219,220
GREENWOOD
  Dick 70,71,73,75
  Effie Belle 118,119,120,121
  Jennie 118,119,120,121
  Lewis 72,73,118,119,120,121
GRIEEL
  Edw C 255
GRIESEL
  E C 245,305,321,322
  Edw C 5,13,15,23,41,66,80,89,123,
  127,137,157,167,203,240,245,268,269,
  305,309,311
GUINN
  Lewis 41,42

HAINES
  Sam 248
HAINS
  H G 255
  Henry G .. 47,51,207,208,256,286,310
HALEPY
  Cooper 33

Index

HALLFORD
  Ida 142
HAMILLON
  E231
HAMILTON
  Alec 307
  Ellan 308,310
  Ellen 307,308,309,310,311
  Mahala 305,306,307,308,309, 310,311,312
  Mary 306,307,308,309,312
  Peter 305,306,307,309,310,311,312
  S H 78
  S H, MD 78
HANCOCK
  C A 228,229,230
  Hattie 227,228,229,230,231
  Hattie L 228
  Lizzie 227,228,229,230,231
HANDCOCK
  Lizzie 229
HANDLEY
  Dave 231
  Mary E 230
  Mrs 231
HANNAH 72
HARDAGE
  Nancy R 100
  Ruth E 99
HARJO 45
  Albert 63
  Alfred 135,136
  Bassta 45,46,48
  Basta 48
  Bastie 47,48
  Hattie 63
  Jemima 47,48
  Jemmima 45,46
  Lila 128,129,130,131
  Lilla 131,132
  Lily 124,125,127,133,134,135,136
  Linda 132
  Lindy 125,126,133,134,135,136
  Malinda 159,160
  Melinda 162,163
  Nancy 134,135
  Rhoda 124,125,127,129,130,131, 132,133,134,135,136
  Roley 45,46,48
  Sallie 324,325,326
  Sandy 128,129,130
  Spana 324,325,326
  Sunday 132
  Tharlip 45
  Winey 124,125,127,128,129,130, 131,132,133
  Wisey 158,162
HARLAN
  John 223
HARRISON
  R P 95,200,201,223,239,240
  Robert P 95,200,239
HARTRIDGE
  Lizie 258
HASKELL
  (Illegible), Jr 244
HAWKINS
  Lizzie 302
  Lucinda 303
HAYNES
  Alice 197
  Sam E 197
HENDERSON
  James 230,231
HENDLEY
  Mamie 228
HICKORY
  Jennie 98,99
  Louina 98,99
  Thomas 98,99
HILL
  Richard J 182,183,184,188
HINKLE
  Oliver C 205,320
HINTON
  J D 142,143
HOLLUBY
  Cooper 35
HOLMES
  C W 278
HOLOBY
  Cooper 31,32
HOSEY
  John B 318,319,320

Index

HOWELL
　Lizzie 302,303
　Samuel Webster 302,303
　Tollie H 302,303
HUGHES
　E B 267,269,270,271
HUNTER
　R O 103

IRETON
　John 231

JACK
　Alice 28,29
　Amy Amanda 28
　John 29
　Mandy Amy 29
JACOBS
　Frank 153
JANWAY
　Preston 303
JEFFERSON
　Moses 12
　Nancy 11
　Nancy W 16
JIMPSEY 73
　Hannah 73
JIMSEY
　Millie 74
JOHNSON
　Rev P 224
JONES
　Annie 209,210,211
　Goliah 300,301
　Jemima 45,47
　Sallie 45
　Washington 45

KA-KO-CON-NEY 267,268,269
KEATON
　Harwood 221,222
KELSEY
　TDanna H 293
KENNEDY
　J L 99
KNOLL
　Dora 307

Sallie 307

LARBAREGH
　Eunice May 224
LAWE
　Canuggee 126
LAWSON
　W A 41
　W H 42
LEADER
　Nancy 301
LEONARD
　B V 142,143,144
LEVERETT
　Bessie 273,274,275
　Kogee 273,274,275
　Walter 274,275
LEVITT
　Bessie 273,274
　Cogee 273,274
　Walter 273,274
LEWALLEN
　Charlie 113,114,115
　John 111,112,113,114
　Louisa 111,112,113
　Lucy 111,112
LEWIS
　Daniel 297,298,299
　Effie 303,304
　Emma 303,304
　Harley 303,304
　Mattie 297,298,299
　Pollie 298,299
　Polly 299
LINDSEY
　Mabel 66,69
LITTLEHEAD
　Willie 269,270,271
LIZZIE 250
LONEY
　James 90
　Jimmie 85,87
　Rachael 86,88,89
　Sam 85,86,87,88,89,90,91
LOWE
　Canuggee 126
　Conuccee 125

Index

LUCAS
  J B 241
LYNCH
  Bob 12
  Robert E 8,9,10,11,14,29,30,98,99

MAGGIE 169
MALLEY
  W F 259
  W R 260
MALOT
  H G 46
MANAHWE
  Cinda 247,253,254
  Ella 247,248,253,254
  John 248,253,254
MANAHWEE
  Cindy 256
  Ella 251,256
  John 251,256
MANLEY
  Arthur 70,71,72,73,74,75
  Martha 220
  Mary 73
  Millie 70,71,72,74,75
  Thomas 70,71,72,73,74
MANN
  Mr 306
MARK
  Willie 320
MARRISON
  Lena 92
MARSHALL
  Alice 146,149
  Arthur 149
  Delphine 146
  Nettie 149
  Nora 149
  T B 149
  Tip 146,149
MARTIN
  Henry 213
  Stebbin 157,158,159,162,163,164
  Stebbin M 157
  Stebin 158
  William T 204,205
  Wm T 205

MARY 73
MATOY
  Anna 287,291
  Annie .. 286,287,289,290,291,292,293
  Charles 286,287,291,293
  Charley 286,289,290,291,292,293
  Chas 288
  John 286
  Martha 286
  Maud 286,287,289,290,292
  Maude 291
MCCALVEY
  Emmit 198,199,200
  Everett 198,199,200,201
  Nora 198,199,200
MCCOMBS
  Jimmie 86,88,89,91
  Joe 85,86,89,91
  Lena 92,93,94
  Mary 273,274,275
  Millie 94
  Sarah 108
  Wm 108
MCCOY
  Delphie 276,277
MCDANIEL
  Henry A 90,91
  Henry L 274,275
MCDERMOTT
  J 1,16,25,31,45,47,71,73,85,93,
  107,109,151,190,201,205,206 211,219,
  229,248,250,252,264,308,314,321,
  322
  Jesse .. 5,12,31,39,44,47,106,169,268,
  269,321,322
MCELVAIN
  B F 201,202
MCGEE
  R C 56
MCGILBRA
  Annie 78
  Lewis 218,219,220
  Nicey 35
  Sanford 218,219,220
MCGILBRAY
  George 30,31,32,33,238
  Jackson 30,31,32,33,34,35

336

Index

Laura 238
Nicey 30,31,32,33,34,35
MCGILBRY
  George 238,240,241,242
  George L 238,240,241,242
  Laura 240,241,242
MCGIRT
  Bettie 300
  Hepsey 67,69
  Minnie 300,301,302
MCINTOSH
  Dve 119
  Henry 119
  Hepsey 119,121
  Jennie 120
  L G 197,198
  Leah 119
  Lizzie 119
  Luke 325
  Susan D 203,204
MCNULTY
  Maude M 296
MEELIE
  Mary 72
MERRICK
  Edward 170,172
MILLER
  J Y 41,45,73,158,167,250
  Lillie 84
MILLS
  B H 279,280
MINUGH
  Alice V 121,122
  C E 122
  Clarence E 121
  Jesse L 121,122
  Jesse Lee 122
  Mrs Elmer 122
MISTA 325
MONAHWEE 250
  Cinda 251,254,255
  Cynda 249,250,252
  Ella 249,251,252,253,254,255, 256,157
  John 249,251,252,254,255,256,257
  John David 249
  Milley 249

MONTGOMERY
  A B 297
  J 298
MOONEY
  Bernard B 277
MOORE
  Cora 172,173,287
  I V 211
  T E 211
MOREY
  Callie D 234
  William 234
MORGAN
  Ed 170
MORRIS
  F B 213,214,215
MORRISON
  Ernest 53,54
  Hence 52,53,54
  Hettie Jane 52,53
  John, Jr 92
  Lena 92,93,94
  Louisa 274,275
  Nancy 52,53,54
MORROW
  J B 241,296,297,317
MORTON
  Joseph C 78
MOSS
  F L 98,104
MULKEY
  Vida 314
MURRAY 190
  Nancy 307,309,311
MYERS
  James B 325,326

NAR-WAL-LA-PE-SE 322
NAR-WAL-LE-PE-SE 318,319,320
NUBBIE
  Geo 180
  Geo, Jr 177,178
  Geo W 178,179
  Geo W, Sr 178
  Geoge W 183
  George 168,169,170,171,172,173, 174,181,182,183,184,186,188

Index

George, Jr 166,167,168,169,170, 172,176,177,178,180,182,183,184,186, 188
George, Sr............................ 168,179
George W 166,173,174,175,176, 177,178,180,181,182,184,185,186,188, 189
Harley Barnett 189
Harlie............... 174,175,180,184,185
Mrs 180
Robert............... 166,167,184,185,189
Robert N 166
Sophia.......166,167,168,169,170,171, 172,173,177,181,182,183,184,186,187
Sophie.................................... 179,188
Willie... 167
Willie E 166,167,174,175,176,180

NUBBY
George, Jr 176
George W 176
Robert... 176
Sophia... 176

NUGGIE
Geo, Jr 179

OSA WAH
George 28

OSAWAH
George 25
Melissa 25
Tommie 25
Tommy 27

OSOWAH
George 26
Melissa 26
Tommy 26

OVERSTREET
John W.. 18

OWAWAH
George 27
Melissa 27

OWEN
Thos H 122

PARRISH
Zera E 305
Zera Ellen 203

PATRICK
Lee.. 319

PAYTON
Blanche Williams 294,295
Clara 294,295,296
L C 294,295

PEACOCK
J L... 239

PEARSON
M E... 21
Mary E... 21

PERRYMAN
Ben 170

PHILLIPS
Betsey... 43
Betsy.........................39,40,41,44
F B 90,91
Louisa 42

PIKE
James B 44

PITTMAN
Lewis 303

PITTS
Drannan 143
Emma 141,142,143
Frank Fields................ 141,142,143
Russell H 141,142

POLK
Cinda 235
Daniel 236
Daniel W 235,237
Ethel 235,236,237
Katie 235,236,237
Lucinda 237

PORTER
Geo M 237,238

POSEY 287
Alex.......27,28,30,31,32,33,42,43,53, 54,60,64,65,66,67,69,70,71,73,74,79, 81,82,85,86,87,88,92,94,111,112,114, 115,116,117,119,120,121,124,125,126, 127,128,130,131,133,134,135,136, 150,154,155,156,157,159,163,174,185, 191,210,211,212,218,219,220,236, 251,255,256,263,325,326,327,328
G A 144
Lily 126

338

Index

Mr 158,286
  Rhoda 126
  Winey 126
POTTER
  Lulu 56

RAIFORD
  Arthur E 110
REED
  Johnson 130
RENEAU
  Walter J 8
REYNOLDS
  Delphie 276,278
  Earnest 275,276
  Ernest 276,277,278
  Joe 275
  Joseph 277,278
  Joseph A 276
  Mrs Joseph 277
RIDER
  Chas 153,154,160,161,162
ROBERTSON
  Andrew Jackson 282,283,284,285
  I W 282,283,284,285
  Lillie 282,283
  Lilly 283,284,285
ROBINSON
  Maysie A 123,124
  Myrtice A 123,124
  Will R 123,124
ROLLETTE
  Arthur 321,322,323
  Hattie 321,322,323
  William 321,323
  Wm 321,322
RUNNELLE
  Ada 190
RUNNELS
  Ada 190
RUSHING
  Frank W 23,109,110,213,214, 217,291,293
RUSSELL
  A J 232
  Maude 233
SANGER

Fannie 242
Fanny 243
Gertrude L 22
Joe C 22
Joseph C 22
Wahnahka 22
Wah-nah-ka 22
SAR-FARTS-CHA 46
SAWYER
  Jas 237,238
SCOTT
  Bettie 119
  Nancy 119
SHANKS
  F E 288
  Fletcher E 288
SHELBY
  David 5,268,269
SIEBER
  John G 226
SIMPSON
  Alice M 94,96,97
  Catherine Elizabeth 94,96,97
  James H 94,95,96,97
SIMS
  E W 6,7,19,20,259,260
SKAGGS
  D C 25,27,28,30,31,32,33,42,43, 53,54,60,64,66,67,69,70,71,74,79,80, 81,82,85,86,87,88,93,94,111,112,114, 115,116,117,119,120,121,127,131,133, 134,135,136,137,151,154,155,156, 157,159,163,174,185,190,191,210,211, 212,218,219,220,229,236,248,252, 254,263,264,327,328
  Drennan C 1,4,27,28,30,31,32,33, 42,43,51,52,53,54,58,59,60,64,65,67, 69,70,74,78,79,81,82,84,87,88,89,93, 94,100,105,106,107,111,112,113,114, 115,116,117,118,120,121,133,134,135, 136,138,140,141,154,155,156,159, 163,174,175,185,192,193,210,211,212, 214,215,216,217,219,220,236,243, 254,263,265,274,289,290,295,299,302, 327,328
  Mr 286
SKEETER

339

Index

Jennie 19
Jensen 6,7
Jenson 19
SMITH
   Dr J C 124
   J C, MD 124
   J P 227
   James 132
   John 251,255
SMOCK
   J C 120
SNELSON
   A J 304
SOLO 318,319,320
STEBBIN 158,165
   Arthur 156,157,158,162,163,164
   Martin 160,161
   Nellie 156,157,158,159,163,164
   Nicey 156,157
   Wisey .. 158,159,162,163,164,165,166
STEBE 158
STEIN
   A J 230
STEPHEN 158
   Wisey 164
STEPHENS
   Martin 160,161
STEPPE 158
STIDHAM
   Timmie 300,301
STINES
   H A 229
STRAWN
   G W 142,143
SULLINS
   J W 145
   W L 145
SULLIVAN
   Minnie 83
SUSAN 249

TAHLOSA 323,326,327,328
   Louisa 323,327,328
   Sally 323,327,328
TARLOSA 326,327
TAR-LO-SHAW 324
TARLOSHAW 324,326

Louisa 324
TAR-LO-SHAW
   Louisa 324
TARLOSHAW
   Louisa 326,327
   Sallie 326
   Sally 323
TAR-LO-SHAW
   Sally 324
TARLOSSA 324,325
   Louisa 325
   Sallie 325
TARREY
   B W 44
TAYLOR
   M D 225
   M D, MD 226
TEBE 158
   Arthur 157,161,162,164,165,166
   Nellie 157,160,164,166
   Stebbin 158
   Wisey . 158,160,161,162,163,164,165
THOMAS
   Harley 59,60
   Louisa 59,60,61
   Lydia 59,60
THOMPSON
   Cinda 254
   March 249
TIGER
   Cassey 245,246,247
   Cooper 4,5,6
   Hannah 279,281,282
   Jane 52,58,190
   Jennie 193
   Johnson 283
   Lesly 153
   Lillie 279,280,281,282
   Nancy 4,5,6
   Salina 4,5,6,18,19,20
   Willie 279,282
TOBLER
   Mariah 197
TOLLESON
   W A 105,200
   W A, MD 105
TURKEY

Index

Barbara 11
Mrs Barbara 10
TURNER 190
K B 237,238
P F 40
Winnie 298

UPTON
 Dan 170

VAN DYKE
 G H 278
VANCE
 B J 242
VANDERPOOL
 J Monroe, MD 146
 James M 147
 James M, MD 146,147,148

WADSWORTH
 Eliza 1,2,3,4
 Eulalie 265,266
 James 1,2,3,4
 Jessie Eulalie 263,264,265,266
 John 1,2,3,4
 Mattie 263,264,265,266
 P J 263,264,265,266
WAITA
 Osie 73
WALKER
 Annie 65,66,67,68
 Jeff 65,66,67,68,69
 John 67
 Johnson 65,66,68,69
 Mabel 66,67,68,69
 Mable 65
 Martha 286
WALTHALL
 Nicholas M 231
 Nick M 231
WASHINGTON
 Aggie 24
 Dixon 24
 Harrie 322
 Hattie 321
 M M 96
 Maggie 24

Mary 318,319
Thomas 318,319,320
Walter 318,319
Willie 318,319
WATERFIELD
 F E 295
WATSON
 Minnie 92,93,94
 Sandy 92,93,94
WATTS
 Anna H 76,77,78
 Louvina 260,262
 Mary 262
 Thomas 262
 W T 78
 William T 76,77,78
 William T, Jr 76,77
WEAVER
 Emma 207
 T T 207
WEBSTER
 Chas E 173
WESLEY
 Lucy 60
WHALEY
 Laura 239
WHITE
 Ellen 308
WHITMAN
 W W 123,124
WILCOX
 C E 95,201
WILEY
 Amanda 261,263
 Bertha 260,261,262,263
 Louvena 262
 Louvenia 261
 Louvina 260,261,262,263
 Monroe 260,261,262,263
WILLIAMS
 J W 305
 Mrs 307
 Mrs B B 305
 Mrs S V 306
 Nat 279
WILLINGHAM
 Lizzie 85,86,87,88,89,90,91

WILLS
- Arthur Rex 223,225,226
- Eunice May 223,226
- Eybuce Nat 225
- Higb S 225
- John 224
- John S 223,226

WILSON
- Earnest 228
- Earnest C 228
- Hattie L 228
- Horace 285
- J E 228
- John 227
- Margarette 228
- R B 227
- Verbena 227

WINSTON
- James A 102

WOLF
- Jackson 80,81,82,83
- Sukey 80,81,82,83
- Timmie Barnet 83
- Timmie Barnett 80,81,82,83

WOLFE
- L M 19

WOODS
- Argethel 7,8,9
- Cora 7,8,9,10,11
- Cora Adams 9
- Lillie 9,10
- Lillie Rosell 10,11
- Willis 7,8,9,10,11
- Willis A 9,10

WRIGHT
- Maysie A 123

YAHOLA
- Jackson 125,127

YELLOWHEAD
- For-co-wee 5

ZIGLER
- Peter J, Jr 232,233

www.ingramcontent.com/pod-product-compliance
Lightning Source LLC
Chambersburg PA
CBHW020241030426
42336CB00010B/577